Side
Hustles

WITHDRAWN

Side Hustles

by Alan Simon

Side Hustles For Dummies®

Published by: **John Wiley & Sons, Inc.,** 111 River Street, Hoboken, NJ 07030-5774, www.wiley.com

Copyright © 2022 by John Wiley & Sons, Inc., Hoboken, New Jersey

Published simultaneously in Canada

For general information on our other products and services, please contact our Customer Care Department within the U.S. at 877-762-2974, outside the U.S. at 317-572-3993, or fax 317-572-4002. For technical support, please visit https://hub.wiley.com/community/support/dummies.

Wiley publishes in a variety of print and electronic formats and by print-on-demand. Some material included with standard print versions of this book may not be included in e-books or in print-on-demand. If this book refers to media such as a CD or DVD that is not included in the version you purchased, you may download this material at http://booksupport.wiley.com. For more information about Wiley products, visit www.wiley.com.

Library of Congress Control Number: 2022934337

ISBN 978-1-119-87013-5 (pbk); ISBN 978-1-119-87014-2 (ebk); ISBN 978-1-119-87015-9 (ebk)

SKY10033767_032622

Contents at a Glance

Table of Contents

Introduction

When you entered the work world, you might have thought you'd do that job — and only that job — until you left that company one day. Until then, your day job (or your night job, if you work evenings) would be your only job.

Not so fast. Tens of millions of people in the United States, and hundreds of millions of people around the world, supplement their primary jobs with some type of business activities on the side. These people all spend at least some of their professional lives embracing the idea of *side hustles.*

I should know, because I'm one of them. My entire professional life has been filled with side hustles.

In 1982, I was a U.S. Air Force computer systems officer, writing software on an antiquated 1960s-era UNIVAC mainframe using an even more ancient 1950s programming language. "Microcomputers" (PCs) were just coming on the market and were all the rage, and I was concerned that by the time my Air Force commitment was up in the mid-1980s, I would be way behind the curve when it came to the newer technology of the day.

I started a computer consulting business on the side, writing PC-based applications for small businesses and not-for-profits in Colorado and Arizona. That side hustle spawned another one when I wrote my first book for McGraw-Hill, *How to Be a Successful Computer Consultant,* which described how to create and operate what we would refer to today as a side-hustle consultancy. That first book led to a revised edition a couple of years later, followed by 30 more technology and business books over the years.

Eventually, my consulting business and those writing projects spawned other side hustles, including university teaching, video courses for Lynda.com (now LinkedIn Learning) and Udemy, and writing novels.

And I'm not the only person in my family who has embraced the idea of side hustles. My wife started an online boutique while she was doing business consulting, and that online boutique led to her latest side hustle: building and maintaining Shopify sites for other small businesses. My parents had a side-hustle mail-order business back in the 1970s, in addition to my dad's full-time job. My father and uncles owned a chain of retail record and video stores in Tucson from the 1970s to the mid-1990s, but one of my uncles started a side business for used records, which, in turn, spawned yet another side hustle selling used CDs. Finally, a century ago, one of my great-grandfathers was sort of a pioneer in the world of side hustles: His day job was owning and running his family produce store, but on the side, he was a bootlegger, making and selling illegal alcohol during Prohibition!

In some ways, a side hustle is like any other job, or running any other small or medium business. But the very nature of side hustles — the fact that you're doing something alongside a full-time job, or perhaps alongside other side hustles that you've got going — presents unique challenges, as well as unique opportunities, above and beyond a "regular" job or self-owned business. Understanding those challenges, and taking advantage of those opportunities, can be daunting as you jump into the side-hustle game.

That's where *Side Hustles For Dummies* comes in.

About This Book

Side Hustles For Dummies helps you make sense of the ABCs — acronym anarchy, buzzword bingo, and complicating confusion — that you frequently find in short articles, blog posts, and online videos about side hustles.

This book is not just a tutorial about side hustles; it also serves as a reference that you may find yourself consulting on a regular basis. You don't need to memorize large blocks of content (there's no final exam!) because you can always go back to take a second or third or fourth look at any particular point during your own side-hustle adventures.

Right from the start, you find out what you should expect from the world of side hustles, as well as see what challenges are lurking. You dig deep into deciding what kind of side hustle will work best for your individual and family situation — or if one even does! — and then wrap your brain around the big picture of how the operational, financial, and legal sides of your side hustle all fit together.

I don't use many special conventions in this book, but you should be aware that *sidebars* (the gray boxes you see throughout the book) and anything marked with the Technical Stuff icon are skippable. So, if you're short on time, you can pass over these pieces without losing anything essential. On the other hand, if you have the time, you're sure to find fascinating information here!

Within this book, you may note that some web addresses break across two lines of text. If you're reading this book in print and want to visit one of these web pages, simply key in the web address exactly as it's noted in the text, pretending as though the line break doesn't exist. If you're reading this as an e-book, you've got it easy: Just click the web address to be taken directly to the web page.

Foolish Assumptions

The most important assumption I've made about you is that you either are seriously exploring the world of side hustles or already have a side hustle going and are looking for additional insights to help you make the most of your efforts.

Perhaps you're driving for Lyft or Uber, or delivering packages for Amazon, or delivering food for Grubhub or DoorDash, in addition to your full-time job. Or maybe the professional side of your life thus far has been limited to a full-time job, but you're getting the itch to do something on the side.

Maybe your satisfaction level with your day job has been on the decline in recent years, and you're thinking about switching careers, but you want to get a better idea of what you're getting into. A side hustle could be the perfect way for you to have your cake and eat it, too: Keep your full-time job and financial security for the time being, while seeing if the grass really is greener doing something else.

Or you could already have a side hustle underway that's going so well that you're thinking about expanding your business. Not quite sure how to take your side hustle to the next level? This book has the answers.

You don't need to already be in the side-hustle game for *Side Hustles For Dummies* to be helpful. No prior business knowledge or experience is assumed, nor do you have to already be laser-focused on one particular side-hustle idea. You'll find all sorts of ideas and plans in these pages to either get you started or keep your side hustle moving along.

Icons Used in This Book

As you read this book, you'll find icons in the margins that indicate material of particular interest. Here's what the icons mean:

TIP

These are the tricks of the side-hustle trade. You can save yourself a great deal of time, and avoid more than a few false starts, by following specific tips collected from the best practices (and learned from painful experiences) of those who preceded you in the world of side hustles.

Side hustles are often filled with detours and roadblocks. Pay particular attention to situations that are called out with this icon.

Occasionally, I take a deep dive into a particular topic related to side hustles, and these sections are identified with this icon. If you're not particularly interested in the nitty-gritty details, you can skim or even skip over these sections.

Some points about side hustles are so critically important that you'll be well served by committing them to memory. You'll even see some of these points repeated later in the book because they tie in with other material. This icon calls out this crucial content.

Beyond the Book

In addition to what you're reading right now, this product also comes with a free access-anywhere Cheat Sheet. There you can find reasons to start a side hustle, categories of side hustles, and ways to avoid conflicts between your side hustle and your day job. To get this helpful content, simply go to www.dummies.com and type **Side Hustles For Dummies Cheat Sheet** in the Search box.

Where to Go from Here

Now it's time to dive into the world of side hustles! If you're totally new to the subject, you won't want to skip the chapters in Part 1, because they provide the foundation for the rest of the book. If you already have a side hustle underway, I still recommend that you at least skim Part 1 to get a sense of how to get beyond all the hype, buzzwords, and generalities related to side hustles.

From there, you can read the book sequentially from front to back, or jump around as needed, using the table of contents and index as your guide. Whatever works best for you is how you should proceed.

1

Getting Started with Side Hustles

Get the straight scoop about the world of side hustles.

Figure out if you're ready to jump into a side hustle.

Find the perfect hustle to match your mindset and your lifestyle.

Chapter **1**

Joining the Side-Hustle Game

I f you're thinking about jumping into a side hustle — or if you've already taken the plunge — you're not alone! According to a study reported on Side Hustle Nation (www.sidehustlenation.com/side-hustle-statistics), 45 percent of working Americans — around 70 million people! — had at least one side hustle going. Even better: Another 60 million were thinking about jumping into the side-hustle game.

Side hustles aren't only popular in the United States either. According to an article paid for by GoDaddy appearing on the *USA Today* website (www.usatoday.com/story/sponsor-story/godaddy/2017/12/12/how-people-side-hustling-around-globe/108532604), 54 percent of people in the United Kingdom, another 54 percent of people in Singapore, and an astounding 77 percent of people in the Philippines had side hustles.

Side hustles are all the rage, all around the world. But what exactly is a side hustle?

Getting Clear on What a Side Hustle Is

If you were to put ten people in a room and ask them to define the term *side hustle*, you would probably get 15 different answers. Instead of having some precise, everyone-is-in-agreement definition for the term, we have a lot of shades of gray and wiggle room in defining what is — and what isn't — a side hustle.

Some people think that a side hustle is limited to activity in the so-called gig economy (see "Seeing the Connection between Side Hustles and the Gig Economy," later in this chapter), filling a services industry type of role on a contract basis, with self-set flexible hours — for example, shuttling passengers in your own car for Lyft or Uber, delivering packages in your spare time for Amazon, shopping and delivering groceries for Instacart, or delivering restaurant meals for DoorDash or Grubhub.

Some people limit the world of side hustles to part-time roles in businesses that operate under the multi-level marketing (MLM) structure. Anything else is, well, something else, but not necessarily a side hustle. (See Chapter 3 for a discussion of MLMs.)

Other people think of a side hustle as being limited to anything where you're compensated on a non-employee basis rather than as a salaried employee. In the United States, that means you file a W-9 form and have your income reported on a 1099 form, rather than being paid a salary (even a part-time salary) on a W-2 basis. To their way of thinking, if you're paid as part of someone else's payroll and receive a W-2 at the end of the year, then whatever you're doing isn't a side hustle. (See Chapter 8 for a discussion of the various business structures for your side hustle.)

Which of these perspectives is correct? Well, a better question to ask is this: Are any of these perspectives too narrow? The answer: Yes, they are *all* too narrow — not necessarily wrong, just too limiting in attempting to define what is and isn't a side hustle.

REMEMBER

A better way to look at a side hustle is to consider an activity to be a side hustle if it's one in which you're *materially invested* (basically, what you've started isn't some passing whim, but rather something you're really, really interested in doing) but it's not your full-time, salaried, career-oriented job. Basically, a side hustle is an activity that is "on the side" of your primary, full-time job and that requires more than a minimal amount of time and energy (at least as you get established).

Now consider a few examples:

>> Meghan is a financial analyst for a Denver-based insurance company. She lives in the south suburbs of the Denver metro area but works downtown. Three or four times a week, if she doesn't need to be back home after work by a certain time, Meghan signs in to an app and becomes an Uber driver, earning a little bit of extra money during her evening commute. Sure, she and her car don't exactly take the most direct route back from downtown to the south suburbs, but a song from way back in the late 1970s by the rock group Supertramp perfect describes Meghan's journey on those Uber-enabled evening drives: She takes the long way home!

>> Jack is a software developer for an app development company based in Scottsdale, Arizona. Jack's employer supports both flexible hours and working from home. As long as Jack and his coworkers meet their deadlines for assigned work, they have a great deal of autonomy for how they manage their time. Taking advantage of his employer's flexibility, Jack teaches a programming class two afternoons each week at a community college campus about 5 miles from his apartment.

>> Bhavna graduated with top honors from a leading engineering school and works as a mechanical engineer at an aerospace company in Seattle. She's very good at her job, but after a couple of years, Bhavna is becoming disenchanted with the aerospace industry and even her chosen engineering profession! If she had a time machine, Bhavna would go back to her college days and study what she belatedly discovered she's really interested in: the world of fashion and retail. No worries, though: Last year, Bhavna started a small online boutique, selling clothing and accessories. She spends a couple evenings a week, not to mention most of her weekends, on a range of tasks for her boutique: finding and buying new products, packing and shipping orders, and doing all sorts of general business management functions. Soon — maybe *very* soon — Bhavna plans to ditch her full-time job and devote all her energies to her boutique.

>> Eric and Brittany had been single-mindedly focused on their respective full-time careers, both before they met as well as after they began dating and eventually got married. Eric is a high school teacher, while Brittany is a drug sales rep for a large pharmaceutical company. When the COVID-19 pandemic hit in early 2020, however, both of their professional worlds turned upside down. Eric continued teaching but solely online because his high school switched over to all-online courses. Brittany's job was eliminated as part of the pharmaceutical company's cutbacks, and she began working 15 to 20 hours a week shopping and delivering groceries for Instacart. As the months went by, Brittany also began delivering meals for both Grubhub and Uber Eats, as well as occasionally driving for Lyft. Eric began doing college entrance exam tutoring on the side, in addition to his full-time teaching. Eric is now wondering if he should quit his full-time teaching job and not only do even more SAT and ACT tutoring, but maybe even do some Lyft or Uber driving.

Pop quiz time!

From the blurbs above, who is in the side-hustle game? Meghan and her Uber driving? Jack and his community college teaching? Bhavna and her online boutique? Brittany and her portfolio of gig-economy jobs? Eric and his college entrance exam tutoring?

If you answered "all of the above," you're absolutely correct. Even though the particulars for what Meghan, Jack, Bhavna, Eric, and Brittany are doing vary at least a little bit from one person to the next, each one of them has already jumped onto the side-hustle bandwagon.

Some side hustles are actually part-time jobs rather than a small business or some gig-economy side work. In fact, you get paid for your side hustle through a regular paycheck — just like most day jobs — rather than in the less-than-predictable manner of most side businesses.

Take Jack, the Scottsdale software developer. Jack doesn't have a side business in the traditional sense. He's not creating and trying to sell instructional videos about software development or other technology-related topics. He does sign class-by-class contracts for each course that he teaches at the community college, but he gets paid through the college's standard biweekly payroll on a W-2 basis while he's teaching. If Jack isn't teaching during some stretch of time — say, the first part of the summer, or during the latter part of a spring semester — then Jack doesn't get paid anything. Basically, Jack is a part-time, on-and-off employee of the community college, rather than, say, an outside consultant.

But is Jack "materially invested" in his part-time teaching? Well, he teaches on a regular basis, most of the year (including at least part of each summer), and has been doing so for the past three years. He spends 10 to 15 hours a week while he's "on the clock" on his teaching gig, between the classroom and other support activities such as grading and holding office hours to meet with his students. And he's doing all this while holding down his full-time job, so you could definitely say that Jack is hustling!

Other side hustles come in what you could think of as a "convenient multipack," packaged with other side hustles.

Take Eric and Brittany. Brittany no longer has a full-time job because her now-former employer laid her off during the COVID-19 pandemic. Instead, Brittany has her own small portfolio of what might otherwise be side jobs for someone who was employed full-time. Does the absence of a full-time job exclude any of Brittany's side gigs — Instacart, Grubhub, Uber Eats, Lyft — from being considered a side hustle? Absolutely not!

REMEMBER

In fact, Brittany's little portfolio of side gigs — yes, that's right, side hustles — in lieu of a full-time job is becoming increasingly common (see "Seeing the Connection between Side Hustles and the Gig Economy," later in this chapter). In fact, notice that Brittany's husband, Eric, is contemplating voluntarily leaving his full-time teaching job and joining Brittany with his own portfolio of side hustles.

Other side hustles are much more like running a regular full-time business rather than a "here and there, whenever you feel like it" side activity. You don't have the leeway to just say, "Nah, I don't feel like packing and shipping a couple dozen customer orders this weekend, I want to go skiing. They can just wait for their jewelry, even if they paid for two-day shipping. I'll get around to filling those orders early next week. . .." Nope!

Bhavna's boutique, which she runs in addition to working her full-time, career-track engineering job, isn't any sort of gig-economy activity that she can sign in to or out of on a moment's notice. Running an online business entails regular commitment and being proactively responsive to her customers' needs: processing and fulfilling orders, restocking inventory, addressing problems with suppliers, handling returns, and all the rest. Although Meghan, Brittany, and anyone else who delivers groceries for Instacart or drives for Uber or Lyft can arbitrarily choose not to engage in those activities if they're too tired or just aren't "feeling it" for a couple of days, Bhavna can't necessarily "go dark" on her business for too long of a stretch.

But does Bhavna have a side hustle going? Absolutely — every bit as much as Brittany, Eric, Jack, and Meghan do.

WHEN WAS THE TERM *SIDE HUSTLE* COINED?

Back in the early '80s when I started my first side hustle, I called what I did a *side consulting business* or described what I was doing as *moonlighting*. The term *side hustle* wasn't used very commonly back then.

However, according to Merriam-Webster (www.merriam-webster.com/words-at-play/words-were-watching-side-hustle), the phrase dates back to the 1950s! So, even though the popularity of the term *side hustle* may seem to be a recent phenomenon, the phrase dates back many decades, just as side hustles themselves do.

Knowing What You're Looking for from a Side Hustle

People start side hustles for a variety of reasons. For many people, money is the prime motivator. But to some people, the financial side of their side hustle is so secondary that it's almost an afterthought.

So, why are *you* interested in a side hustle? Maybe it's money, knowledge, or experience. Maybe you're hoping to make a big career change. Maybe you're looking to monetize a hobby or passion. Maybe you want a safety net in place in case you get laid off. Or maybe you're trying to make ends meet after losing your full-time job. Whatever the reason, a side hustle can be right for you!

Money, money, money . . . money!

Our professional lives are hallmarked by a simple, straightforward equation: Work equals pay. Or, stated a bit more broadly: You put forth effort and provide value, and in exchange, someone pays you for your labors.

Many people are satisfied with what they earn from their full-time jobs, so the idea of making more money from some type of side hustle isn't exactly top of mind.

For many others, however, their full-time jobs may come up short on the financial side. Maybe they make just enough to pay the bills and save a little, but their kids' college tuition is on the horizon in a couple of years, and they're not sure how they'll afford it. Or maybe they want to pay for a wedding or a dream vacation that's been on hold for too long.

Whatever the reason, doing something on the side — yep, a side hustle — may be the answer for how you can have your professional cake and eat it, too. In other words: Continue to hold down a full-time job that provides stability and benefits (even though the financial side isn't quite what you're looking for), while still earning money above and beyond what comes from your job.

CAN VOLUNTEER WORK BE A SIDE HUSTLE?

Take another look at the broad definition of a side hustle: an activity outside of your full-time job in which you are materially invested. Maybe you're materially invested in some type of volunteer work — dog walking a couple times each week at a nearby animal shelter, or being on the board of a local charity that assists homeless veterans. You aren't getting any sort of pay for this volunteer activity, but it certainly takes up a fair amount of your time and needs to be balanced with your full-time job. So, could you think of your volunteer work as a side hustle?

Well, maybe. If you limit the definition of a side hustle to an activity — *any* activity — that fits the "work equals pay" equation, then no, volunteer work isn't really a side hustle. However, if you leave aside the compensation and income aspect of side hustles, you may, indeed, find a great deal of similarity between certain types of volunteer work and certain kinds of side hustles.

But now we're diving deep into the terminology weeds, or splitting hairs, or whatever other metaphor you'd like to apply here. A better way to think of volunteer work and side hustles is that you could combine "traditional" side-hustle activities with your volunteer work to benefit a particular cause. You could, for example, write blog posts or create YouTube videos about your favorite cause, which bring in a little bit of advertisement-sponsored revenue. Or you could create an online retail site in Shopify and sell donated clothes — sort of an online thrift store. You could then (maybe after covering your costs) donate some or even all of your proceeds to your favorite charity. So essentially, you're engaged in some sort of side-hustle activity, but you're forgoing part of the "reward structure" — the income — for a good cause.

Extending your knowledge and gaining experience

Your journey into the world of side hustles might follow that fabled path of least resistance, where you embark on an activity or business that is similar to what you do for your day job, but different enough to scratch that side-hustle itch. I should know — that's exactly how I jumped into the side-hustle game many years ago.

Many years ago, in the early days of my professional career, I was a U.S. Air Force computer systems officer. I was stationed at Cheyenne Mountain in Colorado Springs, Colorado, and was assigned to an office of about ten other officers and civilians who were responsible for writing software for the missile warning defense of the United States. Basically, our software received messages from sensor sites all around the world that detected missile launches and then used some head-spinning math to figure out if this alert was just a test launch by "the other side" or if (cue the ominous music) they had just started World War III.

A pretty cool-sounding job, right? This was in the early and mid-'80s, at the height of the Cold War, and you could say that business was good for the missile launch detection mission and expanding the functionality of our software to support new and upgraded sensor sites. Only one problem: Our software was written in an ancient programming language called JOVIAL that was already obsolete and was only used in certain military-oriented applications and systems. Well, make that two problems: Our JOVIAL-written software ran on antiquated UNIVAC mainframe computers from the '60s and '70s. (In fact, our UNIVAC was so out of date that the university where I went to school — Arizona State — had retired its UNIVAC two years earlier because it had become too obsolete for academia!)

The early and mid-'80s were also when so-called "microcomputers" — what we know as personal computers today — were hitting the market and quickly becoming wildly popular, not only for home use but also in business. Wouldn't it be great to get some experience in this hot new area of computer technology, even if the hardware and software of my full-time job was light-years behind what was coming to market? I was almost certain that I wasn't going to stay in the Air Force past the four years that I owed in exchange for my college scholarship, and when I reentered the civilian world, I would be four years behind so many other people in the tech field.

I bought my first personal computer and started a little application development and computer training side business, aimed at small businesses and not-for-profits in Colorado Springs and in Arizona, where I had gone to college and lived before going on active duty. And of course, I crammed and crammed and crammed, learning as much as I could about these new-fangled microcomputers and then-modern PC programming languages and software development frameworks.

Soon enough, I landed my first consulting project at a local tourism-oriented business. That first project was a doozy! I learned the hard way how packaged software development frameworks didn't always work as advertised and were often full of bugs (as we refer to software problems in the programming trade). I had to program a lot of workarounds into the customer's system to prevent the applications from blowing up, or to help them get back up and running if their application suddenly and abruptly terminated. I think I sized and priced the job at about 150 hours and wound up putting an extra 30 or 40 hours into the project that I didn't bill for to handle all the complications.

But I learned a ton! And I learned even more on the next customer's project, and the next one after that. Fast-forward to when I got ready to leave the Air Force and started looking for a job. Everything I learned during four years of doing software projects (and also some computer training) on the side — in other words, my first side hustle — really helped me get the perfect job and jump-start my civilian tech career.

Was I trying to make some extra money above and beyond my Air Force salary? Of course! Back in those days, junior officers didn't make a whole lot of money. So, I was absolutely after money!

But even more than the additional income, my primary motivation was the knowledge and experience that I gained from my side-hustle consulting and software business. Could I have just bought a PC and taught myself modern programming skills and microcomputer administration without starting a side hustle? Sure. But my thinking at the time was — and still is, even with 40 years of hindsight — that if I didn't force myself to spend all those hours behind a keyboard because I owed finished applications to my clients, I might not have had the motivation to do more than a perfunctory amount of self-learning. And I almost certainly wouldn't have run into all the unforeseen software hiccups for which I had to find workarounds, which served me well even in my full-time Air Force job, not to mention when I became a software product developer after leaving the Air Force.

TIP

You can do the same thing that I did so many years ago, no matter what your full-time job is or what industry you currently work in: Start a side hustle to learn new skills, and make some money at the same time for your efforts!

Jumping onto a different career track

Maybe you've been in your career field for 10 or even 20 years, but you're at the point where going to work every day is starting to be harder and harder. True, you're making decent money. But the days drag, and you can't *wait* until the workday is over.

Or maybe you wound up with the job of your dreams, but those dreams turned out to be more of a fantasy. Sure, you knew about the crushing hours and the wearying travel, but you were actually looking forward to the fast-track lifestyle on the road toward that big-time paycheck. Now, after only a year or two, you're asking yourself, "What in the world was I thinking?"

You're not quite ready to hit the ejection seat without a new job. You could start interviewing for jobs with a better work–life balance. But one message that has come through loud and clear every time your boss tells you that you need to work all weekend and miss a family event: You really want to be your own boss.

REMEMBER

A side hustle can be the perfect gateway between your current career path and something — anything — that is totally different. Not sure exactly where your passions lie? Try out one side hustle that fits your available time and passions. If it works, great: You can work on taking that particular side hustle to the next level and turning it into a full-time business (see Chapter 15). If that one doesn't do it for you, no problem — try another one, all the while still trudging along at your full-time job.

Or, if something miraculously happens for the better in the realm of your full-time job — say, you wind up interviewing with and then accepting a new job in your current career with better hours and a much lower stress level — you can either keep your side hustle going or slowly unwind and stop doing your side gig (see Chapter 14).

Profiting from a hobby or passion

TIP

Whether it's sports memorabilia, Pokémon cards, stamp and coin collecting, scrapbooking and crafting, gardening, homebrewing, or winemaking — or any one of dozens of other hobbies — there's probably an opportunity for you to monetize your hobby by adding on some sort of side hustle.

Todd started collecting baseball and other sports cards when he was a kid and collected them all through high school. When he went away to college, he tossed all his cards — carefully, of course! — into the closet of his old room at his parents' house. Fortunately, Todd's mother didn't throw out all his sports cards when he moved away, as many of Todd's friends' mothers did. Almost 20 years later, Todd rediscovered his old cards during a Thanksgiving visit to his parents' house.

What did Todd do next? Sure, he began buying current cards for his personal collection at the local big-box retailers and also at hobby shops. But he also discovered something interesting: Some of his childhood cards were now worth a fair bit of money! He began reading blogs and listening to podcasts about the investment and speculation side of sports cards. He began bargain-hunting on social media, at swap meets and flea markets and estate sales, and anywhere that he might find cards for sale. If he found a good bargain, he would buy cards — sometimes lots of cards — with the intention of flipping them for a modest profit.

Then Todd had another idea. Sure, there were already lots of podcasts and YouTube channels about sports card collecting and investing. But he had some interesting and unique ideas about topics that he didn't see covered anywhere else. By the time baseball season was underway, Todd's YouTube channel was up and running. Several months later, Todd had more than 1,500 subscribers. At that point, he applied for YouTube's Partner Program so he could begin monetizing his

YouTube presence. (Just in case you're not familiar with the term *monetizing*, it means "to make money from" and it's a key element to many side hustles.)

Fast-forward six months to October and World Series time. Each of Todd's videos was now generating a large number of views, and he was pulling in a couple thousand dollars a month from ad placement revenue.

Todd had taken his newly rediscovered passion — sports card collecting — and turned it into not one, but two side hustles: sports card investing and flipping, and also monetized videos about the hobby he had rejoined after being away for 20 years.

Playing defense

The signals are crystal clear: Your job is in jeopardy!

Maybe the overall national economy hasn't been that great for the past six months and seems to be slipping into recession. Or maybe the economy is just fine, but your employer made a couple of serious missteps and profits are way, way down — and rumors of layoffs are swirling through the office.

Whatever the reason, you can read the writing on the wall: Losing your job may be in your near-term future — and even though you've been a top-notch performer, there's nothing you can do about it.

Or is there?

A side hustle can help you "play defense" and cushion the blow of being laid off, should that unfortunate turn of events actually come to pass. If you're already doing something on the side, great! You can ratchet up your efforts and try to earn even more money from your side hustle than you already are. Driving 10 or 15 hours a week for Uber? Ramp that up to 20 or 25 hours, if you can make the schedule work with your full-time job. And then if you wind up getting laid off, you can immediately start driving 40 or 50 hours a week to help make up for the loss of your full-time salary.

Or maybe you've already maxed out the number of hours or level of effort you can put into your current side hustle, but you can add another side hustle if your schedule has — unfortunately — been "freed up."

TIP

If you were fortunate enough to receive a severance package when you lost your job, and if you're also receiving unemployment insurance payments, great! But don't procrastinate with your side hustles! Sure, you may need to take a week or two to process your job loss, but get back on that proverbial side-hustle horse as soon as possible!

At the first inkling of a possible job loss, if you don't already have a side hustle underway, take a long, hard look at some ideas that you think you could make work. Because the last thing you want is to not only lose your job, but to be totally powerless when it comes to your own financial fate.

Activating your financial emergency response plan

The worst has happened: You've lost your job, for one reason or another. Even more than that: You now find the traditional world of full-time employment so distasteful that you cringe every time you think about heading out on the interview trail. Even the thought of receiving and accepting a job offer, rejoining the same grind that you just left, makes you queasy. Maybe this isn't the first time you lost your job, and in your mind, you're about to jump right back onto the same treadmill that inevitably ends with your being whooshed off the back, tumbling onto the floor. If so, a side hustle may be just the ticket: a way to earn money while being your own boss.

Seeing the Connection between Side Hustles and the Gig Economy

According to Investopedia (www.investopedia.com/terms/g/gig-economy.asp), the term *gig economy* refers to an economic climate where "temporary, flexible jobs are commonplace and companies tend to hire independent contractors and freelancers instead of full-time employees." (Investopedia also goes so far as to claim that "a gig economy undermines the traditional economy of full-time workers who often focus on their career development.")

What's relevant in this definition for understanding the concept of side hustles is the reference to "independent contractors and freelancers." When Meghan takes the long way home from downtown Denver because she goes on the clock with Uber, she's functioning as an independent contractor rather than as an employee of Uber. If you take a step back and look at the big picture of the ride-sharing business, one of the points of contention is that Lyft, Uber, and other ride-sharing companies use independent contractors to compete with taxi companies, limousine services, and airport shuttles.

From Meghan's sort-of-microeconomic point of view, she has a little side hustle going a couple times a week to earn a little extra money. From the big-picture, macroeconomic view, however, Meghan's side hustle "enables" the gig-economy concept and has helped disrupt longstanding business models.

THE "GREAT RESIGNATION" AND SIDE HUSTLES

A somewhat surprising byproduct of the COVID-19 pandemic and its disruption of global business has been the so-called "Great Resignation" of 2020 and 2021.

The early stages of the pandemic, in spring and early summer of 2020, saw massive job loss in the United States and around the world. U.S. unemployment peaked at 13 percent in May 2020 and may actually have been a point or two higher than what was officially reported (www.pewresearch.org/fact-tank/2020/06/11/unemployment-rose-higher-in-three-months-of-covid-19-than-it-did-in-two-years-of-the-great-recession) before beginning to drop back to more "normal" levels in the latter part of 2020 and into 2021.

Normally, high unemployment levels lead to workers exhibiting three perfectly natural behaviors:

- Those who are lucky enough to avoid being laid off often cling to the security of their current jobs for dear life, doing everything they can to avoid joining the ranks of the unemployed.

- When an economic recovery arrives and picks up steam, many people continue to cling to their jobs. Maybe they do so out of gratitude for being able to keep their jobs, or perhaps they saw the financial and personal toll on others who weren't as fortunate and did lose their jobs.

- Many of those who do find themselves unemployed — temporarily, they hope — do everything they can to find new jobs and then likewise cling to those jobs and do everything in their power not to again lose that job security.

But 2020 was different. Maybe the extreme safety net measures taken by governments all around the world made this severe downturn different from previous ones. In the United States, for example, state-level unemployment payments were boosted by additional federal government money that came through the Pandemic Unemployment Assistance (PUA) program. The bottom line was that for many people, unemployment during the early stages of the COVID-19 pandemic wasn't as disruptive and painful on a personal or family basis as it might otherwise have been.

With some of the lost-my-job pressure reduced, many of those newly unemployed workers started dabbling in a little bit of this or a little bit of that during their now-free time. Others who kept their jobs were working at home with far greater schedule flexibility than they had ever had before. Many people enjoyed another side benefit of working from home: saving one, two, three, four — or maybe even more! — hours a day by not having to commute to and from an office. And what did many of those folks do with their now-free time? They also dabbled in a little bit of this or a little bit of that.

(continued)

(continued)

Stated another way: Lots of people picked up the side-hustle habit during the spring and summer of 2020.

By the autumn of 2020, COVID infection rates were dropping along with the unemployment rate. Largely due to the extraordinary measures taken by governments around the world, the business world didn't collapse during the worst of the pandemic. Now, recovery was on the horizon, and many companies began refilling the positions they had terminated earlier in the year.

But tens of millions of people in the United States, and tens of millions more around the world, had a taste of the world of side hustles and were now rethinking the very idea of rejoining the full-time workforce.

Even more people eyeballed side hustles from the security and stability of their careers and decided to ditch full-time work in favor of a portfolio of side hustles. An October 2021 study by leading consultancy McKinsey noted that 19 million workers had quit their full-time jobs since April of that year (www.mckinsey.com/business-functions/people-and-organizational-performance/our-insights/great-attrition-or-great-attraction-the-choice-is-yours)! Where would a person head after quitting a full-time job? For many, the answer is crystal clear: the world of side hustles!

Jobs with lower wages and even lower satisfaction levels — not to mention traditionally high turnover — have been particularly hard hit by the Great Resignation. Many of these jobs were in the service industry: restaurants, retailers, cleaning- and repair-oriented businesses, and others. But surprisingly, according to a September 2021 *Harvard Business Review* article (https://hbr.org/2021/09/who-is-driving-the-great-resignation), "resignation rates are highest among mid-career employees." Maybe even more surprising: "resignations are highest in the tech and health care industries."

And so, the Great Resignation got underway during a climate when most experts would have expected otherwise. People still needed to make money somehow, though, which is a large part of the reason that so many people jumped onto the side-hustle bandwagon for the first time beginning in 2020.

Suppose, however, that Lyft, Uber, Instacart, DoorDash, Grubhub, and other similarly structured companies didn't have a large pool of independent contractors to drive, deliver groceries or meals, or perform other services. Say these companies had to hire full-time employees. Basically, their business models would fall apart. The primary utility they provide is *brokering* between those who are available to provide certain services and those who want to take advantage of those services.

But the nature of those services is unpredictable and subject to peaks and valleys. Many of these services are also very short-term in nature — maybe a 45-minute drive to the airport or an hour's worth of grocery shopping and delivery. Large portions of the so-called gig economy are built around short-duration "service matchmaking" between an ever-changing pool of providers and those who need those services, at least at the moment.

Even longer-duration services fall under the gig economy. Going on a two-week summer vacation, but not taking the two family dogs? No problem: Use Rover or another pet-sitting service, and you can find someone to stay at your house and take care of Fido and Spot for the two weeks. After your vacation is over, you head back home and your pet sitter heads off to a new gig — or, you could just as accurately say, to a new client for their pet-sitting side hustle.

REMEMBER

The key point is that side hustles and the gig economy are made for each other. In the United States and in much of the world, traditional employment and career notions are being turned on their heads. Companies are foregoing the idea of hiring full-time or even regular part-time employees in lieu of independent contractors who can come and go with little or no disruption to business operations. And many people are turning their backs on full-time jobs and careers in favor of less secure but more flexible, shorter-duration independent contractor assignments.

Recognizing That Side Hustles Are For Everyone

Side hustles are for everyone! Nobody is too young, or too old, to jump into the side-hustle game. You might need a particular background — interests or expertise, or maybe even academic or other credentials — for some types of side hustles. But even if you don't have a particular background, you have lots and lots of other options available to you.

Consider Ravi, who is just beginning his senior year of high school. Ravi is sort of a financial prodigy and has been dabbling in Bitcoin and other cybercurrencies ever since he was a freshman. Last summer he started a subscription-only blog aimed at other teenagers looking to learn more about cybercurrencies. So far, Ravi has nearly 300 subscribers, with more people signing up every day.

Ravi's sister Maira, a junior at the same school Ravi attends, also has an entrepreneurial focus. Ever since her freshman year, she has been creating YouTube videos with fashion tips. This year, she expects to make close to $15,000 in ad-sharing money from her videos.

Ravi's and Maira's next-door neighbor Paula has been living in the same house for the past 40 years and is now the last remaining original homeowner from when the development was first opened. Paula was a college professor for most of her professional life, but she retired five years ago. After six months of reading and going for long walks, Paula started to get a little restless. She had always been high-energy, filling her days with not only teaching and other university-related tasks but also several hobbies, most notably scrapbooking and stamping. She still spends a fair bit of her time with those hobbies, but now she also makes YouTube videos from which she earns some decent money from placed ads.

Kelsey just turned 50 and retired from her city's public school system after 25 years teaching elementary school. With a lot of free time on her hands, Kelsey is a constant presence at garage sales, swap meets, flea markets, and church bazaars all around her city. She looks for great bargains in older toys, children's books, nostalgic Americana such as old signs and posters, and other items that she then sells on eBay and other websites. She spends around 15 to 20 hours a week buying and listing items and packing and shipping what she sold. Kelsey doesn't make a killing, but she does make a fair bit of money to supplement her teaching pension.

REMEMBER

Your side hustles may — and probably will — evolve over time, along with your interests and experiences. I'm a great example of this proposition. My side-hustle journey began with doing small business PC applications on the side and teaching people about then-new microcomputers. After 40 years in the technology world, I'm ready to leave databases and analytics and other techie stuff behind. I may still write a tech book or two, or do some data- and analytics-oriented videos every now and then. But I'm much more energized writing novels or doing videos about my lifelong hobby of baseball and sports cards or writing about non-tech topics . . . like side hustles!

Chapter **2**

Surveying Your Options

You're all-in on the side hustle game — or at least the concept. But how do you even get started?

You can do an online search for "best side hustles" or "side-hustle ideas" or a similar term, and you'll wind up with hundreds of results, many containing dozens of ideas. How do you make sense out of this information overload? How do you find the needle in the haystack: the side hustle that's a great fit for you?

TIP

Fortunately, you can follow a methodical, step-by-step process that will help you narrow down thousands of different side-hustle ideas into a small subset that matches your interests, abilities, and goals. Specifically, you need to consider and evaluate

>> Various topical areas available to you to focus on for your side hustle

>> How to flesh out and add substance to your initial topical area

>> Various venues or formats through which you can enter the side-hustle game

>> How your side hustle should relate to your full-time job or career or possibly other side hustles that you already have underway

>> Financial considerations on both the moneymaking and money-spending side of your side hustle

>> Time considerations, including the highly valued — and often misunderstood — concept of "passive income"

>> Whether you need special skills, training, or licensing for your side hustle

You can then mash the results of each of these areas together, and — presto — that overwhelming list of hundreds or thousands of side-hustle ideas is now magically narrowed down for you to make your final side-hustle decisions.

Your Side-Hustle Topical Area

Cooking!

Photography!

Fashion!

Baseball cards and sports memorabilia!

Gig-economy work, such as delivering takeout meals, providing rideshare services, or shopping and delivering groceries or other items!

Sports and exercise!

Travel!

Finance!

REMEMBER

You have hundreds, maybe even thousands, of different topical areas — think in terms of "subjects" or "focal points" — available to you for your side hustle. Before you even *think* about making other critical decisions such as whether you should try to actually sell products or services versus make money from free content accompanied by online advertising, or whether you should do your side hustle on your own or partner up with somebody else, you first need to decide what topic or subject you want to use as the foundation for your side hustle.

Ask yourself some very basic questions:

>> What am I interested in?

>> What do I know a lot about?

>> Is there something that I know only a little about right now, but would like to learn a lot more about and maybe make some money from that new knowledge?

>> Besides what I'm interested in and know, is there some sort of generic activity that I can spend time doing just to make some extra money?

TIP

In general, side hustles fall into two major "buckets" that you should consider:

>> Side hustles built around an area of interest to you that you'd like to *monetize* (make money from), at least to some extent

>> Side hustles that aren't necessarily interesting or exciting to you, but that still present a way for you to earn extra money beyond what you earn from your full-time job or other side hustles that you already have going

Cindy majored in mechanical engineering in college. These days, she lives in Seattle and works for an aerospace company. She enjoys her full-time career, but on the weekends she really wants to forget her day job and enjoy the Seattle party and music scene. While Cindy was in college, she worked weekends as a bartender in one of the most popular bars near campus. Just because Cindy graduated and now has a "grown-up job" as a mechanical engineer doesn't mean that her bartending days need to be in the past. Cindy makes an important decision: She's going to do some sort of side hustle related to bartending!

Miguel was an accounting major during his college days in Boston. He stayed in Boston after graduating and is now a staff accountant at a large consumer products company. If you were to look at Miguel's and Cindy's résumés, at first glance the two of them would seem to have very little in common other than being fairly recent college graduates. But if you were to get to know Miguel and Cindy, you would learn that just like Cindy, Miguel also worked as a bartender during college and, likewise, has a continuing passion for the "mixology arts."

Miguel, like Cindy, has a pretty straightforward 9-to-5, Monday-through-Friday work schedule. With his evenings and weekends almost always free, Miguel makes an important decision just like Cindy did: He's going to do some sort of side hustle related to bartending.

Will Miguel wind up doing the same sort of bartending-related side hustle in Boston that Cindy does in Seattle? No! Why? Stay tuned, because selecting "bartending" as their respective side-hustle interest is only the first of many key decision points along the pathway toward finalizing all the specifics of a side hustle.

In the meantime, Cindy's father, Sandy, has been a sports fanatic for his entire life. When Sandy was growing up many years ago, he played baseball, soccer, football, and basketball year-round. He also collected sports cards and memorabilia all the way from elementary school through high school. Eventually, though, Sandy's interests shifted, and he stuffed all his baseball cards, football cards, autographs, and other sports collectibles into a dozen cardboard boxes. Originally, those cardboard boxes were stashed in the basement of his childhood home, but eventually they wound up in the attic of his current house, all still sealed tightly. In fact, Sandy hadn't even looked at any of his old sports cards or other collectibles for years — until the start of the COVID-19 pandemic, when all of a sudden sports cards became wildly popular again. Now working from home, Sandy went up to the attic one Saturday, brushed away a bunch of cobwebs, and found and opened all those long-ignored boxes — and he was instantly overcome by a flood of nostalgia. Cindy had told her father about her own side-hustle ideas, which sparked a few of their own in Sandy's mind. Cindy may be thinking about a side hustle related to bartending, but Sandy has a few ideas for side hustles related to baseball cards and sports memorabilia.

At the start of the COVID-19 pandemic, Lori's hours working in a mall clothing store were cut way back. Fortunately, she kept her job because the store also has an online presence, and Lori was able to work from home packing and shipping orders for the store's suddenly booming online business. But instead of working 40 hours a week, Lori was now working only about 20 hours a week, sometimes even less.

Unlike Cindy, Sandy, or Miguel, Lori doesn't have any particular area of interest to turn into a side hustle. Still, she wants to — actually, she *needs* to — earn some extra money to supplement her weekly pay, which is now about half of what it used to be. Fortunately for Lori, many of the gig-economy delivery-oriented jobs went sky-high in popularity as people hunkered down in their homes. She signed up with Instacart and soon began spending about 20 or 30 hours a week shopping for groceries and other goods and then delivering those products to people's homes.

In Lori's case, you know exactly what she's doing for her side hustle: working as an independent contractor for a gig-economy company, doing shopping and home delivery. But what about Cindy? Or Sandy? Or Miguel? You know that Cindy and Miguel are interested in bartending as their respective side hustles, while

Sandy wants to do something related to sports memorabilia. But exactly what kind of side hustles will they wind up doing?

REMEMBER

Cindy, Sandy, and Miguel all fall into the first of the two main side-hustle areas: choosing some topic that's interesting to them as the foundation for their respective side hustles. They need to work their way through the progression of decisions covered in this chapter, and so far they've only reached Step 1: selecting a topical area.

Lori's side hustle falls into the second area. She's simply looking for some sort of flexible side hustle that doesn't require any particular skill or passion, but from which she can still earn money above and beyond her regular paycheck.

REMEMBER

Even if Lori's hours at the mall hadn't been cut, she could still head down this second side-hustle path. In fact, after businesses began reopening, the mall clothing store where she works — which, fortunately, was able to stay in business — increased Lori's in-store schedule back up to 40 hours per week. Does Lori need to quit her Instacart side hustle? Absolutely not! She may scale back the number of hours she signs in and does shopping and delivery; or maybe she'll keep the same level of Instacart activity but do more on the weekends and when she's not working at the mall than she did when her day-job hours were cut.

Figure 2-1 illustrates the two main side-hustle "families" along with some great examples of specific side hustles for each one. Note, though, that Figure 2-1 only includes a small number of examples of specific side hustles. Plus, Figure 2-1 only includes the topical areas, not how to flesh out those subjects or topics into specifics, as you'll see in the next section.

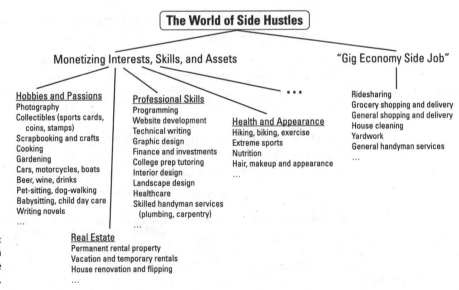

FIGURE 2-1:
The two main side-hustle families.

Running with Your Side-Hustle Idea

Choosing a topical area of interest for your side hustle is only the first step. You then need to add substance and detail to your first idea and decide what *exactly* you're going to do for your side hustle. You might do one or more of the following:

>> Perform some sort of service on a contract basis.

>> Sell some type of product, and maybe make the product as well.

>> Build online content to provide information.

>> Build online content to monetize yourself.

>> Monetize an asset.

>> Take on a part-time job as your side hustle.

Cindy and Miguel have both decided that a bartending-related side hustle is around the corner. Cindy decides that she's going to do some bartending on the weekends for private parties. Miguel, however, decides to create a series of videos that he'll upload to either YouTube or TikTok.

Contracting to perform a service

Many side hustles involve performing some kind of service, such as:

>> Doing hair, nails, or makeup for other people

>> Doing a little bit of part-time plumbing, electrical work, or other skilled handyman-related tasks

>> Walking dogs, doing pet-care visits during the day, or staying overnight at someone's house for pet sitting

>> Helping people pack their household goods and do a local move

Many gig-economy side hustles are service-related:

>> Using your personal vehicle to provide ridesharing

>> Shopping for and delivering groceries

>> Delivering restaurant meals to people's homes

TIP

For many service-oriented side hustles — grocery shopping and delivery or pet sitting, for example — you don't need to make a significant upfront financial investment. Even if you're providing, say, local moving services, you can still get into the side-hustle game without shelling out big bucks for a box truck large enough to move a household's worth of furniture and boxes. You can set your side-hustle business up where every time somebody hires you, you head to Hertz, U-Haul, or some other place that rents moving trucks by the hour or by the day, and bill your customers for the cost.

Cindy has decided that she's going to be a weekend bartender, mostly for home parties. She may need to purchase a few supplies to have on hand — a couple of bottle openers, a few corkscrews for wine, and maybe some drink stirrers — just in case the place where she's bartending doesn't have what she needs. But for the most part, Cindy's side hustle involves performing some specific service — bartending, in her case — for some defined period of time.

Selling products (and maybe making products as well)

REMEMBER

When it comes to selling products for your side hustle, there are typically two different paths you can take:

» Buying products from manufacturers or wholesalers

» Making your own products that you'll then sell

No matter which product-sale path you choose, chances are, you'll need to make a larger investment in your side hustle — both initially and on an ongoing basis — than you would if you were instead doing weekend bartending like Cindy or doing ridesharing through Uber or Lyft. Make sure your side hustle business plans (see Chapter 4) take these financial considerations into account!

Tasha and Breanna both absolutely love fashion, and both are intensely interested in starting some sort of side hustle. Tasha decides that she's going to provide personal-shopping services, helping other people choose stylish clothes and accessories to fit their budgets. Basically, Tasha will be providing contract services — the same side-hustle family as what Cindy will be doing for her bartending gigs.

Breanna, on the other hand, is thinking bigger. She wants to build a website that she'll use to sell women's clothes and fashion accessories. She'll find the right suppliers for print T-shirts, blouses, pants, skirts, denim jackets — you name it! Then she'll put their products on her website and, hopefully, bring in customers through social media marketing. Basically, Breanna's side hustle is almost indistinguishable from any other online retailer, other than the fact that she'll be running her online boutique during evenings and on weekends when she's not doing her day job.

Sarah also has a thing for the latest fashions, and she's also very interested in starting some sort of a side hustle. Just like Breanna, Sarah really likes the idea of building a website and selling products. Unlike Breanna, however, Sarah doesn't plan to search for suppliers for what she plans to sell. Sarah started making jewelry back in college — initially just for herself, but eventually a piece here and there to sell to her friends. Back in college, she just sold her jewelry to friends at cost (basically, she didn't make any money — she just charged her friends for the cost of the materials).

Now, though, Sarah wants to turn her jewelry-making into an ongoing side hustle. She designs about a dozen bracelets, another dozen rings, some earrings, and some necklaces for her initial product offerings. She makes a couple of each item to have on hand and plans to custom-make new items as orders come in (at least for now).

Providing information

Miguel, the accountant in Boston, wants to do something related to bartending for a side hustle. Miguel isn't interested in actually doing bartending, building a website to sell bartending supplies, or anything along those lines. He's after Internet stardom! (Well, sort of. . . .)

Miguel's side hustle will be creating a series of short videos — each one about five minutes long — that he'll post on YouTube, TikTok, or some other video site. Each video will show Miguel making some sort of unique craft cocktail (an espresso martini in one video, special margaritas in another video), tasting and rating the latest vintage of popular wines, or demonstrating new bartending-related items (cocktail shakers, glasses, wine openers, and so on).

Miguel's side-hustle aspirations involve more than just trying to become known as "that cocktail and wine guy" or a similar tagline. He wants to make money from his side hustle, just as Cindy will do from her bartending services. In Miguel's case, he plans to earn money from:

>> Ads placed alongside his videos after they become fairly popular

>> Affiliate marketing payments from products he uses and discusses in his videos

Miguel's coworker Mark also has the same idea: to create and upload videos that he'll then try to monetize through ads. Mark, however, knows next to nothing about bartending. In Mark's case, accounting not only is his day job, but will also become the foundation of his soon-to-be-launched side hustle. Mark plans to create a series of videos that he'll publish on YouTube covering accounting do's and don'ts for people doing a side hustle. (Talk about meta!)

About a year passes, and Mark's side-hustle accounting videos are doing fairly well. Every so often, someone emails him and asks if he has an actual course in accounting that's available for purchase. Mark soon figures, "What the heck, I'll try it!" He creates new accounting-related videos but now, instead of uploading them to YouTube, he packages them into a beginner's course and an intermediate course that he publishes on Udemy. He sets a list price of $44.99 for each course, and before long, he's earning a couple thousand dollars a month from his Udemy courses.

REMEMBER

If your side hustle is going to involve creating content — say, videos — you have two main avenues available to you:

>> Online courses that you sell to viewers who sign up

>> Free content that you post on YouTube, TikTok, or some other video service that you monetize through ad-related revenue or affiliate marketing links

TECHNICAL STUFF

If you head down the paid-course road, you typically earn money in several ways. People can directly purchase your course, with the financial transaction being a simple, straightforward "they pay the price upfront, then they can watch." Most online learning sites, however, also have some type of subscription service where customers pay a flat fee every month and get access to as many courses as they want during that month. If your course is available through a subscription service (like Udemy or LinkedIn Learning), the service will figure out how much to pay you (and all the other content providers) at the end of each month or reporting period. They usually use some sort of formula where they

>> Calculate your course's percentage of the total minutes watched for all videos during the month (or reporting period).

>> Take the total dollar (or other currency) amount available for the courses during the reporting period, after they take their cut.

>> Multiply your course's percentage by the total amount available to determine how much money your course earned that month.

WARNING

Different course hosting platforms may do their calculations differently, so before you point your own side hustle at a platform's subscription host, make sure you're crystal clear how your payments are determined, along with any "gotchas" such as whether the hosting platform is permitted to offer your course for free for some period of time with no payments due. Likewise, on the direct payment side, the hosting platform may be permitted to put your course on sale or change the price at any point without consulting you, reducing your earnings every time a course is sold. You may well make more money when your course has a temporarily reduced price because online learners often wait for sites such as Udemy to put courses on sale — and significantly more course purchases happen during these sales. Still, you'll make less money when your course is priced less than it normally is, so be aware of what hosting site companies are and are not permitted to do with your content.

Monetizing yourself

You've probably seen videos on YouTube or Vimeo where someone builds content that is, basically, that person doing or saying something to grab your attention: singing (sometimes pretty badly!) or lip-synching popular songs, for example. Or maybe you've seen videos where someone shows off their latest expensive fashion purchases. And of course the Internet is filled with dogs, cats, and other animals acting silly or just looking adorable.

All these types of videos, and thousands of others, are built around the premise of grabbing and holding your attention, and then getting you to follow or subscribe to the YouTube channel. Along the way, the creative people who uploaded that content can make money from ads placed along with their videos.

Mark and Miguel, both of whom plan to enter the side-hustle game with videos that they hope to monetize, have another co-worker named Max who is also intensely interested in creating and uploading video content. But although Mark and Miguel both intend to create videos that convey information (small business accounting for Mark, and bartending for Miguel), Max intends to monetize, well, himself.

Max decided that he's going to record himself walking or biking all over Boston and sharing his observations about interesting people he notices, the buildings that he passes, and whatever else he feels like talking about. Will his videos build a following to the point where Max can make a little bit of money from them? He thinks so. Max is a pretty funny guy, and his running commentary will basically be a standup comedy routine — at least that's what he intends.

Monetizing an asset for your side hustle

If you own real estate, you can turn that asset into a side hustle. You can also monetize other assets into side-hustle money:

>> Renting your boat (anywhere from a fishing boat to a yacht!) to vacationers

>> Renting your luxury sports car to someone looking to put the finishing touches on an extra-special occasion

Cindy and Tasha plan to earn money from their respective side hustles from what they do (bartending in Cindy's case, and personal shopping for Tasha). Breanna and Sarah will make money from what they sell. Miguel and Mark will make money from what they know and communicate. Max's side-hustle goal is to monetize himself. Hu and Min, however, plan to make side-hustle money from what they *own*.

Hu and Min have been married for 20 years. Ten years ago, Min received a ginormous financial windfall when the software company where she worked at the time went public, and her stock options were suddenly worth a whole lot of money. Hu and Min talked it over, and decided to buy a vacation house in northern Arizona after she cashed out her stock windfall. Fortunately, both of their jobs allowed them to work remotely, so every summer they would pack up their house in Phoenix and escape the 110-degree temperatures for a few months.

Five years ago, Hu received a job offer based out of New York City that he couldn't turn down, so the family moved across the country. They kept the house in northern Arizona, however; they just don't spend summers there anymore. Instead, they decided to turn that vacation house into rental property. Initially, they worked through a northern Arizona real-estate agent who would list their house for rent for the entire summer. Eventually, though, they decided to list the house on Airbnb for rentals lasting anywhere from one day to an entire month — and year-round now, because their vacation home was close to one of northern Arizona's ski areas for winter rentals and near some spectacular hiking trails for spring and summer rentals.

The part-time job side hustle

In Chapter 1, I introduce you to Jack, a software developer in Scottsdale, Arizona, who decides to do a little bit of side hustling alongside his full-time job. Unlike Brian and Keith, Jack doesn't want to actually start a small side-hustle business. Jack's side hustle is teaching programming classes two afternoons each week at the nearby community college campus.

WHAT'S THE DIFFERENCE BETWEEN AN ASSET AND AN INVESTMENT?

Is real estate an investment or a side hustle? Answer: Either or both!

What about cryptocurrency: An investment or a side hustle? Another answer: Once again, either or both!

Sometimes you'll find a very fine line between investments and side hustles. Take real estate, for example. If you invest in a property that you plan to rent out, either for someone to live there or for a constantly revolving parade of guests courtesy of Airbnb or Vrbo, then:

- You are definitely investing in real estate.

- You are *also* doing a side hustle that will involve time and effort but will also earn you money.

Suppose, though, that you plop some of your investment money into a *real-estate investment trust* (REIT; basically, using your money and other investors' money to buy real-estate assets) that will become part of your portfolio. You certainly want to keep an eye on the value of that REIT investment, but — and here's the important part — unlike a house or condo that you buy and then rent out, an investment in a REIT is mostly "passive." Until you decide to cash in that REIT, it's just another asset in your portfolio rather than an investment that you actively do something with.

Or suppose that you buy a second vacation home up in the mountains or near a beach, but you have enough money that you don't need to rent out that vacation home or otherwise try to monetize that real-estate asset while you own it. You may sell the vacation home at some point down the road, or maybe you'll keep it in the family and pass it down to your children or grandchildren. But along the way, only you, your family, and your friends will visit and stay there. In this case, a vacation home is definitely a real-estate investment, but it doesn't really fill the bill as a side hustle.

What about cryptocurrency? Suppose you really like the investment potential of Bitcoin, Ethereum, and other cryptocurrencies, and you decide to allocate around 5 percent of your investment portfolio to crypto. Investment? Sure! Side hustle? Nope!

Now suppose you also start recording and uploading videos in which you offer your thoughts about the cryptocurrency market, the underlying blockchain technology, the world of decentralized finance (DEFI) that includes blockchain technology and cryptocurrencies, and similar topics. Initially you intend to make money from ads placed with your videos; if your videos get popular enough, you may start a small cryptocurrency advisory service on the side.

Now ask the questions again in light of your expanded approach to cryptocurrency.

Investment? Still a resounding "yes." Side hustle? Well, because of your videos and ideas for making money above and beyond trading Bitcoin and other cryptocurrencies, the answer is also "yes."

Wait a minute: Doesn't it sound more like Jack is taking on a part-time job than starting a side hustle? Well, just like real estate (see the nearby sidebar), there's a big gray area when it comes to part-time jobs and side hustles.

In Jack's case, you could argue that his teaching gig fits the description of a side hustle:

>> He'll make some money from his efforts.

>> He needs to balance the time he spends on his teaching gig with the time requirements for his full-time job, being careful to avoid any conflicts.

>> He can adjust his teaching load to more or fewer classes as his time and energy level permit (with enough advance notice to the community college, of course).

TECHNICAL STUFF

The one main difference between the software development–oriented side hustles that Brian and Keith are doing and Jack's teaching is that Jack probably doesn't need to set up any sort of "side-hustle company" for his college teaching. Most likely, the college will pay him as a part-time employee on a W-2 basis; in the United States, that means Jack is a part-time employee rather than a 1099 independent contractor. (See Chapter 7 for all the details about how to form the legal structure for your side hustle.)

But other than this W2-versus-1099 distinction, Jack's teaching features all the characteristics of a side hustle.

Drilling into your side-hustle topical area

Remember Sandy, who rediscovered his childhood sports memorabilia? He noticed that baseball cards, football, and basketball cards, along with all sorts of sports memorabilia, suddenly became wildly popular at the beginning of the COVID-19 pandemic. Many people were working from home, and many others unfortunately lost their jobs (but fortunately, millions of them started side hustles!). Overall, people were at home much more than before and had a lot of time on their hands, as well as surprisingly flexible work and personal schedules. For whatever reason, lots of people either discovered sports cards and collectibles for the first time or, as with Sandy, rediscovered their long-forgotten collections.

So, it's settled: Sandy has selected his topical area and is going to start a side hustle related to baseball cards primarily, but also including other cards from football and other sports along with other types of sports collectibles.

But exactly what kind of side hustle is this?

Sandy could, under the general umbrella of "sports cards and collectibles side hustle," focus on any of the following:

>> Just baseball cards

>> Baseball, football, basketball, and soccer cards — but basically only sports cards

>> "Game-used" memorabilia, such as uniforms and hats, or balls and baseball bats

>> Autographs

>> Old sports books, almanacs, yearbooks, scorecards, and similar items

TECHNICAL STUFF

But wait! Sandy isn't even close to being done with his narrowing down and filtering. He decides to focus on baseball cards. But what kind? The baseball-card world is divided into different eras:

>> Vintage (basically, older cards from before around 1980)

>> The so-called "junk wax" era from the mid-1980s to the mid-1990s

>> Modern and ultra-modern cards that came after the "junk wax" era ended

Sandy decides to focus on vintage cards. However, stop me if you've heard this before, he still has some more narrowing-down to do! He could specialize in:

>> Individual cards

>> Cards for specific baseball teams

>> Unopened packs and cases of old cards (yes, they still exist)

>> Complete sets for a given year

Even if you don't know the first thing about baseball cards and sports collectibles — and don't care in the least about them, either! — you probably get the idea. Of course, Sandy isn't limited to only one particular subcategory, or sub-subcategory, or sub-sub-subcategory, or. . .. But Sandy's chances for side-hustle success go way up if he hasn't cast too wide of a net. Whether he plans to buy and then *flip* (sell quickly) vintage baseball cards, start a podcast about jumping back into the sports collectible hobby, or provide advice to other returning collectors to help them get the most value when they sell their collections, the more focused Sandy is, the better off he'll be.

TECHNICAL STUFF

Sandy can also head right for the techie world for his sports collectible–related side hustle by focusing on *non-fungible tokens* (NFTs), a hot new area in the sports marketplace (as well as the art world and other areas of society). An NFT is a unique "digital asset" (basically, an online image, audio clip, or video) that uses blockchain technology to essentially make that digital asset behave as if it were a physical "piece of something" that is actually owned by someone. Sandy obviously doesn't have any NFTs stashed away in those cardboard boxes up in his attic, but as he jumps into a sports-collectible side hustle, he absolutely could find something interesting and potentially lucrative related to NFTs.

TIP

If you don't have a clue about blockchain or NFTs and you'd like to learn more, check out *Blockchain For Dummies*, 2nd Edition, by Tiana Laurence (Wiley) or *NFTs For Dummies* by Tiana Laurence and Seoyoung Kim, PhD (Wiley).

Sandy began his side-hustle planning the right way: by first selecting some area of interest and then narrowing that area down. No matter what your side hustle is going to be, you'll almost certainly find yourself following the same narrowing-down steps. Table 2-1 shows a few different side-hustle topical areas and then, for each one, some of the underlying narrowed-down subcategories.

TABLE 2-1

Side-Hustle Topical Areas and Example Subcategories

Side-Hustle Topical Areas	Example Subcategories
Beauty and appearance	Haircutting and hairstyling, women's haircutting and hairstyling, hair blowouts, manicures and pedicures, eyebrow microblading, laser hair removal
Health and exercise	Outdoor biking, stationary biking and spinning, hiking, weightlifting, resistance training, martial arts
Home-design services	Furniture layout, kitchen remodeling, home exteriors, backyard design, firepits
Fashion	Women's clothing, vintage women's clothing, jewelry and accessories, vintage jewelry

Even if you're doing the "just something to earn extra money" version of a side hustle rather than trying to monetize an interest or hobby, you still need to do at least a little bit of narrowing down. Suppose you've decided to do some gig-economy delivery service. Do you want to also do shopping and then deliver what you buy at the supermarket or at other stores? Maybe you just want to pick up food from restaurants and deliver the food to homes, with no shopping involved. Making this particular decision will help you decide between, say, an Instacart side hustle versus doing something with DoorDash or Grubhub. Or you may want to just deliver packages for Amazon.

REMEMBER

You can "package up" as many different side-hustle ideas as you have time for or that make sense for you. You aren't even limited to ones that are closely related to one another, such as baseball and football cards, or hair and eyebrow microblading. Be careful not to spread yourself too thin, especially as you're first getting started in the world of side hustles.

Taking Your Side Hustle to Market

You've selected your side-hustle topical areas to focus on, and you've decided what sort of side hustle to do (providing a service, selling something, delivering content, or monetizing an asset). Guess what: Your decision-making still needs to march ahead! Now you need to decide how you're going to take your side hustle to market and how you're going to reach prospective customers.

You could

>> Go to market totally on your own.

>> Leverage an online marketplace.

>> Join a multilevel marketing (MLM) organization.

Going to market on your own

You can start, build, and run a side hustle that is structurally identical to a full-time business. Breanna went down this particular side-hustle road for her online boutique. She built a simple website and Shopify store and is doing her own social-media marketing. She lined up her suppliers and set aside a spare bedroom in her house to serve as a warehouse and shipping area. She processes customer orders as they come in and then packs and ships each outgoing package herself.

Breanna's brother Brian is also in the side-hustle game, but he has taken a different route than his sister did. Brian is a software engineer who wants to do a little smaller-scale contract software development for his side hustle. So, whereas Breanna is selling physical products for her side hustle, Brian is providing a service for his.

But other than the product-versus-service and fashion-versus-tech differences, Brian's side hustle is very similar to Breanna's. He also built his own website and has been doing online targeted ads to drum up business. Basically, Brian's side hustle mirrors that of his sister in terms of going to market as a microcosm of a larger business.

Leveraging an online marketplace

Rather than try to market and advertise your side hustle totally from scratch, you can get a head start by posting your services on an existing online marketplace that's widely known and that your potential customers frequently visit to find providers for what you're selling.

Keith is a software engineer at the same company where Brian works, and he also wants to start a software development side hustle. Keith, however, doesn't have the patience to set up his own website or to do his own targeted marketing on social media to try to find business.

Instead, Keith lists his services on Fiverr, an online marketplace where people and businesses come to find contractors for software development, video editing and production, graphic design, market research, writing a business plan, or other professional services.

REMEMBER

Many people like Keith use online marketplaces such as Fiverr, Upwork, Freelancer, Guru, and other sites as the foundation for their side hustles.

Online marketplaces aren't limited to professional services side hustles, either:

>> If you do dog walking or pet sitting for your side hustle, you can list your services on Rover, Holidog, or Puppy Friends Social Club.

>> If you provide home-related services, you can go to market through Angi or Thumbtack.

>> If you do freelance hair styling or tutoring, or provide dance lessons, you can post your services on the aforementioned Fiverr under the "Lifestyle" category.

TECHNICAL STUFF

Suppose Sandy decides his sports collectible–related side hustle will be to help other people figure out how much their long-forgotten vintage card collections are worth. Sandy could list "Vintage Baseball Card Appraisal and Valuation" on Fiverr under "Lifestyle" services. In fact, if you happen to be a Pokémon collector, you're in good company with other side hustlers who post that they'll help you figure out how much your Pokémon collection is worth. Another side-hustle free-lancer posts that they'll appraise Peanuts (the comic strip with Snoopy, Charlie Brown, and their friends) collectibles. If you can imagine a product or service, odds are that you can come up with a related side hustle!

Multilevel marketing organizations

MLM organizations — also called *network marketing* companies — are *the* most controversial topic in the world of side hustles. Some people swear that MLMs are the absolute best way to do a side hustle, while others swear *at* MLMs and regret the day they ever signed up for one. So, what's the story with MLMs?

Suppose you're interested in selling exercise clothing, activewear, and leisurewear for a side hustle. You could do what Breanna did:

>> Build your own website or storefront.

>> Decide which specific products you want to sell.

>> Find suppliers for the products you want to sell.

>> Figure out the tricks of social-media advertising to reach potential customers.

>> Pack and ship orders if you're handling your own inventory.

On the other hand, you could find an MLM that markets the type of activewear and leisurewear that you want to sell and then join that MLM.

WARNING

You don't just sign up with an MLM, however. The term *multilevel* is part of the name for a reason. You typically become part of the sales network for someone who is already a member of that company (thus, the significance of the work *net-work* in *network marketing*). Further, as illustrated in Figure 2-2, that network is constructed in multiple tiers, or levels, thus, the name *multilevel marketing*.

If you join an MLM, you make money from selling products to other people. But you also make money by bringing other people into the company and typically by receiving a small portion of the sales made by each person in your network. Basically, the larger your network, the more money you can make from products that other people sell.

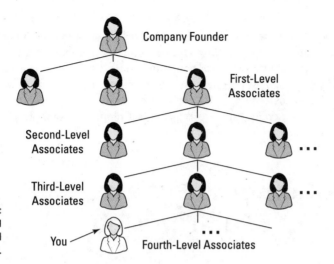

Company Founder

First-Level Associates

Second-Level Associates

Third-Level Associates

FIGURE 2-2:
A typical MLM hierarchical structure.

You → Fourth-Level Associates

WARNING

The pyramid-like structure of the typical sales force within a multilevel marketing company is why many people view MLMs as a "pyramid scheme." The full story is somewhat murkier. If an MLM company has a viable product that its independent contractor sales associates — basically, a whole bunch of people doing side hustles — offers and sells to the public, then despite the pyramid-like structure the MLM likely isn't a pyramid *scheme* in the classic financial fraud sense. But the key is that the company does need to have real products or services that you and others actually sell.

You need to do your homework and determine

>> How to figure out if a given MLM's compensation model is good for you

>> Whether you can make any money if you're way, way down the sales ladder

>> How sales territories are allocated

>> If you're required to purchase a monthly allocation of products, or if you can purchase products as you sell them

From a side-hustle perspective, MLMs have some interesting advantages and possible disadvantages. On the plus side, you can find an MLM for almost anything that you want to sell for your side hustle: clothing, health and wellness products, cleaning supplies, cooking-related products, makeup, and even (ahem) "adult" products. If you can imagine something, you almost certainly can find an MLM to join!

WARNING

One possible drawback, however, is that if you join an MLM, much — maybe even most or all — of your selling will be to family members and friends. Before you head down the MLM road for your side hustle, think about the possibility of constantly pushing new products on your friends and family, or dealing with them as dissatisfied customers, or telling your sister or a parent that the automatic payment on their credit card was rejected last month. . .. Yeah, might not be a whole lot of fun.

Deciding Whether to Pursue a Side Hustle Related to Your Full-Time Job

When I first jumped into the side-hustle game, I stuck with something very close to my day job as an Air Force computer systems officer by starting a small computer consulting and software development firm. I also began teaching and again stayed with tech topics for the classes that I taught. Then, when I wrote my first book, I once again stayed close to home, synergy-wise, and authored a book called *How to be a Successful Computer Consultant* (McGraw-Hill).

Your side-hustle adventures may also have a high degree of synergy with your day job.

Jack, the Scottsdale software developer who is doing part-time community college teaching, aimed for synergy with his side hustle, as did Mark, the Boston accountant who is creating a series of small business accounting videos that he'll try to monetize.

But what about Mark's coworker Miguel, who will also be creating and uploading videos that he hopes to monetize, but whose videos are about bartending and related topics? Accounting . . . bartending . . . nope, not even close!

Your side hustle can be closely related to what you do for your day job, or it can be totally different. Miguel opted for the totally-different fork in the road, as did Cindy, the Seattle mechanical engineer (though in Cindy's case, she'll actually be doing bartending).

TIP

If you're trying out a side hustle to experiment with or begin the journey to a career change (see Chapter 1), then "something different" is a pretty good strategy for your side-hustle efforts. Or you may be like Cindy and Miguel, who enjoy their respective day jobs (for now, at least) but just want to do "something different" and make a little bit of money at the same time.

In my case, I eventually got burned out writing business and tech books, but I enjoyed the process of writing. Because I read a ton of fiction when I was a traveling consultant, I shifted my writing efforts away from the technology books to novels. For about 15 years, my side hustle writing business and tech books not only earned a little bit of extra money, but also helped establish credibility in my day job. I reached a point, however, where I had maxed out the career benefit from business and tech writing, so it was time to switch to what I enjoyed more, which was writing novels.

TIP

You can follow the same strategy: Have some synergy between your full-time career and your side hustle at first, but eventually shift your side hustle to provide a break from your day job. Or you could head right for the "something different" road right from the very beginning.

Show Me the Side Hustle Money!

Earlier in this chapter, I introduce you to Lori, who began doing gig-economy side-hustle work at Instacart when her hours at her full-time job were cut back. One of the main reasons Lori headed for the gig-economy side of the side-hustle world was the predictability of what she would make in exchange for her efforts. She was fairly confident that she could do 20 hours a week, maybe even a little more; and she knew what Instacart paid and what she could expect from customers' tips in addition to her contract pay.

Likewise, Jack, the Scottsdale software developer, is absolutely certain how much money he'll make from his community college teaching side hustle — the payment amount for each class is right there in his teaching contract.

Some side hustles come with highly predictable incomes. In Jack's case, he knows exactly what he'll make; in Lori's case, she's highly confident of the range in which her income will fall each week, and she knows that if she decides to work extra hours one week and fewer hours another week, she'll make more or less money, respectively.

But what about Cindy, the part-time weekend bartender? Cindy's side-hustle income is less predictable than Lori's or Jack's. She won't necessarily have a bartending gig every weekend, so in any given month, she could make more or less than she makes in another month, depending on how busy she is (or isn't).

What about Miguel and his bartending videos? Or Mark and his accounting videos? Or Max and his hiking-and-biking-comedian-around-Boston videos? All three of these guys work together during the day, yet any one of them could be wildly successful with his side hustle while the other two could flop miserably and make little or no money. Or two of them could be successful; or perhaps *none* of them will be successful!

Some side hustles come with highly predictable incomes, or at least a high confidence for the range of money you can make, while other side hustles could wind up bringing you anywhere from no money at all to literally millions of dollars! So, how do you align your side-hustle selection with your financial needs?

TIP

If you *need* your side hustle to help you cover monthly expenses or to meet some specific financial obligation, then choose one that comes with "guaranteed" — or at least predictable — income. Think of these types of side hustles as having "lockstep income" — in other words, the income you make from your side hustle moves more or less in lockstep with the effort that you spend on that side hustle.

You don't necessarily need to do a gig-economy job or a part-time job in pursuit of predictable income. Most of the time, a real estate–oriented side hustle such as a second home that you lease out, or a condo at a resort location that you rent through Airbnb or Vrbo, can also provide somewhat predictable income.

But what about the various monetized videos that Miguel, Mark, and Max plan to do? Or whatever Sandy decides to do related to his recently rediscovered sports cards and memorabilia? True, none of those side hustles could turn out to be a winner . . . or each could bring in ginormous amounts of money!

REMEMBER

Many side hustles are built around the concept of *passive income,* which is actually a widely misunderstood concept. Many people think that the term *passive* means "no work required" — sort of like a side-hustle version of the old Dire Straits song "Money for Nothing." Actually, passive-income side hustles *do* require work, but that work and the resultant income do not typically occur in lockstep with one another.

Dhiraj creates a techie course that he uploads to Udemy. He spends three solid months on the course: recording and then editing the videos, creating assessments, producing the MP4 files, and then uploading everything to the account that he creates on the Udemy platform. As shown in Figure 2-3, Dhiraj spends 200 hours from the time he begins work on his course until the course is published. During that time, he makes absolutely no money at all from the course.

The course starts slowly, but over the next three months (until the six-month point) Dhiraj pulls in $2,500. Not bad, especially because during those first three months that the course is active, he does almost no additional work! Basically, he's sitting back and letting the money roll in, which means that he has now crossed the threshold and is earning passive income.

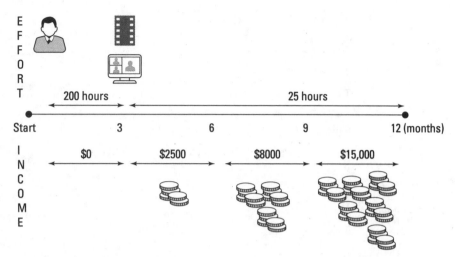

FIGURE 2-3:
A successful passive-income side hustle.

Over the next six months, Dhiraj pulls in another $23,000 ($8,000 in the second three months that the course is active, and then $15,000 during the following three months). During this entire time (refer to Figure 2-3), Dhiraj is still doing almost no work; in fact, he spends only about 25 additional hours after the course is published answering emails from people who purchased the course or maybe doing a small update here and there to include some new topic and keep his course fresh and up to date.

REMEMBER

You have absolutely no ceiling on how much money you can make from passive-income side hustles, especially when you have more than one going — at least in theory. Max, Mark, and Miguel could conceivably bring in tens or hundreds of thousands of dollars *each month* if their respective videos catch on and the advertising and affiliate marketing money starts rolling in.

However, those three guys — Max, Mark, and Miguel — could also theoretically make little or no money from their videos. In fact, the same fate could befall Dhiraj and his adventures into online course development as a side hustle. Figure 2-4 shows a different outcome for Dhiraj's course on Udemy.

Dhiraj still spends 200 hours of his time creating and publishing his course. Now, though, instead of $25,500 in income *just in the first year* (and with momentum on his side, probably indicating an even better second year!), he brings in only $325 for the entire year. At least as of the first year, Dhiraj earns less than $2 per hour for all the time that he put into his side hustle. Not good!

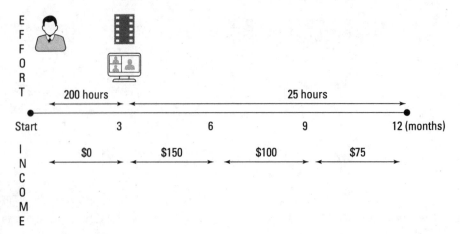

FIGURE 2-4:
An unsuccessful
passive-income
side hustle.

WARNING

Passive-income side hustles can be big winners or big losers (or somewhere in between). Sometimes, no matter how much planning you do or how good an idea seems, something just doesn't "click" and you wind up spending a ton of time for very little money in return. Other times, though, you could hit the jackpot and that upfront effort will really pay off as the money rolls in for months or even years to come.

You also have financial considerations on the investment and expense side of your side hustle. Suppose you want to start an online boutique and sell leisure-wear. You could line up suppliers — many of whom will have minimum order amounts — and set aside a bedroom in your home as a "warehouse" where you'll stash all the inventory that you buy from your suppliers. Be prepared to spend a fair amount of money on inventory! And ask yourself what will happen if your sales estimates are incorrect and you're stuck with all that inventory that you just paid a bundle for?

Alternatively, you could find suppliers who do *drop shipping*, where the suppliers themselves actually pack and ship the orders and you never have to stock — and more important, preemptively purchase — the products that you hope to sell. You'll typically make less with drop shipping than you would by fulfilling your own orders, but you also have a lot less money at risk if your side hustle comes up short of what you thought it would, sales-wise.

REMEMBER

As you refine your side-hustle selections, take both the income and the expense side of the financial picture into consideration.

Your Side-Hustle Clock and Calendar

Some side hustles have fairly rigid schedules. Jack can't just decide on the fly what days of the week or time of the day he'll teach his community college classes next semester. Cindy's day job limits her to weekends for her bartending gigs.

Other side hustles give you far more flexibility, at least when it comes to when you'll record videos, or pack and ship orders for your online boutique, or spend many hours handcrafting jewelry.

REMEMBER

You need to match up any calendar and clock constraints from your day job, or your life in general, with whatever is required for a specific side hustle. Look at more than just specific time blocks that you are and aren't available, though. Also look at the amount of time you need to spend on your side hustle, as well as the "cadence" of tasks that you may need to do on a regular basis.

Max, Mark, and Miguel all plan to create online videos that they'll then monetize for their respective side hustles. Miguel decides to do a new bartending-related video every week. Mark, however, figures that a new small business accounting video every two weeks is enough for his intended audience and fits better with his available time to record, edit, and polish the videos before uploading and publishing them. Max, on the other hand, settles on a far more fluid schedule for his "monetizing himself" videos. Some weeks, he'll do two or three videos, and then he may pause for a couple of weeks until he does another two or three.

WARNING

If your side hustle will involve regularly creating content — videos, a podcast, blog posts, and so on — make sure that your overall schedule gives you enough time to create your content every week, or every two weeks, or whatever interval you've settled on. If your schedule isn't that flexible, or if your day job is one of those where you may unexpectedly need to jump on a plane on short notice, you should probably steer clear of a side hustle where you can't meet your commitments to produce content, or fill customers' orders, or otherwise treat your side-hustle business like, well, like a real business.

You also need to be honest with yourself about how your energy level aligns with the time you've set aside for your side hustle. Back in the 1990s and early 2000s, I would typically have two or even three active book projects at various stages at any given point. Because I was spending most of my time traveling, I allocated every hotel night to writing — at least on paper. But you know what? Sometimes, after a really long and stressful day, I would go back to my hotel after dinner, sit down at the desk, open my laptop, and not be able to string together two coherent sentences.

TIP

Give yourself at least a little bit of cushion in your overall schedule when it comes to scheduling your side-hustle work. Don't think to yourself, "Every single night I will . . ." or "I'll spend 12 hours every weekend doing. . . ." You *will* have days or evenings when you just won't have the energy, so be careful when you're planning your side hustle to take this reality into consideration.

Figuring Out Whether You Need Special Skills or Licensing for Your Side Hustle

You can jump headfirst into some side hustles with absolutely no prerequisites at all. Interested in starting an online boutique? Go for it! Weekend bartending? Start pouring the drinks!

For other side hustles, though, you may need special skills or even need to be licensed by some governmental agency to certify that you are, indeed, qualified to do whatever that particular side hustle calls for.

For example, Shauna and Miranda have been friends since high school. Both are interested in doing infusions and other skilled medical treatments for people in their homes — a growing business in general, and one that is perfect for a side hustle.

Shauna graduated from nursing school and not only has ten years of experience as a hospital nurse, but also has all the up-to-date licenses required by the state where she lives.

Miranda? Well, she has a business degree and has been a sales rep for one of the big pharmaceutical companies for the past ten years. Miranda may be interested in providing home health-care services as a side hustle, and she may even turn out to be skilled at giving injections and similar treatments, but she doesn't have the formal educational background or the licensing to legally be able to provide those services. Miranda's story may be an extreme one, but you get the idea.

Many — maybe even most — side hustles have no formal licensing requirements of any kind. Others do, though. Just because you're interested in health care, for example, doesn't mean that you can just start a side hustle giving home infusions or providing similar services.

Even if you're not thinking "health-care side hustle," you still need to be aware of any licensing requirements. Suppose you want to make and sell homemade wine. Guess what? Most states in the United States require you to have a license for anything related to the manufacture and sale of alcohol.

REMEMBER

Make sure you carefully check to see if your side hustle idea has any city, county, state, or even federal licensing requirements. If you plan to do business on an international basis, check for any export or import licenses or requirements or any work visas that you may need (see the nearby sidebar).

Filtering and Finalizing Your Side-Hustle Short List

Maybe you began with a relatively simple "Hey, this side–hustle stuff sounds pretty good!" But I made you run the gauntlet through one decision point after another. Trust me, though: By taking the time to methodically evaluate all the key decisions and factors covered in this chapter, you'll be in much better shape when it comes to a side hustle that's a good match for your interests and expertise.

Cindy and Miguel both began with "bartending" as the theme of their respective side hustles. Now, after stepping through the decision points:

>> Cindy is going to do weekend bartending and will advertise her services on several local marketplace websites. She doesn't need to make any significant investments, and she can reliably figure on about $1,000 in extra income each month from four or five gigs at the most.

>> Miguel is going to take a chance on ad-supported and affiliate marketing videos that he'll post on YouTube and TikTok. He doesn't need to make too much of an investment beyond a new webcam and a few backdrops for the spare bedroom that he'll turn into a home video studio. He needs to study up on social-media advertising and different ways to draw attention to his videos. But Miguel is perfectly aware that he could be doing all this for little or no money if his videos don't go viral.

Sometimes you may pass through one of the decision points covered in this chapter without a clear-cut "do this, don't do that" answer. Breanna is definitely going to start her boutique. Even though she has a decent amount of savings available for her side hustle, does she really want to put a ton of money into buying inventory and turning her house into a warehouse and distribution center? Or should she do drop shipping instead?

Breanna's problem is that the products that she really, really likes are only available through traditional wholesalers with minimum order quantities, and aren't available from a drop shipper. What to do, what to do. . ..

Breanna decides on a compromise solution. She'll initially set up her store with a mix of drop-shipped products and a few of the nicer buy-and-stock ones. If her store catches on and her inventory actually does sell, she can shift more toward buying inventory that she'll pack and ship herself. If, however, her boutique side hustle turns out to be a flop, she won't be stuck with a ton of inventory that she'll then have to unload.

As you filter your side-hustle options, you may find yourself left with a package of several that you want to try together, such as:

>> Paid video courses that you publish on Udemy or Skillshare along with other videos that you post to YouTube from which you'll hopefully make money through advertising

>> Blogging about the same subjects for which you did videos

>> Registering with a speakers' bureau to try to land conference presentations and maybe keynote addresses, also about the same subjects from your videos and your blog

At this point, you're almost done with finalizing what you should do for your side hustle. You have one final step, and it's a big one: making sure that your side hustle is a good match for your personality (see Chapter 3).

Chapter 3

Determining Your Side-Hustle Personality

Your chances for success go way, way up if you devote your energies to a side hustle that's a good match for your personality and motivations. On the other side of the equation — as you can probably guess — a mismatch between almost any side hustle and your personality and motivations is going to be frustrating at best and a disaster at worst.

Understanding Your Personality

Are you an extrovert who loves to constantly meet and engage with new people? Or are you sort of shy and more of an introvert?

Do you tend to persevere through one tough challenge after another, and somehow always find a way to make things work? Or do you tend to surrender when things get particularly difficult, and move on to some other activity?

When people criticize you, do you take it personally? Do you get defensive? Do you immediately fire back with angry words, either in person or online? Or are you more along the lines of "Oh, who cares — it's their problem, not mine."

By now, you may be wondering: Where is this chapter headed? This is starting to sound like some sort of personality quiz you would run across on Facebook or maybe in a Psychology 101 class in college.

REMEMBER

Matchmaking between your personality and the world of side hustles is critically important. The better you understand your personality — *really* knowing what makes you tick — the better you'll be able to pick a side hustle that's a solid match for how you think and how you act. And on the other side of the equation, you can avoid side hustles that may sound interesting at first but really aren't a good match for you, at least when it comes to key facets of your personality.

Before you commit to a side hustle, you need to have a crystal-clear understanding of:

>> Whether you're mostly extroverted or introverted

>> Whether you have a multitasking mindset or get easily sidetracked

>> How much of a self-starter you are

>> Whether you can keep working when you're exhausted

>> How well you can add substance and depth to a fuzzy concept

>> Whether you prefer to work on your own or with others

>> Your ability to deal with rejection and criticism

>> Whether you're one of those people who refuses to admit defeat (which can be both good and bad)

>> What happens when you actually fail at something

>> Whether some of your favorite things throughout your life eventually became not a whole lot of fun, and what you did then

>> Whether you're more of a visual person or the written word resonates more with you

Extrovert or introvert?

You probably have a pretty good idea whether you're extroverted or introverted. When you go to social or business events, are you perfectly comfortable chatting with people you didn't previously know? Are you one of those people who can easily walk up to a group of folks and effortlessly insert yourself into the conversation?

Or, on the other hand, do you dread parties and business gatherings where you don't know many people? Or even those where you *do* know people? Are you more comfortable on your computer or going for a walk by yourself?

For some side hustles, it doesn't matter whether you're introverted or extroverted. For others, though, if you're not one of those outgoing, highly social people, you're almost certainly going to have some challenges ahead of you.

TIP

But first things first: Where do you fall on the extrovert–introvert continuum? For now, don't worry about figuring out which sides hustles fit best with which personality type or whether your side-hustle ideas (see Chapter 2) match up with your personality. Just keep it simple: Focus on the extrovert-versus-introvert question, and be totally honest with yourself.

How many balls can you juggle?

How good are you at multitasking? At your day job, do you often switch back and forth between different assignments? If your full-time job involves sales, can you simultaneously work with three or four different customers, all at different stages of the sales cycle? If you're an accountant, can you work on tax returns or quarterly filings or other accounting-related documents for a bunch of different clients at the same time?

How about at home: Can you feed the dogs while paying bills online and straightening up your living room and also emptying the dryer, all at the same time?

Some side hustles fit the one-task-at-a-time mold and don't require much (or any) multitasking. Other side hustles, however, require you to juggle and switch back and forth among a whole lot of tasks. Likewise, some people are expert multitaskers, while others are much more comfortable starting a task and then working on nothing else until they're done — and only then moving on to the next task.

Where do you fit when it comes to multitasking?

Can you give yourself that kick in the pants to get going?

Are you a self-starter? Do you hop out of bed each morning, ready to tackle the day? Can you keep that enthusiasm going all day long?

When you're at work, do you take a look at what's scheduled for the day and then get right to it? When you get home, do you immediately dive into whatever less-than-enjoyable tasks are awaiting you, because you know they need to get done, so you may as well get them out of the way?

Or are you one of those people who really can't get going at work in the morning until your boss assigns you the first task of the day? And then, when you finish that assignment, do you usually wait until your boss tells you what to do next? When you get home, you know the dishwasher needs to be emptied and a load of laundry needs to be started, but do you think to yourself: "Well, maybe later, I had a long day at work and besides, there's no real sense of urgency."

You can dabble in some side hustles here and there, a little bit at a time. With other side hustles, though, procrastination is basically a mortal sin, and no matter how tired or frazzled you are, you need to get busy doing whatever needs to get done — right now!

So, are you a self-starter, or do you need someone else to give you that proverbial kick in the pants to get you started?

Working past the point of wanting to stop

It's after midnight. Your alarm is set for 6 a.m. You're absolutely exhausted, and all you want to do is climb into bed and grab a few hours of sleep before you have to get up for work tomorrow. However, your to-do list for the day isn't quite finished yet. Do you take a deep sigh, yawn a couple times, and figure "Well, I gotta get this done" and get back to work? Or do you shake your head and tell yourself, "I'll get to it tomorrow."

REMEMBER

If your side hustle has a somewhat rigid schedule or cadence, you'll often find yourself plopping into your chair or starting your webcam or doing something along those lines even if the clock tells you that midnight has come and gone, and you're only going to get a couple hours of sleep that night. Or maybe you had to spend three or four hours extra at work on a given day, but you still need to record a podcast and write a blog post that both need to drop tomorrow morning.

Other side hustles are more forgiving, schedule-wise, and don't come with a rigid schedule that may require you to work past the point of exhaustion one or two days a week, or maybe even more frequently. To help you find the right side hustle, ask yourself: "Will I be able to keep plugging away to honor my side-hustle commitments even if I can't keep my eyes open?"

Painting your side-hustle picture

As a side hustler, you need to be the type of person who can take a high-level idea — almost a sound bite — and methodically proceed through the refinement steps in Chapter 2 to get down to a very specific idea for your side hustle. And there's the good news for you: Chapter 2 guides you through those key steps and decision points to go from a fuzzy concept to a refined, crisp side-hustle idea.

In Chapter 2, I introduce you to Sandy, who recently rediscovered his childhood sports cards and collectibles. Sandy not only enjoys looking through his old baseball cards, programs, and autographs, but also has decided that he wants to do some type of side hustle related to his cards and memorabilia.

But exactly what?

Sandy started with an impulse of "I want to do a side hustle related to my sports collectibles," but to turn that fuzzy concept into reality, he needs to add a ton of substance to that initial impulse.

TECHNICAL
STUFF

Does Sandy want to buy cards and collectibles and then sell them? Suppose that Sandy thinks — for now, at least — that he wants to try a buy-and-flip sports collectible side hustle. Where will he find these collectibles: Online? Yard sales? Estate sales? What's his budget? How big of a backlog of cards and collectibles does he want stashed in a spare bedroom before he stops buying until he can sell what he has? Where will he do his selling: Online? Okay, then on Facebook Marketplace or eBay or Amazon? Or on a sports collectible-specific site such as COMC or PWCC? Should he hold, pack, and ship his own merchandise, or should he ship the cards that he intends to sell to one of the dedicated marketplaces for safekeeping (referred to as a "vault" in the sports memorabilia world) and then have that company fulfill his orders?

Details, decisions; more details, and more decisions; even more details, and even more decisions!

WARNING

If, however, you aren't exactly a detail-oriented person, then the recipe presented in Chapter 2 may not be much help. If you're not really into following a step-by-step, progressively detailed methodology, you may get frustrated or lose interest before you get to the level of detail sufficient for your side hustle.

However, you can still jump into the side-hustle game, though probably with a different idea that requires far less detail work and decision-making.

Breanna, who I also introduce in Chapter 2, knows for certain that she wants to do an online boutique for her side hustle. But to turn that initial high-level idea into an actual side-hustle business, she needs to proceed down a similar path through numerous details to decide on her:

>> Specific products

>> Pricing strategy

>> Website or storefront technology

>> Social media marketing strategy

>> Supplier model (holding inventory versus drop-shipping)

As with Sandy, Breanna needs to methodically refine her initial impulse to "do a boutique side hustle" into all the sometimes tedious details that will turn an idea into something real. And, also like Sandy, if trudging through details isn't quite her thing, she needs to be crystal clear that her side hustle adventures may be better directed elsewhere.

Collaborating (or not)

Are you thinking about jumping into the side-hustle game on your own? Or are you contemplating the idea of partnering with a friend or relative? Either approach will work, but if you're thinking about going the partnering route, you need to make sure that your personality is a good fit for going into business with one or more other people.

You're also not locked into either going solo or partnering forever. You can always start off on your own, and then later, if you get to the point where you really need someone to keep juggling all those side hustle balls, explore the idea of partnering.

For example, Breanna flies solo when she first launches her boutique. Sure, handling all the technology, supplier relationships, order fulfillment (packing and shipping), returns and refunds — everything! — on her own is a ton of work. But she can handle all her side-hustle tasks on her own — at least at first.

After her first six months in business, Breanna's boutique is pretty successful — maybe even *too* successful! She approaches her friend Janet, who recently told Breanna that she was also thinking about starting a boutique.

"Here's an idea," Breanna tells Janet. "Why don't we partner together on my boutique? I could really use some help?"

Breanna has always worked well with others. In her day job, almost everything she does is as part of a three- or four-person team. She also spends a lot of time volunteering — well, at least she did until she started her side-hustle boutique — and for the past ten years she has almost always been on some committee, working closely with several others people. Breanna knows with all the certainty in the world that collaborating with others is part of her DNA.

Jim, however, has a totally different mindset when it comes to collaborating. To be perfectly blunt, Jim doesn't "work and play well with others." He's opinionated; he bristles when anyone at work even hints that one of Jim's ideas isn't absolutely brilliant; and he takes only a split second to go from zero to irate.

Whatever Jim decides to do in the world of side hustles — and he definitely has a few ideas — he would be much better off working almost totally on his own. Jim could be every bit as successful as Breanna with her boutique or Sandy with his sports cards, but he really should avoid any side hustle where success depends on close cooperation and collaboration with other people.

You hurt my feelings!

Are you one of those people who couldn't care less what others say or think about you? Or are you absolutely crushed if someone posts a snarky, dismissive comment to one of your social media posts?

Some side hustles require you to be able to brush off criticism — especially unfair or really mean criticism! Suppose your side hustle is built around YouTube or TikTok videos in which you are, essentially, monetizing yourself by detailing your travels, demonstrating makeup techniques, or just documenting your lifestyle in your quest to become an influencer. We've all seen the handiwork of Internet trolls or observed nasty back-and-forth flaming in comments to social media posts. Unfortunately, trolling and flaming are part of the online world. If your side hustle may expose you to criticism — some of which is particularly nasty and maybe even unfair — you need to have the temperament to be able to withstand that not-so-nice feedback without taking it personally.

TIP

Look deep inside yourself, and think about your social media activity, performance reviews at your day job, or any other situation where someone has provided you with feedback of any type — whether you wanted that feedback or not. How have you reacted negatively, especially to harsh and maybe unfair words?

This fight isn't over!

When your back is against the wall. . . .

When all hope is lost. . . .

When everything looks bleak. . . .

Pick your favorite cliché, but think about this critically important question: How do you react when things aren't going your way and failure looks to be inevitable? Do you instinctively look for some way — *any* way — to negate that "inevitable" defeat and somehow save the day? Or do you figuratively (or maybe even literally!) curl up into a ball and meekly accept defeat and failure?

Not to be too blunt, but whatever side hustle you decide to try may turn out to be far more difficult than you envisioned. Basically, your worst-case scenario from your planning (see Chapter 4) may well come about — and then what?

Some side hustles just don't work out the way you planned. For example, maybe:

>> Your online boutique has been up and running for almost a year, but you're still not making any money, and sales have been dropping for the past couple of months.

>> Both of your video courses covering web development programming tips have been live on two different learning platforms for more than six months, but so far only a handful of people have taken your courses.

>> Your YouTube channel featuring cute farm animal videos doesn't have anywhere near enough subscribers to qualify for advertising revenue, and the number of views for each newly released video has been pretty low for the past couple of months.

>> You've had a listing on Upwork for your graphic design services for more than a year, but so far you've only landed three side-hustle gigs, and one of them turned into a total nightmare with the most difficult client in the history of difficult clients!

Think about your current day job, past full-time or part-time jobs, and even your personal life. When difficulties or even imminent failure are staring you in the face, do you surrender and call it quits? Or do you take a deep breath and figure out a way to turn those lemons into lemonade?

REMEMBER

Many side hustles — particularly those where you are, essentially, creating and running a business of some type — are best suited for people who have successfully dealt with difficult circumstances in the past and have somehow found a way to sidestep imminent failure. Does that sound like you?

If not, don't despair — you're not shut out of the side-hustle game. Many of the gig-economy side hustles (such as ridesharing or doing contract delivery services) don't require you to be able to keep forging ahead, or adjusting your strategy in some way while facing extremely challenging circumstances. You just need to understand your own personality so you can direct your side-hustle efforts along the best path for you.

Shaking off failure

It's official: Your side hustle is a bust. Yeah, maybe you kept trying and trying until you ran out of money or finally decided to call it quits. But the truth is that your online boutique, or your video courses, or whatever your side hustle was turned out to be a failure.

Now what?

Maybe you're a charter subscriber to the old adage of "If at first you don't succeed, try, try again." Maybe when you didn't make the freshman soccer team, you went to soccer camp the next summer, and what do you know, you made the varsity team! Or maybe you didn't get into any of the top-tier colleges to which you applied, but after your stellar undergraduate career at a state university and then two really successful years in the workforce, every one of those colleges accepted you when you applied to graduate school!

And then, there's your day job. Maybe you were passed over for a promotion last year (rather unfairly, you thought). But instead of quitting in a huff, you buckled down and performed even better over the following year. This time, you not only got that promotion, but also got a pretty big raise and a nice stock-option package, too.

REMEMBER

No matter how resilient and persistent you are in the face of challenging times (see the previous section), sometimes your side hustle will fail. If you're the type of person who can get past failure, do your best to diagnose what went wrong, and try again, you can try a riskier side hustle where failure is a distinct possibility.

If, however, you take failure as a personal shortcoming, or if failing at something really drives you into a serious depression, you should direct your side hustle efforts more toward less risky activities, such as gig-economy contract jobs or other activities where you won't beat yourself up over not having achieved some specific side-hustle objectives.

Sorry, not interested anymore!

Do you get bored easily? If so, then side hustles may not be for you. No, I'm not trying to scare you away from a side hustle — I'm just telling it like it is.

Your side hustle needs to be a commitment, not a whim. Sure, you can drive for a couple weeks with Uber and then call it quits because you've lost interest in doing ridesharing. Or you could deliver groceries for Instacart for only a couple days and never go back into the world of gig-economy contract jobs.

However, if you're thinking about doing a series of YouTube videos or starting an online business or buying investment real-estate properties that you'll lease or do short-term rentals through Airbnb or Vrbo, you need to have a little bit more "staying power" with your side hustle to justify all the time you'll put in to get underway.

Maybe you're like Johann, who changed majors three times in college. When Johann was in elementary school, he begged his parents for guitar lessons and dutifully went each week. . . until he got tired of the guitar. Then he started playing soccer and was pretty good at it . . . until he lost interest in the sport. Then there was the volunteer work at the local animal shelter, two or even three times a week . . . for about six months. And on the career side, Johann has changed jobs five times in the past seven years, each time because (stop me if you've heard this before) he lost interest and wanted to do something else.

WARNING

Hey, some people like Johann get bored easily, and often. That's okay! But some side hustles pretty much require you to be able to stick with a particular idea for a while to really get things going. If you decide to start an online storefront to sell your own handmade jewelry, your side hustle may not start making money for six or nine months, or maybe even longer. Along the way, if you get bored making jewelry or keeping your Shopify site up to date with all your inventory and new products, or doing social media marketing, or setting up a booth at local arts-and-crafts festivals, or the other couple dozen things you need to do for your side hustle, well, if you get so bored that you lose interest and decide to quit your side hustle, you'll have wasted months of time and maybe hundreds or even thousands of dollars!

Sometimes, trying to monetize a hobby and turn scrapbooking or stamp collecting or coin collecting into a side hustle can have a really bad outcome.

Take Sandy, who wants to monetize his recently rediscovered interest in his childhood sports cards and collectibles hobby into a side hustle. Maybe Sandy's side hustle, whatever the details turn out to be, will be successful; or maybe he won't succeed, and he'll just sort of retire from the side-hustle game.

WARNING

Maybe, however, Sandy's side-hustle experiences will be so "painful" that he gets turned off from the very idea of sports cards and memorabilia, even as just a hobby. True, Sandy's collectibles have been stashed away in sealed cardboard boxes for decades. But after rediscovering all those old treasures, wouldn't it be a shame that Sandy's failed attempt to start some type of a sports collectible side hustle wound up totally ruining any enjoyment he may have gotten from rediscovering his childhood hobby?

So, how about it? Do you easily get bored and lose interest in hobbies, jobs, or even people? If so, then be careful about the world of side hustles. Stick with gig-economy types of side hustles that you can ease into and out of at will, instead of trying to start a business that requires a sustained level of interest over a long period of time.

The picture or the thousand words?

TIP

If your side hustle involves conveying information in any way to the world at large, make sure the method you choose for presenting your content aligns well with what you're most comfortable with. If you like writing, blogs and books may be in your future; otherwise, maybe videos and slides are more your forte.

Bart and Mia both majored in business supply chains in college, and both work in the logistics organizations of their respective full-time employers. Mia absolutely loves writing; in fact, she originally was going to be an English major in college with an emphasis in creative writing.

Bart? Well, to be honest, Bart has always had difficulty writing anything longer than the typical email. Writing has always been very difficult for Bart.

Bart and Mia each want to start some sort of side hustle related to their full-time jobs working with supply chains. Mia decides that she's going to write a weekly blog and maybe even author and self-publish a book about emerging technologies for global supply chains.

Bart, on the other hand, is self-aware enough to realize that blogs and books aren't exactly within his personal skillset. Is he shut out of the side-hustle game? Absolutely not! Bart decides to record a series of videos about supply-chain technology that he'll post on his new YouTube channel. If he's successful and gets enough subscribers, he'll be able to monetize those videos through advertising.

And then, if the YouTube videos get popular enough, he may create and record a course or two that he'll upload to Udemy or Skillshare and try to sell.

What about you? Are you the reincarnation of Shakespeare or Hemingway when it comes to writing, or do you just like writing? Are you more of a visual person who finds it much easier to create a Microsoft PowerPoint presentation than write a document in Microsoft Word?

Personality, Meet Side Hustle

Digging into what makes you tick may seem a bit tedious, but not only is doing so critically important, but also that self-insight is only the beginning of aligning your personality with a possible side hustle. Your next steps:

>> Identify key personality factors of a side hustle that interests you.

>> Match up your personality self-assessment with the side-hustle personality factors.

>> Look for potential problem areas or even deal breakers.

In the following sections, I offer some examples of how other people followed these steps to arrive on the side hustles that are right for them. You may not be interested in these specific side hustles, but you can use the examples to assess your own personality and the side hustle that interests you to see if you're a good fit.

Creating and monetizing travel-related lifestyle videos

Both Omya and Jason are interested in the same side hustle: recording and uploading a series of travel-related lifestyle videos to YouTube and trying to monetize their YouTube channels through advertising and affiliate marketing revenue.

Omya diligently walked through the personality evaluation criteria described earlier in this chapter, and came up with the self-assessment that you see in Table 3-1.

Jason also did a deep dive on his personality, and Table 3-2 shows what Jason came up with.

TABLE 3-1

Omya's Side-Hustle Personality Assessment

Criteria	Omya's Traits
Extroverted or introverted	Extroverted
Multitasker	Yes
Self-starter	Yes
Can work beyond exhaustion	Yes
Can add substance to a fuzzy concept	Yes
Works well with others	Yes
Handles rejection and criticism well	Yes
Refuses to admit defeat	Yes
Deals well with failure	Yes
Loses interest easily	No
Visual or written	Mostly visual, some written

TABLE 3-2

Jason's Side-Hustle Personality Assessment

Criteria	Jason's Traits
Extroverted or introverted	Introverted
Multitasker	Yes
Self-starter	Yes
Can work beyond exhaustion	Sometimes
Can add substance to a fuzzy concept	Sometimes
Works well with others	Sometimes
Handles rejection and criticism well	No
Refuses to admit defeat	Yes
Deals well with failure	Not sure
Loses interest easily	No
Visual or written	Mostly visual, some written

With their self-assessments behind them, Omya and Jason both turn their attention to the personality criteria associated with the side hustle they're interested in. Even though they both worked independently — and in fact don't even know each other — they both arrived at the same conclusions, as shown in Table 3-3.

TABLE 3-3 ## Key Personality Traits Relevant to a Travel/ Lifestyle Video Side Hustle

Criteria	Ideal Traits
Extroverted or introverted	Extroverted
Multitasker	Yes
Self-starter	Yes
Can work beyond exhaustion	Yes
Can add substance to a fuzzy concept	Yes
Works well with others	N/A
Handles rejection and criticism well	Yes
Refuses to admit defeat	Yes
Deals well with failure	N/A
Loses interest easily	No
Visual or written	Mostly visual, some written

So far, both Omya and Jason each have two independent sets of data points. Now comes the time for each of them to match up their respective personality factors with what they've determined to be relevant for their prospective side-hustle idea. Table 3-4 shows both Omya and Jason in the same table so you can see a side-by-side comparison.

Scrolling down each row of the table, you can see that for the most part, Omya's personality seems to fit pretty well with what's important for trying to monetize travel/lifestyle videos. Jason, on the other hand, has a couple "hot spots" that you see in bold in Table 3-4:

>> **Jason is fairly introverted, and he knows it.** Travel/lifestyle videos tend to require the "star" to be outgoing and engaging. Omya, for example, wouldn't just be pointing a video camera at sites in Paris or Florence or Vancouver or wherever she is in any given video. She needs to be an integral part of every

single video: gleefully eating gelato in front of the famous Trevi Fountain in Rome, or nervously shuffling along the Grand Canyon SkyWalk and its glass walkway, or schussing through the snow somewhere in the Swiss Alps. But for Jason, trying to become an Internet star is an incredibly unsettling proposition.

» **Jason is sensitive to criticism.** The thought of Internet trolls making fun of one of his videos has his stomach in knots.

TABLE 3-4 ### Matching Omya's and Jason's Personality Traits with Those of Their Side Hustle

Criteria	Ideal Traits	Omya's Traits	Jason's Traits
Extroverted or introverted	Extroverted	Extroverted	**Introverted**
Multitasker	Yes	Yes	Yes
Self-starter	Yes	Yes	Yes
Can work beyond exhaustion	Yes	Yes	Sometimes
Can add substance to a fuzzy concept	Yes	Yes	Sometimes
Works well with others	N/A	Yes	Sometimes
Handles rejection and criticism well	Yes	Yes	**No**
Refuses to admit defeat	Yes	Yes	Yes
Deals well with failure	N/A	Yes	Not sure
Loses interest easily	No	No	No
Visual or written	Mostly visual, some written	Mostly visual, some written	Mostly visual, some written

REMEMBER

The bottom line: Creating and trying to monetize travel/lifestyle looks to be a pretty good idea for Omya, but Jason should probably direct his side-hustle efforts elsewhere. He may have methodically walked through all the steps described in Chapter 2 to settle on the idea of travel/lifestyle videos, but this final check — making sure that he has the right personality traits to help set himself up for success — has turned up a few red flags and potential deal breakers.

Making and selling craft jewelry

Breanna and Kylie live in separate parts of the United States and don't know each other, but just like Jason and Omya, they have the same idea for a side hustle. In Breanna's and Kylie's cases, however, they're both interested in making craft jewelry and building Internet storefronts to sell their respective products.

Just like Omya and Jason, Breanna and Kylie are proceeding down the initial steps of their respective side-hustle journeys the right way. They've both stepped through the refinement process described in Chapter 2, and now it's time for each of them to do their side-hustle personality assessments. Table 3-5 shows what Breanna has come up with, while Table 3-6 shows the results of Kylie's self-analysis.

TABLE 3-5 **Breanna's Side-Hustle Personality Assessment**

Criteria	Breanna's Traits
Extroverted or introverted	Extroverted
Multitasker	Yes
Self-starter	Yes
Can work beyond exhaustion	Yes
Can add substance to a fuzzy concept	Yes
Works well with others	Yes
Handles rejection and criticism well	Yes
Refuses to admit defeat	Yes
Deals well with failure	Yes
Loses interest easily	No
Visual or written	Mostly visual, some written

Both Breanna and Kylie independently come up with the critical traits of making and selling craft jewelry online, as shown in Table 3-7.

Finally, Table 3-8 matches up both Breanna and Kylie with their side-hustle aspirations, and just like the travel/lifestyle videos for Omya and Jason, you can see some critical differences between the two aspiring side hustlers.

TABLE 3-6

Kylie's Side-Hustle Personality Assessment

Criteria	Kylie's Traits
Extroverted or introverted	Extroverted
Multitasker	No
Self-starter	Sometimes
Can work beyond exhaustion	No
Can add substance to a fuzzy concept	Sometimes
Works well with others	Yes
Handles rejection and criticism well	Yes
Refuses to admit defeat	Yes
Deals well with failure	Not sure
Loses interest easily	No
Visual or written	Visual

TABLE 3-7

Key Personality Traits for an Online Craft Jewelry Side Hustle

Criteria	Ideal Traits
Extroverted or introverted	N/A
Multitasker	Yes
Self-starter	Yes
Can work beyond exhaustion	Yes
Can add substance to a fuzzy concept	A bit
Works well with others	N/A
Handles rejection and criticism well	A bit
Refuses to admit defeat	Yes
Deals well with failure	N/A
Loses interest easily	No
Visual or written	Mostly visual, some written

TABLE 3-8

Matching Breanna's and Kylie's Personality Traits with Those of Their Side Hustle

Criteria	Ideal Traits	Breanna's Traits	Kylie's Traits
Extroverted or introverted	N/A	Extroverted	Extroverted
Multitasker	Yes	Yes	**No**
Self-starter	Yes	Yes	**Sometimes**
Can work beyond exhaustion	Yes	Yes	**No**
Can add substance to a fuzzy concept	A bit	Yes	**Sometimes**
Works well with others	N/A	Yes	Yes
Handles rejection and criticism well	A bit	Yes	Yes
Refuses to admit defeat	Yes	Yes	Yes
Deals well with failure	N/A	Yes	Not sure
Loses interest easily	No	No	No
Visual or written	Mostly visual, some written	Mostly visual, some written	Visual

Breanna looks to be in pretty good shape, with solid alignment between her personality and the key traits for her desired side hustle. Kylie, on the hand, has a few red flags that could start her off with the proverbial two strikes if she continues with the idea of an Internet craft jewelry side hustle:

>> For one thing, Kylie has enough self-recognition to acknowledge that she's not the best multitasker in the world and sometimes has difficulty being a self-starter.

>> She has never been known to stay up until all hours of the night to finish incomplete tasks, either for work or in her personal life — she has more of a "it can wait until tomorrow" personality. Thinking ahead, will she be able to stay awake an extra couple of hours to craft a bracelet or a set of earrings that a customer ordered with next-day shipping? Or to process a half-dozen orders that came in earlier that day, all of which need to have labels and postage printed and boxes packed? She's honestly not sure, now that she really gives the question some thought.

TIP

As with Jason and his aspirations, Kylie can certainly play in the side-hustle game, but she may be better suited toward a different idea, even if she stays with her overall theme of craft jewelry. In fact, she realizes, maybe she could create videos of herself making and wearing jewelry and try to monetize those videos. Or maybe she could build a course for Udemy or some other learning platform for people who may also want to learn how to do custom jewelry for themselves.

REMEMBER

Just because some very specific side-hustle idea may fail your final personality assessment doesn't mean you need to go totally back to the drawing board. Sometimes a slight pivot here or there, staying with the same theme that you began with, will yield a slightly different but similar overall idea that could be a big winner for you!

Finding the right gig in the gig economy

Even if your side-hustle aspirations are more in the gig-economy space than trying to build a small-scale business of some type, your personality assessment still comes into play.

Carl has already decided that he wants to "do some kind of gig" for a side hustle. He has a ton of options available to him, such as:

>> Ridesharing

>> Shopping and delivering groceries and other goods

>> Doing restaurant meal delivery

>> General "assistance" such as running errands for people who are short on time or may have difficulty getting around

Carl initially thinks that doing ridesharing for Uber or Lyft (or maybe both) is the way to go. Table 3-9 shows what Carl came up with for his side-hustle personality assessment.

Tables 3-10 and 3-11, respectively, compare Carl's traits with the personality characteristics for ridesharing and delivery services, both of which fit the classic gig-economy side-hustle mold.

For the most part, ridesharing and delivery-related side hustles are similar in their personality characteristics, with one important distinction, at least for Carl: Carl is incredibly introverted, almost to the point of being socially awkward. He has tremendous trouble talking to or being around someone he doesn't know for more than a minute or two. He's been working on this personality trait, but at least for now, he dreads the thought of regularly interacting with strangers.

TABLE 3-9 **Carl's Side-Hustle Personality Assessment**

Criteria	Carl's Traits
Extroverted or introverted	Extremely introverted
Multitasker	No
Self-starter	Mostly
Can work beyond exhaustion	Sometimes
Can add substance to a fuzzy concept	Sometimes
Works well with others	Sometimes
Handles rejection and criticism well	No
Refuses to admit defeat	Yes
Deals well with failure	Not sure
Loses interest easily	No
Visual or written	Mostly visual, some written

TABLE 3-10 **Matching Carl's Personality Traits with a Ridesharing Side Hustle**

Criteria	Ideal Traits	Carl's Traits
Extroverted or introverted	Extroverted	**Extremely introverted**
Multitasker	N/A	No
Self-starter	Sometimes	Mostly
Can work beyond exhaustion	Sometimes	Sometimes
Can add substance to a fuzzy concept	N/A	Sometimes
Works well with others	N/A	Sometimes
Handles rejection and criticism well	Low	No
Refuses to admit defeat	N/A	Yes
Deals well with failure	N/A	Not sure
Loses interest easily	N/A	No
Visual or written	N/A	Mostly visual, some written

TABLE 3-11

**Matching Carl's Personality Traits with a
Delivery Service Side Hustle**

Criteria	Ideal Traits	Carl's Traits
Extroverted or introverted	**N/A**	**Extremely introverted**
Multitasker	N/A	No
Self-starter	Sometimes	Mostly
Can work beyond exhaustion	Sometimes	Sometimes
Can add substance to a fuzzy concept	N/A	Sometimes
Works well with others	N/A	Sometimes
Handles rejection and criticism well	Low	No
Refuses to admit defeat	N/A	Yes
Deals well with failure	N/A	Not sure
Loses interest easily	N/A	No
Visual or written	N/A	Mostly visual, some written

Ridesharing through Uber or Lyft wouldn't be the best option for Carl, at least for now. Maybe someday in the future, if he can overcome his severe introversion, he could try out ridesharing, but the more he thinks about it, the more almost terrified he is by the idea of strangers getting into his car several times a day and riding with him for 20 or 30 minutes, or even longer.

Should Carl forget his side-hustle aspirations? Definitely not! He could easily stop by restaurants, pick up orders with only minimal interaction with the staff, and deliver those meals to homes and offices.

TIP

Even with gig-economy side hustles, you should take the time to make sure that your personality aligns well with what you have in mind. Suppose your day job comes with almost no interaction with other people, which is driving you nuts because you're one of the most sociable people around. You're starved for social contact! If you want to do some type of gig-economy side hustle, then unlike Carl, ridesharing would probably be a better bet for you than something like delivery services, where you'd have little or no interpersonal contact.

2

Getting Your Side Hustle Up and Running

Get your side-hustle ducks in a row.

Dip a toe into the side-hustle pool before jumping in.

Take your side hustle to the next level.

Get the business side of your side hustle humming along.

Put your side-hustle finances in order.

Keep track of all your side-hustle activities.

Share your side-hustle proceeds with the taxman.

IN THIS CHAPTER

» Letting the ideas flow

» Diagramming your value chain

» Sizing up your risks

» Identifying your best-case and worst-case scenarios

» Pulling it all together into your business plan

Chapter **4**

Putting Your Plans Together

You're pretty sure now what you want to do for your side hustle, and you've made sure that your personality is a good match for your aspirations. So far, though, you're still side hustling at 30,000 feet — in other words, your side hustle is still more concept than action. But now it's time for the rubber to hit the road!

Before you start building a website, or signing up for a gig-economy job, or designing your social media ads that you'll use to catch people's attention, you need to get your side hustle ducks in a row.

Ready? Let's go!

Starting with Free-form Brainstorming

If you're not a fan of rigid, structured planning, I have good news and bad news for you and your side hustle. First, the bad news: Eventually, you'll have to fit your plans into a structured format to make sure that you've dotted all your *i*'s and crossed all your *t*'s.

The good news, though, is that you should start your side-hustle planning with stream-of-consciousness brainstorming that will encourage you to let ideas flow. Spreadsheets? Templates? Nope! Just let your mind run free!

TIP

In fact, at the earliest stages of your planning, the less structure and constraints you put on generating ideas, the better. But if you're looking for a good starting point, you can begin with the five *W*s and that hanger-on *H* that you may remember from your earliest school days:

>> What your side hustle will be

>> Who will be involved in your side hustle

>> Where your side hustle will operate

>> When important milestones and other time-related aspects of your side hustle will occur

>> How you'll turn your side hustle ideas into reality

>> Why you even want to do this side hustle

Whatcha gonna do?

TIP

If you've reached the planning stage for your side hustle, here's some good news: You've already settled on the *what*. You started with a fairly general topical area, such as "fashion and clothing" or "sports cards and memorabilia" or "bartending" (see Chapter 2). Then you refined that overall concept into, say, "building and running an online boutique where I'll use drop-shipping suppliers" or "finding bargain-priced sports collectibles that I can sell at a profit" or "creating a YouTube channel with a series of ten-minute videos about bartending-related topics that I'll try to monetize."

Surprise! You already began your brainstorming the moment you came up with an idea and started spending some time refining and fleshing out that concept. So, you're ready to forge ahead with your brainstorming. Wasn't that easy?

Who's there?

Now you need to decide if you're going to fly solo with your side hustle or if other people will be involved. If others will be part of your side hustle, what exactly will they be doing?

TIP

Start by contemplating three important questions:

>> Do you want to do your side hustle totally on your own?

>> Can you do your side hustle totally on your own?

>> Even if you can do your side hustle totally on your own, would you benefit from having someone else involved?

Breanna plans to start an online boutique. She'll definitely interact with other people — suppliers, customers, someone to build her Shopify site, an accountant — but as for the boutique itself, well, it's her idea, and she's all-in on going solo.

Now Breanna contemplates the second question: Sure, she wants to do her own side hustle, but *can* she, or is there too much work for one person? Are there critical aspects of running the business side of her side hustle that she doesn't really know well enough to do on her own?

Breanna decides that by finding a Shopify developer on Fiverr or Upwork, and by farming out the tedious bookkeeping and all her tax filings to her accountant, she doesn't *need* a partner or a full-time employee for her boutique.

Still, though, would Breanna be better off if someone else were heavily involved in her boutique anyway? Breanna has already done the side-hustle personality check (see Chapter 3) to confirm that she's a self-starter and that she knows she'll work until well past her normal bedtime to get her side-hustle work done. She doesn't have a history of quickly losing interest in new ventures or hobbies. Breanna doesn't need anyone simply for morale or "cheerleading" purposes; she's totally confident that she'll stick with her side hustle and doesn't need anyone else to give her a little extra "oomph."

Location, location, location!

You need to identify all locations where you'll operate your side hustle. If you're like most people jumping into the world of side hustles, you'll start off working out of your house or apartment, even if you can't help but dream of the day when your side hustle has outgrown your spare bedroom or your dining room table.

For example, when Breanna lets her mind run free, she can easily envision her boutique growing into a full-time business with a physical retail location adjoining a large warehouse area, where dozens of her employees are hard at work filling hundreds or even thousands of online customer orders every day.

But what about the here and now? Breanna can dream all she wants, but she knows she'd be throwing money away leasing any sort of warehouse facility. Like most side hustles in their early days, Breanna will run hers out of her house. She has a spare bedroom that she'll convert into a combination warehouse/office. Sure, it'll be pretty crowded in that room, and Breanna tends to be a little bit claustrophobic, but for now, she'll take the prudent route and run her side hustle out of her house.

Drafting your timeline

Quick: What does the next month look like for your side hustle? How about the next two months? When will you be up and running? When will you start bringing in money? When do you think you'll turn a profit?

WARNING

You'll definitely need to dig into the details of your timeline when you get into the more formal part of your planning (as discussed later in this chapter). Right now, though, don't get too far ahead of yourself or too far down in the weeds. Just jot down your initial thoughts, your first impulses, to get a sense of what your timeline looks like.

How now, brown side-hustle cow

You know that saying "The devil's in the details"? In other words, you need to flesh out dozens or even hundreds of steps that you'll take to turn a concept into reality. In other words, *how* will you actually take your side hustle to the real world?

For example, Breanna doesn't plan to make any jewelry or sew any clothing. Instead, she'll buy clothing, jewelry, and any other items that she decides to sell from various wholesalers.

But will Breanna preemptively buy dozens of fashion T-shirts, doing her best to guess what sizes she needs to order and stash in her spare bedroom that she's using for her warehouse? Or will she find suppliers who will *drop-ship* (basically, fill and send orders directly to customers without Breanna ever having to even handle the merchandise)?

As Breanna refined her "fashion" concept into ever-more-detailed ideas, a lot of the "how" aspects of her side hustle were fleshed out, so she should be well along her way for this part of her brainstorming.

Still, maybe she didn't quite get to the critical decision point on filling orders herself (and, thus, receiving and storing inventory). Or maybe Breanna hadn't yet thought about her social-media marketing strategy: Advertise on Facebook? Run Google Ads? Try search engine optimization (SEO)? All of the above?

Okay, but why?

In Chapter 1, I describe how people embark on a side hustle for a variety of reasons. Are you trying to monetize a passion or hobby? Are you looking for an escape path from a full-time job that you hate? Are you looking to expand your knowledge and skills, and trying to make some money in the process?

Whatever your motivations for starting a side hustle are, make sure that at the planning stage you're crystal clear and totally honest with yourself about why you've steered yourself onto the side-hustle highway.

Before you dive into (fair warning!) the tedious side of your planning, do a last check while you're letting your mind run free: Why are you thinking about this particular side hustle? If you can't articulate a good answer to yourself, then pause and *really* think about it before you get too much further. You want to make sure that you aren't acting solely on an impulse that has taken on a life of its own, and that you don't stumble into some side hustle that will eventually make you miserable.

For example, is Breanna venturing into Side-Hustle Land in the hopes that within the next two years, she can leave her full-time job and turn her boutique into a full-time business? Or is she looking to monetize one of her long-time passions?

Jack is a software developer in Scottsdale, Arizona, who is thinking about teaching on the side. For Jack, the good news is that he doesn't need to expend a whole lot of brain power on the what, who, when, where, and how aspects of side-hustle teaching, because all those facets are pretty well set in stone. But *why* is Jack contemplating teaching as a side hustle? Is he just looking for a little extra money? Is he thinking about going back to school to get a PhD and then jump onto some university's tenure track as a full-time faculty member? Is he thinking about teaching topics that are slightly different from the techie stuff he works with every day, "forcing" himself to learn to be able to teach?

Doing the brainstorming two-step

Should you a) do your brainstorming on your own, or b) bounce ideas off of others and gather a whole bunch of feedback? The answer: Both!

Start by brainstorming on your own. Why? Initially you want to let the ideas flow without any undue outside influence from others. After all, this is *your* side hustle. Even if you'll eventually rely on others for advice on a regular basis, or bring other people in as partners or employees (see Chapter 13), you need to make sure that you can wrap your head around key aspects of your side hustle.

TIP

Go for a couple of long walks. Plop down on a lounge chair in your backyard or by the pool at your apartment. Do a couple of miles on your treadmill or stationary bike. Whatever works best for you when it comes to getting those creative juices flowing, get yourself into a good place, both physically and figuratively, and do your brainstorming.

Eventually, though, take the ideas and preliminary decisions that you came up with and bounce them off other people.

Suppose that Breanna decided that she's going to pre-purchase inventory from various wholesalers and then pack and ship customer orders herself. This way, she can make more money for every item she sells versus drop shipping. She has big, big — gigantic! — plans for her boutique, even while it's still just a side hustle. So, why cut into her profit on each and every item that she sells?

Makes sense, right? But Breanna's friend Diane has had the nickname "One thing's wrong Diane" ever since she was in high school. Almost every time someone tells Diane about some a job opportunity or plans for a vacation or even a new relationship, Diane listens and then says something along the lines of "Okay, but what about. . . ." And you know what? More often than not, Diane has a pretty good point to make that a friend or relative of hers hadn't yet considered!

Diane may sound like a downer. But when it comes to being a sounding board when a friend, like Breanna, is barreling down the train track, Diane is a great resource. Finishing up your brainstorming with a couple of other people who, like Diane, have a natural ability to zero in on possible problems or even just something that you hadn't yet thought about can really help you fine-tune your plans, even while you're still at the brainstorming stage.

Transforming Your Initial Brainstorming into Your Value Chain

In the world of big business, consultants and business analysts spend a lot of time figuring out an organization's *value chain*. In the simplest terms, a value chain is all the interconnected activities that you need to orchestrate in your business to bring whatever you're selling to your customers.

Okay, hold on a minute: You're getting ready to do a side hustle, not work on your MBA or go to work for a consulting firm or a Fortune 500 company. What's with all this fancy business school lingo?

REMEMBER

You can apply the basic concept of a value chain to not only help you figure out the critical aspects of your side hustle, but also help you avoid skipping over very important decision points.

Figure 4-1 shows how you can diagram your side hustle's value chain, using the same kind of model that big-time consultants use for their clients, called an *organization diagram*.

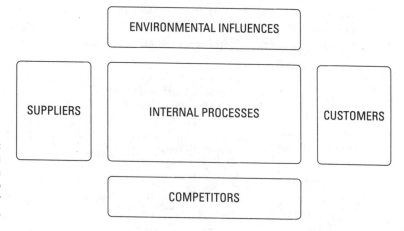

FIGURE 4-1:
Using an organization diagram to document your value chain.

TECHNICAL STUFF

If you really want to dig into the down-and-dirty details of how to use an organization diagram to document your side hustle's value chain, see the book *Business Process Change*, 3rd Edition, by Paul Harmon (Morgan Kaufmann Publishers).

In the middle of your diagram, you have your *internal processes* — basically, the major functions that you'll need to sew together to make your side hustle actually operate.

To the left of your internal processes, you'll find your suppliers, and to the right of your internal processes, you'll see your customers. Basically, if you go left-to-right across your diagram, you'll see how raw materials or products or jobs make their way into your side hustle, followed by what happens inside of your business, and then how you reach and then sell or provide services to your customers.

Your side hustle doesn't exist in a vacuum, however. On the top of your diagram, you'll document the most significant *environmental influences* that are likely to impact your side hustle. Think in terms of "major trends" such as more people shopping online or some new technology that has a direct bearing on your side hustle, or even some overall economic or societal factor (such as the start of the COVID-19 pandemic or the easing of pandemic-related restrictions) that could impact your side hustle.

Finally, on the bottom of your diagram, you'll list the competitors to whatever you're doing for your side hustle.

TIP

Think of "competitors" in a general sense. Sarah, who is creating a custom jewelry side hustle, doesn't need to list every single person or company who is also doing custom jewelry. But she can list major categories of competitors such as "other online boutiques" and "people with booths at arts-and-crafts fairs."

Want to see a value chain in action? Take a look at Figure 4-2, which is what Sarah came up with as she transitioned her free-form brainstorming into a much more formal, end-to-end blueprint for her custom jewelry side hustle.

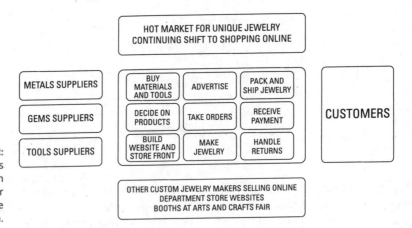

FIGURE 4-2: Sarah's organization diagram for her side-hustle value chain.

Sarah has identified three major types of suppliers that she'll need for her side hustle:

>> Places where she'll go to buy silver, copper, gold, and other metals that she needs for her jewelry

>> Places where she'll buy emeralds, sapphires, rubies, and other gems

>> Places where she can buy the tools that she needs to make her jewelry

REMEMBER

Will she be able to go to, say, one supplier for both metals and gems? Perhaps. At this stage of her side hustle, she doesn't need to identify specific companies or people as her suppliers; she can stick with "categories" of suppliers and then fill in the details later.

On the right side of the diagram, Sarah can get away with just having a large box labeled "Customers" to document that she'll be selling her jewelry to, well, customers. Down the road, though, suppose that Sarah's side hustle gets large enough that she winds up selling her jewelry not only to individual customers, but maybe to other businesses who buy dozens of pieces at a time that they, in turn, resell. At that point, she would adjust her diagram to reflect both "individual customers" and "business customers" because very likely, her internal processes will be at least slightly different for these two different types of customers. For now, though, she can keep her diagram on the simple side.

On the top of the diagram, Sarah documents the environmental influences that have significant impact on her side hustle. She's identified two:

>> From everything that she has read and studied, the market for unique custom-made jewelry is hotter than ever.

>> Not unsurprisingly, more people are shopping and buying online than ever before.

At the bottom of her diagram, Sarah identifies the major categories of businesses against which she will be competing for business. Sarah is hardly alone when it comes to selling custom jewelry online; plenty of other side hustlers and more than a few full-timers are doing exactly the same thing, so she starts with "other custom jewelry makers selling online." Who else is a competitor? Nordstrom, Macy's, Nieman Marcus, and all the big department stores also sell jewelry online. Finally, even though Sarah is selling only online for now, prospective customers also go to arts-and-crafts festivals and buy custom-made jewelry there.

What about the core of Sarah's side hustle? In the middle of her diagram, she shows the nine major high-level business functions that she needs to do as part of her side hustle, starting with buying materials and tools and continuing all the way through receiving payments from customers and handling returns. She'll need to flesh out each of these processes, listing exactly how she'll find the suppliers from which she'll buy her materials, and how she'll ship her orders (FedEx? UPS? U.S. Postal Service?), and what her return policies will be. But for now, she has documented that she *will* be doing these various functions and that she *will* need to work out the details.

How about another example? Sandy's side hustle is buying baseball and other sports cards, and then selling those cards for a profit. Figure 4-3 shows Sandy's value chain.

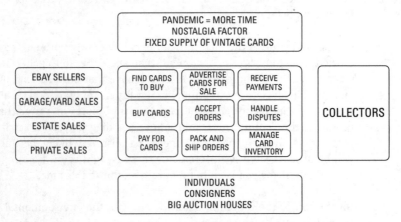

FIGURE 4-3: Sandy's organization diagram for his side hustle.

At first glance, Sandy's value chain looks very similar to Sarah's. Both Sandy and Sarah will buy "things" from "somewhere" that they will sell to customers (though in Sandy's case, he uses the term *collectors* for his customers, because he'll be selling to sports card collectors). Their specific environmental influences at the top of their respective diagrams differ from one another, as do their competitors, but both Sandy's and Sarah's side hustles are impacted by environmental influences, and they both have competitors.

REMEMBER

Inside their side hustles, however, you start to see a few significant differences. Even though both Sarah and Sandy need to reach prospective customers, take orders, collect money, and handle issues such as a dispute over a specific baseball card's quality (Sandy) or a customer returning a necklace (Sarah), Sarah will be making everything that she sells, while Sandy is acting as more of a middleman and won't be doing anything to what he buys and then resells.

If Sandy and Sarah fleshed out their respective side hustles, you would see more and more differences between the two. But for planning purposes, they're both at the right level of detail for now.

What about gig-economy side hustles? Isn't this whole value-chain thing overkill if you're not going to be buying and selling products, or making anything, or trying to monetize videos?

Well, sort of. But at the same time, your side hustle still has a value chain, even if you're going to be providing services rather than selling products. Take a look at Figure 4-4, which shows Cindy's value chain for her side hustle that will consist of doing weekend bartending gigs.

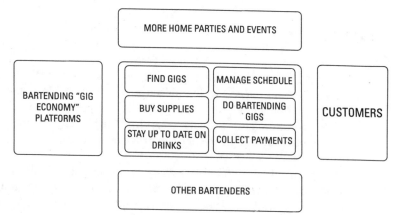

FIGURE 4-4: Cindy's organization diagram for her side hustle.

Notice that Cindy still has one main supplier that will be crucial to her success — the side gig platforms such as GigSmart and Gigsmash.com where Cindy will list her bartending services and through which people will find and then hire her.

Even beyond making note of the platforms that will supply her with bartending gigs, Cindy also documents that she sees a bright future for her side hustle because of people holding more home parties and events (maybe with an easing of pandemic restrictions?).

As for competition, Cindy technically isn't directly competing for business against anyone. True, on GigSmart, Gigsmash.com, and other platforms where Cindy will have a listing, so too will dozens or even hundreds of other bartenders for hire. But Cindy won't find herself in any sort of drink-making competition, facing off against two or three other people as they all compete against one another to bartend at somebody's party coming up in a couple of weeks. Still, she does note on her diagram that "other bartenders" are, in the larger sense, her competitors.

Notice also that the inside of Cindy's side hustle is a little bit simpler than Sandy's and Sarah's are. Cindy's has six major functions, starting with finding gigs and ending with collecting payments. Still, she needs to document these "buckets" of tasks because eventually she'll note, for example, that if she gets hired through her listing on one of the gig-related platforms, she gets paid by the platform (after they take their cut) rather than directly by the people for whom she did the bartending.

REMEMBER

Details, details, details. . . . But hey, even if a side hustle is a very small business, it's *still* a business. And you don't run a business of any type without digging into and fleshing out these details during your planning.

Risky Business

One of the first movies that actor Tom Cruise made was the 1983 film *Risky Business.* In the movie, Cruise played a high school kid named Joel who puts together a one-night-only side hustle at his parents' house offering (ahem) "adult entertainment" to make enough money to pay for the damages that he accidentally caused to his father's expensive sports car.

Joel encounters all kinds of risks setting up and then doing his one-night side hustle. You, too, will likely encounter a lot of risks, even if your particular side hustle idea won't be anywhere near as risqué as the one that Tom Cruise's character sets up in that classic film.

Sarah has done her brainstorming, both on her own and using a couple of her best friends for I-swear-I'll-give-you-my-honest-opinion feedback. She took her somewhat loosey-goosey brainstorming ideas and fleshed them out into the value chain that you see documented in Figure 4-2. So, now what?

WARNING

Sarah will face plenty of risks all along the yellow brick road from Sarah's suppliers to her customers, and covering everything that Sarah needs to do on the inside of her side hustle. Not only does Sarah need to think through and then document as many risks as she can, but she also needs to come up with a *mitigation strategy* to counteract each one.

Table 4-1 shows some of the risks that Sarah identifies for her custom jewelry side hustle, along with how she plans to counteract each one and keep her side hustle from running into trouble.

Even if you're doing gig-economy side jobs, you should still think through and jot down your risks. Suppose you're thinking about doing ridesharing. The more you drive, the more money you'll make, right? But also the more you drive, then statistically the greater the chance of your being in a car accident, simply because you've spent significantly more hours on highways and city streets.

TABLE 4-1 **Sarah's Risks and Mitigation Strategy for Her Custom Jewelry Side Hustle**

Risk	Mitigation
Supply-chain issues (suppliers out of materials, gems, tools)	Have backup suppliers.
Supply quality issues	"Two-strikes" policy — if a supplier has quality issues more than once, move on to a backup supplier.
Difficulty finding customers online	Take social media marketing course and test out various channels (Facebook, Instagram, Google Ads) with different types of ads.
Supply costs go up	Try to increase prices to cover costs, but be prepared to drop a product if it can't be made profitably.

WARNING

And then, if you're in an accident while you have a passenger in your vehicle, guess what: lawsuit time! You need to increase your auto insurance to make sure you're covered, and maybe even pay for a special *rideshare insurance* policy (see www.nerdwallet.com/blog/insurance/best-ridesharing-insurance). So, even if you're "only" doing ridesharing services, you *do* have risks, and you *do* need a mitigation strategy for each risk that you should get into place before you start your side hustle!

The Best of Times, the Worst of Times

If you think that this whole planning process is getting increasingly tedious and too detail-oriented, I have good news for you: Just like when you started your planning with free-flowing brainstorming, you can go back to letting your mind run free — at least for a little bit.

Take a look down the road, maybe a year from now, maybe two years, or maybe longer. Picture the absolutely best-case outcome for your side hustle. *Everything* falls in your favor. You don't make a single mistake, and you don't get caught blindsided by an economic downturn or any other environmental change. Competitors? Yeah, they're out there, but you have more business than you can handle anyway!

Breanna already touched on her "best of times" vision during her brainstorming, even if she didn't realize it at the time. When confirming that she needed to start her boutique with a warehouse and office in her spare bedroom, she also could clearly picture a time when her side hustle had grown into a full-time business with a physical retail location adjoining a large warehouse area, where dozens of her employees would be hard at work filling hundreds or even thousands of online customer orders every day. That's a great aspiration for Breanna, and as she proceeds with her planning, she can keep this vision in mind and think about what needs to happen to make that dream a reality.

But at the same time, Breanna also needs to throw a bucket of ice cold water on her vision by asking herself: What's the doomsday scenario here? If everything goes wrong, what's the worst that can happen?

At a high level, the answer to the "worst of times" question is pretty straightforward: Breanna's business might eventually cease to exist, and she will have lost a bunch of money. But she needs to dig a big deeper: What exactly would have to go wrong to bring about her colossal failure? How about:

>> Selecting and buying a bunch of products that only a handful of people (or maybe nobody at all!) wanted to buy

>> Setting prices either too high (nobody bought her jewelry) or too low (she sold a lot, but wound up losing money for all her time and effort)

>> Choosing the wrong suppliers who delivered late, sent her poor-quality gems, or maybe even took her money and didn't even deliver anything

>> Spending a lot of money on social-media advertising but getting very few views and even fewer clicks

Okay, that's depressing enough. Breanna needs to keep going with her list of everything that might go wrong for the sake of completeness, but you get the idea.

REMEMBER

Use this little exercise as a checkpoint for everything that you've done so far in your planning, and also for your remaining steps. First, look at your sun-always-shining vision of side hustle utopia and ask yourself:

>> **How realistic is this vision?** Can you actually see this fantastic future happening, or are you out in La La Land envisioning a totally unrealistic future?

>> **Even though you're starting your side hustle off on a small scale, are you paying attention to what it will take to eventually grow into what you're envisioning?** Are you serious about tedious-but-necessary aspects of your side hustle business such as record keeping (see Chapter 9) and professionally handling your business finances (see Chapter 8)?

>> **On the other side of the coin, are you just "doing a part-time job" to earn a bit of extra money, and you're perfectly fine with ridesharing or doing delivery services and don't have any particular future side hustle aspirations?**

Then think about your doom-and-gloom picture in the context of the risks and mitigations that you've jotted down. Something would have happened to bring about failure, but what? Take a look at your risks, and if you now realize that you missed something, add it to the list along with how you intend to mitigate that newly added risk.

REMEMBER

Chances are, the future of your side hustle will fall somewhere between "total failure" and "rip-roaring success." You're trying to tilt the odds in your favor to land closer to the "success" side of the continuum than to the "failure" side.

Building Your Business Plan

Okay, back to the more formal side of your side hustle planning. Time to pull together your official side hustle business plan.

TIP

Think of all of the results of all the planning steps that you've done so far as pieces of an overall puzzle that you need to put together to create a recognizable picture. If you've ever done a jigsaw puzzle, you know that you typically start with a little portion of the overall puzzle in, say, the top left corner. Then maybe you shift to working on the bottom right side; then move to somewhere in the middle; and so on.

Your business plan is like a jigsaw puzzle. You have your brainstorming, your value chain, your risks and mitigation, and then both your glorious-days and disaster-days scenarios. Along the way, you've double-checked your side-hustle ideas against your personality. But these are all sort of the same as puzzle pieces, and it's time to connect all those pieces.

When it comes to business plans, you have a little bit of a challenge on your hands: If you put 10 people in a room, you'll get 20 opinions about what a business plan should look like!

You've probably come across this same problem when you worked on your résumé, with one person telling you to structure your résumé one way, and another person indignantly disagreeing and insisting that you write your résumé a totally different way!

REMEMBER

I have some good news for you when it comes to trying to make sense out of all the different guidance you'll find for how to write a business plan. For a side hustle, you have a lot more leeway in the order of topics that you cover — and even what you do and don't include — than if, say, you're putting together a business plan in search of a large bank loan or millions of dollars of venture capital investment.

Maybe someday, if your side hustle really hits its stride and starts growing toward your best-of-times scenario, you'll have to worry about making sure that your business plan matches the structure that a bank or private equity firm or some venture capital company insists on seeing. For now, though, think in terms of pitching your side hustle to yourself — an audience of one. Are you painting a cohesive and compelling picture of how to get your side hustle going?

TIP

If your side hustle is a gig-economy job such as delivery services or ridesharing, you can probably skip over the whole business-plan stuff. However, if your gig services are along the lines of pet-sitting or bartending or doing handyman work — basically, if you're setting up a small-business structure even though you plan to land gigs from side hustle–oriented platforms — you should at least jot down bullet points for most of the business plan sections.

Your side hustle business plan should include the following sections.

A short overview and a really short elevator pitch

By now you should be to clearly articulate exactly what your side hustle is going to be, so write it down! In fact, write it down twice!

Start off your business plan with both:

» A one-paragraph (two paragraphs at most) highly summarized version of *every* key aspect of your side hustle

» A single-sentence elevator pitch that summarizes your summarized version (got that?) even more!

TECHNICAL STUFF

Having an *elevator pitch* means being able to describe an idea so persuasively in about the duration of the typical elevator ride that the person to whom you're talking is crystal clear about the most critical or unique aspects of your concept.

Sarah's business plan starts with:

> I will design, craft, and sell custom-made jewelry. I will build a Shopify site that I will promote using online marketing and advertising techniques such as Facebook and Instagram ads, Google Ads, and short demonstration videos on YouTube and TikTok that will link to my site. I will run the business out of my house. I've lined up primary and backup suppliers for all materials and tools.

Then she adds her elevator pitch:

> I will sell custom-made jewelry from my Shopify site that I will promote through a variety of online ads.

As Sarah works her way through the rest of her business plan, she can refer back to this section and adjust the wording as necessary. For now, though, she has placed a stake into the fertile side-hustle soil and is ready to start planting.

Your time commitment

Your business plan is for a side hustle, so you need to be crystal clear with yourself exactly how much time you plan to spend on your venture. Plus, if you have specific time constraints such as "only evenings after work" or "only on weekends" or "only on Wednesday evening and all day Saturday," you need to go on the record for these constraints.

REMEMBER

As you go through the rest of your business plan, you now have an "official statement" that describes your available time that you can use as a sanity check for your side hustle's details.

TECHNICAL STUFF

For example, suppose you plan to do software development on the side. However, because of extra hours you need to work at your full-time job, you only have about 15 hours a week available for your side hustle. You can certainly take on a little bit of software development here and there, but you'll need to focus on shorter-duration tasks such as building template-based websites or doing some light software configuration rather than heavy-duty application development.

If you don't have a full-time job and instead have a portfolio of several different side hustles, documenting your available time is still important to help make sure that your side hustles don't clash with each other with conflicting demands for your time.

Your schedule and major milestones

How long will it take Breanna to line up her wholesalers for clothing and accessories?

How many bartending-related videos will Miguel create before he uploads his first batch to his YouTube channel?

How many community college classes will Jack teach during the first semester of his side hustle?

At what point does Sandy plan to branch out from buying baseball and sports cards into other sports collectibles?

When and under what circumstances will Breanna move her boutique out of her house into a separate business facility? And will that facility be for warehousing only, or will she also open a retail business?

Whatever your side hustle is, you have a longer-term plan in mind. Maybe your longer-term plan is built around expanding your business, or maybe you have no intentions of growing your business at all and you just intend to get a little business up and running and keep it going. No matter what your timeline looks like, document it all in your business plan along with key milestones and decision points along that timeline.

Key players in your side hustle

Who exactly are Breanna's wholesale suppliers? Who are her key points of contact — the actual people — at each one of those wholesalers?

Sandy will try to sell his higher-value sports cards and collectibles through an auction house rather than on eBay, but which auction house? More than one?

Sarah's metals and tools suppliers, the gig job sites that Cindy will use to land bartending jobs, the video-editing service that Mark will use to edit and polish his small business accounting videos . . . you get the idea.

REMEMBER

No matter what your side hustle is, and even if you're going solo, you'll almost certainly be involved with other people and companies at some point. Write all these details down in your business plan, including any designated backup companies or services that you may switch to at some point.

Your customers

You need to identify who will comprise your *target market* (the people to whom you'll try to sell your products or watch your videos or take your course, or for whom you'll provide weekend landscaping or bartending services, or whatever your side hustle is).

Sometimes, your target market can (and should) be as broad as possible. After all, if you have a potential customer out there somewhere in the world, why not try to attract that person to your business? For example, Breanna will sell clothing and accessories online to "the world at large" — basically, anybody who wants to place an order on Breanna's website for a blouse or leisurewear or a necklace can do so. Breanna might get to know some of her regular customers, but for the most part these customers will be anonymous to her.

In other situations, you should narrow your target market to better focus on catching the attention of a person or another business even more likely to be in your side hustle "sweet spot." For example, Sarah's customer base will be the same as Breanna's, at least initially. At some point down the road, Sarah may wholesale her jewelry to other online and in-person retailers for them to retail. At that point, Sarah needs to go back and adjust her business plan to more precisely target certain customers — maybe not specific names of people and businesses, but at least descriptions of the types of retailers to which she'll sell her jewelry.

Startup money, budget, and financial projections

Chapter 8 discusses the financial aspects of your side hustle in detail: how much startup capital you'll need, how to budget, how to forecast sales and expenses, and more. Your business plan needs to include the key aspects of the financial side of your side hustle.

TIP

Pretend that you're pitching your side hustle to an investor, and you also happen to be that investor. Convince yourself that you have all your financial ducks in a row.

How you'll operate

The inner portion of the organization diagram that you use to document your value chain (refer to Figure 4-1) contains the high-level business processes through which you'll operate your side hustle.

Now it's time to add more detail to each. For example, Sarah's value chain (refer to Figure 4-2) has nine internal processes: buying materials and tools, deciding on her product list, building her website and storefront, and so on. Sarah needs to take each of those nine boxes and decompose its process into the underlying steps that she'll do. She can simply list the steps as bullet points or a numbered list.

Risks and mitigation

Remember those risks and mitigations that you pulled together (see Table 4-1)? You can drop that table right into your business plan.

However, now is a great time to take a fresh look at those risks and, for each, list how you intend to counteract and neutralize the risk. As you've been working through your business plan, you may have come across a new risk or two, or come up with a new mitigation strategy for a risk that you've already documented. So, spend a little bit of time and take a fresh look at your list, and make any necessary updates.

TIP

You can check out *Creating a Business Plan For Dummies* by Veechi Curtis (Wiley) for much more information about business plan structure and content, especially if your side hustle really catches on and you're looking to take it to that mythical "next level."

IN THIS CHAPTER

» **Identifying the questions you need answered**

» **Defining success versus failure from your test-drive**

» **Factoring in the fun factor**

» **Setting the duration of your test-drive**

» **Looking at some example side-hustle test-drives**

Chapter **5**

Taking Your Side Hustle for a Test-Drive

So far, your journey into side-hustle land is in great shape. You've transformed your initial high-level concept into a very specific side-hustle idea (see Chapter 2) and then made sure that your personality is a good match for your planned side-hustle adventures (see Chapter 3). Your side-hustle ducks are now in a row to get up and running (see Chapter 4).

So, now you're all set to hit the side-hustle highway at full speed, right?

Well, sort of.

Before you hit the throttle and kick your side hustle into high gear, you really should take your side hustle out for a test-drive.

When you buy a car, you take the car out for a test-drive, right? You want to see for yourself how comfortable the car is for you and your passengers, how it steers, how fast it accelerates, and what the braking is like. If you're a smart car shopper, you do your test-drive *before* you write a check or take out a gigantic car loan — basically, before you make a huge commitment.

Test-driving your side hustle should follow the same model as taking a car out for a test-drive. You want to:

>> See if, even after all your planning, you still have some big unknowns that you need to figure out before proceeding.

>> Decide how long you need for a meaningful test-drive for your side hustle.

>> Know in advance what defines a successful test-drive versus one that tells you that your side hustle may not be as rewarding as you originally thought.

>> Determine if you're having fun and if the time you devote to your side hustle will turn out to be enjoyable — at least to some extent — or if it will be a total downer for your mental state.

Questions, Questions, and More Questions

Your side-hustle plans may be in place, but chances are, you still have a few — or maybe more than a few! — big questions that you need answered. You probably made a number of assumptions in your side-hustle planning. How good of a job did you do with those assumptions? Before you jump big time into your side hustle, you need answers to questions such as the following:

>> Those suppliers that you lined up — will they deliver the quality products they say they offer? Will they fill the orders in the time frame that they promise they can? Will they be as friendly and cooperative as they claim if they ship you defective merchandise that you need to return?

>> You're convinced that your YouTube videos will be wildly popular and generate a decent amount of advertising revenue. Will they? Will you be able to draw enough subscribers to your channel? Will viewers like and "upvote" your videos, or will you actually wind up with a bunch of "downvotes" and maybe a lot of really nasty comments indicating that people don't particularly like your content?

>> You sign up to do ridesharing or delivery services with a new company that promises almost all your trips will be in your part of town. Will that actually be the case? Or will you really wind up driving through rush-hour traffic and bad weather to a distant part of your metro area?

» Your friends and family tell you that they absolutely love the jewelry you make, and they've been telling you for the past couple years that you should try to sell your products at arts-and-crafts fairs and online. Will other people like your jewelry as much as your friends and family say they do? Can you really make enough jewelry in your spare time to make it worthwhile to try to sell some? And if you price your jewelry to give you a reasonable profit for your time and effort, will potential customers think that your prices are too high?

» Your side hustle will be buying bargain-priced collectibles at garage sales and from estate sales, and then "flipping" those items online for a profit. But will you actually find the right items at the right price? And if you do find what you think are good buys, will they actually sell at a profit on eBay and other sites, or will you wind up having to sell at a loss?

No matter what your side hustle idea is, go back through everything you did to get your plans in place. What assumptions did you make about suppliers, customers, pricing, or how long you need to make your products? You think you understand the ins and outs of advertising on Facebook, Instagram, and other social media, but will your ads generate enough clicks or even be seen?

REMEMBER

Write down a comprehensive list of every single question for which you want a concrete answer, and then methodically work your way through that list as you proceed with your side hustle test-drive.

Establishing Success Criteria for Your Side-Hustle Test-Drive

When you take a car out for a test-drive, you usually have a good idea what will make you want to buy the car, as well as what will make you hand the keys back to the salesperson with a firm "No thanks, not for me." The car was or wasn't comfortable, it accelerated like a champ or went from 0 to 60 in about as long as it takes to cook dinner, and so on.

Before you even begin your side-hustle test-drive, you need to establish very specific criteria for what defines success versus failure, or at least success versus "Wait a minute, I need to take a closer look at this whole idea."

Depending on your specific side hustle, "success" during your test-drive could mean

>> Reaching or exceeding a specific amount of sales

>> Reaching or exceeding some specific number of clicks or views for online content

>> Not exceeding a specific total cost that you set as your budget for products that you're making or buying

>> Recording, editing, and uploading some target number of videos to validate that you can create online content at the pace that you've decided your side hustle requires

What about side-hustle test-drive failure? Basically, reverse each of the preceding success criteria:

>> Your sales short of the target that you set — maybe way short.

>> Not many people are viewing your videos or clicking links on your website that could earn you affiliate marketing revenue.

>> You blow your budget buying or making products, which means that your profit margins will be far less than you thought — or maybe you wind up losing money even if you can sell a large number of products.

>> Recording, editing, and uploading some target number of videos takes way longer than you had thought, and it's far more difficult than you had envisioned.

How Much Fun Are You Having?

Some side hustles can be lots of fun, especially if you're monetizing a long-time hobby. Did you collect baseball and sports cards as a kid? Jumping back into the hobby by going to trade shows and garage sales and scouring the Internet to find reasonably priced cards that you can resell for a profit can be a lot of fun. You get to check out hundreds or thousands of classic old cards, even if you only purchase a tiny fraction of what you actually look at. Maybe you then start doing a podcast or create a YouTube channel about your hobby experiences, and you not only make a little bit of extra money, but you also make new friends who share your interests.

Maybe you've been into exercise and health ever since you were a teenager. Now you're side hustling in the exercise and health realm by teaching yoga classes on the weekend, and you're getting ready to launch a YouTube channel for your yoga classes, as well as a small online storefront to sell "athleisure" clothing. So far, you're only making a little bit of money — barely enough to cover your costs. But you're having a blast!

On the other side of the coin, say that you're a software developer by trade, and you decide that you're going to blog about software tips and tricks and maybe even write a book about so-called best practices for a programming language called Python. You write a blog every Friday during the two-month period that you've designated for your side-hustle test-drive, and you also write the first three chapters of your planned book. But along the way, you discover something that you didn't know before: You hate writing! Do you really want to keep forging ahead, committed to doing something every single week that you really dislike? Maybe, or maybe not.

Your side-hustle test-drive is an important checkpoint for you to really see if you enjoy — or at least can tolerate — key aspects of your side hustle:

>> Your focal point (such as health and exercise, sports memorabilia, fashion, or real estate)

>> Exactly what you're doing for your side-hustle focal point (for example, selling products, creating and monetizing online content, gig-economy work, teaching, and so on)

>> Whether difficulties and challenges in your side hustle really take away from your overall enjoyment or are just bumps in the road that you can easily deal with

Deciding How Long Your Test-Drive Should Be

Will one month be long enough to test out your online boutique side hustle? Probably not. What about two months? Three months? Longer?

What about trying out ridesharing, or some delivery service gig? Do you think you'll have a pretty good idea about the good and bad points after a week or two? A month?

Just as your test-drive for a new car will be for a finite amount of time, your side-hustle test-drive should also be "time-boxed" just long enough for you to get the answers to your big questions, to decide if side-hustle success is likely on the horizon, and to see if what you're about to jump into is really as enjoyable as you thought it would be.

Checking Out Some Side-Hustle Test-Drives

Side-hustle test-drives are like side hustles themselves: They come in lots of different shapes and sizes. Take a look at the following examples to get an idea of what a test-drive might look like for a side hustle that you're interested in pursuing. Even if your side hustle doesn't neatly fall into one of these categories, you can draw upon the examples to see how you can do your own customized test-drive.

Creating videos to monetize online content

Miguel's side hustle is creating and uploading weekly 5- to 10-minute videos to YouTube about drink recipes, wine tastings, and home beer brewing. When it comes to all these bartending-related topics, Miguel definitely knows his stuff. For his side-hustle business planning, he already wrote a list of 100 different videos that he knows he can create, so he's confident that he won't run short on content, at least for the next two years. He's ready for a test-drive, so here he goes!

Questions that Miguel needs to answer

Miguel has a couple of pretty big unknowns when it comes to his side hustle:

- » Can he really record, edit, and publish one high-quality video every single week?

- » Miguel has his witty, engaging dialogue for a bunch of his videos already "written" in his mind, but when he actually records his videos, will he really be as polished and professionally approachable as he sees himself?

- » Miguel knows that online content success almost never happens overnight and that building an audience takes time, but will he actually be able to reach the number of subscribers that he'll need to start monetizing his content?

Miguel's test-drive success criteria

Miguel keeps it simple: He directly aligns his success criteria with each of these key questions and unknowns.

The first item — recording, editing, and publishing one high-quality video every week — comes with a very straightforward yes-or-no answer. At the end of his test-drive, Miguel either achieved this goal — and, thus, addressed that big unknown — or he didn't.

Miguel's second unknown — if his final edited videos will feature a smooth-talking, engaging star, rather than someone awkwardly stumbling through a painful five or ten minutes of video — doesn't come with as clear-cut of an answer as his first item. Miguel will certainly take a close look at each of the videos that he creates, but is he really the best judge?

Miguel decides to enlist several of his friends who swear that they'll give him honest — maybe even brutally honest — feedback about his videos. If every third word Miguel utters is *um*, they'll let him know. If Miguel has a tendency to wander off on a tangent and leave his viewers wondering "what the . . .?," they'll let him know. If Miguel habitually inserts obscure pop-culture references that are more distracting than engaging, they'll let him know. If Miguel has a tendency to forget a step or two and then try to backtrack on the fly, yep, they'll let him know.

Miguel's "critical review team" will give him a thumbs-up or thumbs-down on how polished of a social media star he really is, along with specific suggestions for where Miguel can improve his on-camera performance. They'll also critique the video quality, the backdrops and settings that Miguel uses, everything!

The third unknown that will help establish whether Miguel's side hustle test-drive was successful — whether he can build an audience — is much less within his control than the first two. Miguel can study up on social media marketing and advertising. He can precisely target Google and social media ads to try to steer people to his videos. But will people actually find and watch his videos? And if someone does find and watch one of his videos, will that person then subscribe to his YouTube channel? Miguel will learn the answers to these critical questions by studying the results of those first videos he publishes. He'll find out

>> How many people begin watching his published videos (which will be a great indicator of how effective Miguel's social media advertising is)

>> If people watch his videos to the end or only watch for a few seconds and then stop viewing

>> How many of his viewers actually subscribe to his YouTube channel

REMEMBER

Metrics! Statistics! Numbers! Miguel needs to dig into the data from his test-drive to be able to figure out if those polished and well-edited videos are actually resonating with his target audience.

The duration of Miguel's side-hustle test-drive

Miguel carefully considers all the unknowns and questions that he needs to address. How long does he think he'll need to be able to determine success — or lack thereof — for each one?

Miguel thinks about it and then thinks some more. And then he decides to designate a four-month test-drive for his side hustle. Why?

>> Four months will mean about 17 videos. By then, he'll know for sure if he can actually create, edit, and then upload one video every single week.

>> Four months will also give him enough time to "find his voice" and see if he can meet the level of quality that he knows is essential to build and hold an audience. Miguel knows that his first couple of videos will almost certainly be less polished than his later ones, simply because he's never done these types of videos before. His friends will give him the brutally honest feedback that he needs and that he has requested, and he'll edit out anything really terrible before he uploads to YouTube. But even his first couple finished products are likely to be a bit rocky. By the end of four months, though, Miguel will be able to tell if this type of side hustle is a good match for him.

>> Four months is also sufficient time for Miguel to see if his number of views and the number of subscribers to his channel is on an upward trajectory. Four months may still not be enough time for him to hit the number of subscribers and meet the other criteria he needs to be able to monetize his videos. But Miguel knows that he started from a big, fat zero, and he can certainly chart the trajectory from where he began to where he ends up at the four-month point. If Miguel is closing in on meeting the monetization criteria, and if viewer engagement (the number of "likes" and comments on each video, for example) is steadily improving, then he can declare that his test-drive has been successful for this evaluation item.

Is Miguel having fun?

When Miguel first came up with his idea for weekly bartending-related videos, the whole concept seemed as if it would be a lot of fun. Now, after spending four whole months of late nights and weekends recording and re-recording; editing and then editing some more; uploading and then fixing upload problems, well, is Miguel having as much fun as he thought? Only he can answer that question.

Where does Miguel go from here?

Four months have flown by, and Miguel's side hustle test-drive has hit the finish line. Now what?

Miguel looks at all the things that he was checking out during his test-drive, and what he learned. Suppose that:

>> Even though Miguel struggled a little bit as he created and edited his first four or five videos, the process quickly became much smoother as time went on. By the final month of his test-drive, Miguel was taking about half the time to create, edit, and upload each video that he did at the beginning. The verdict? Success!

>> Truthfully, Miguel's first couple of videos were a bit rocky, quality-wise. Fortunately, Miguel practices what he preaches and is a quick learner. When he friends gave him the brutally honest feedback that he asked them to provide, he took their advice to heart and, with a lot of practice, began doing a much better job on each of his videos. The verdict? Success!

>> Viewer engagement definitely improved during the duration of the test-drive, but Miguel still fell short of where he had hoped to be. He has 400 subscribers to his YouTube channel as opposed to his 700 subscriber projection. So, failure? Maybe not. Miguel studies the analytics available to him and sees that he ended the first month of his test-drive with only 20 subscribers, had only 50 by the end of the second month, and had 100 at the end of the third month, but he gained 300 subscribers during the fourth month, so his trajectory is looking pretty good, at least for now. He also sees that many of his earlier videos only had 20 or 30 views until a couple of weeks ago, but now most of them have hundreds of views, which means that new subscribers (and probably other YouTube users who aren't subscribers) are going back to take a look at these earlier videos, which will increase Miguel's "watch hours" (critical to being able to monetize his channel). The verdict? Maybe not total success at this point, but not a failure, either!

Miguel has one more key test-drive item to grade: Is he having fun? Well, mostly. The videos were a real chore for the first month, but now that he's recording them with fewer takes and he can edit and upload them in about the half the time that he originally took, the whole side hustle isn't the drudgery it started out to be. True, he's not making any money yet, but he doesn't start recording his latest video with "Oh man, here we go again — I guess I gotta do this" swirling around in his head, either. The verdict? Miguel will give the "fun factor" a thumbs-up.

Taking all this information into consideration, Miguel makes the decision on his bartending video side hustle: Forge ahead! He can just keep doing exactly what he's been doing: Uploading one new video each week, and maybe bumping up the social media advertising aimed at his target audience to try to gain more viewers and subscribers.

What might have brought Miguel to a different conclusion? Suppose that:

>> Instead of creating and uploading 17 videos by the end of his test-drive, he was only able to complete 9 videos, so about one every two weeks instead of weekly.

>> Despite the coaching from his friends, Miguel's videos just aren't all that good. Viewers are posting lots of snarky comments about Miguel and his delivery style, which certainly won't help build a loyal, long-term subscriber base.

>> Miguel only reaches 100 subscribers in four months, far short of his target of 700.

>> Miguel has to admit to himself that even though he started this side hustle with a lot of enthusiasm and some pretty lofty goals, he isn't having any fun at all.

If one or more of these evaluations were true, maybe it would be time for Miguel to look for a different side hustle.

Making and selling your own products

Sarah wants to start an online boutique side hustle like her friend Breanna. Instead of buying products from wholesalers that she'll then sell, however, Sarah will make her own jewelry that she'll post on her storefront to sell. Yep, you've got it: Sarah has bitten off a pretty big side-hustle chunk, so her test-drive is critically important.

Questions that Sarah needs to answer

Sarah needs to figure out:

>> If orders come flooding in — which, of course, is a good thing — can she keep up with the demand, given that she has to make each piece of jewelry that she's going to sell?

>> After covering the cost of her materials and other business costs (such as her website and social media marketing), will the amount of money Sarah makes from her boutique be worth the time that she'll spend on all aspects of her business, even beyond making the jewelry?

>> At heart, Sarah is an artist, which is why she chose custom jewelry as the focal point for her side hustle. Will she be able to keep up with the business side of her side hustle — record-keeping, sales tax filings, invoicing, banking, and everything else covered in Chapters 7, 8, 9, and 10?

Sarah's test-drive success criteria

Just as Miguel did, Sarah aligns her test-drive success criteria with those big, big questions that she needs to answer. Which means:

>> Sarah has already decided on a two-week maximum turnaround to fill any order. She expects to receive somewhere between five and ten orders a day when her business gets going. Will she be able to meet the two-week turnaround time, or will she need to contact customers to tell them that their orders will take longer to complete and ship?

>> Sarah will tally up all her costs throughout the test-drive period, and also add up all her income. She'll keep track of how many hours she spends making jewelry, as well as how many hours she spends running her business. Then she'll do the math and figure out how much money she's actually making per hour. She doesn't have any set hourly rate in mind. But she does want to see if, say, she winds up netting only about $2 or $3 per hour for all that time, to see if it's worth continuing.

>> Hiring someone to run the business side of her side hustle isn't really doable right now, so Sarah knows that she has to do all the administrative and financial stuff herself. By the end of the test-drive, has she done a decent job keeping good records? Has she filed her monthly state and local sales tax forms on time? Looking ahead to income tax time next year, will she have a nightmare on her hands trying to reconstruct her side-hustle income and expenses?

The duration of Sarah's side-hustle test-drive

Sarah realizes that getting her Shopify storefront up and running will take about a month. She also knows that social media marketing takes a while to get going and fine-tune. She also needs to line up main and backup suppliers for the materials she needs to make her jewelry.

The good news for Sarah is that unlike Miguel and his YouTube videos, she doesn't have any sort of "production quota" to her jewelry side hustle. Her business model calls for custom-making jewelry only after somebody orders something. She'll have a few of each item on hand as samples of her work, but she's already made most of those items even before officially starting her side hustle. Eventually, she'll preemptively make additional pieces to take to local arts-and-crafts festivals; but that part of her side hustle will be down the road a ways.

So, if Sarah needs, say, two to three months to get her Shopify site going and for her social media marketing to start to yield results, from that point on, she can basically wait for orders to come in and then make and fulfill those orders one by one. Sarah has a fair amount of flexibility when it comes to the duration of her test-drive. On the one hand, if very few people wind up ordering jewelry, she probably doesn't want to keep running her Shopify site and other Internet services that cost her a couple hundred dollars every month; that would be just throwing away good money. On the other hand, if she can cover her business and tech costs with at least a few orders, then theoretically she could keep her side hustle going indefinitely, which tends to muddy the waters.

Still, does Sarah want to keep a side hustle alive that really isn't doing much business? As long as her business exists, she still needs to handle all those financial and administrative tasks that she really doesn't like to do. Sarah decides: "One year; I'll give this side hustle one year. If I'm up to my target of five to ten orders on average every day, and if I can stay on top of the work and meet my two-week turnaround, and if I'm making at least a little bit of money, I'll declare my test-drive a success and update my plans for the second year."

Is Sarah having fun?

Sarah also tells herself: "At the end of a year, if I can honestly tell myself that I enjoy this little jewelry business even though I need to spend a lot of time doing it, I'll feel good about keeping it going if all my other criteria look good."

Where does Sarah go from here?

One year passes and just like Miguel, Sarah takes stock at the end of her test-drive:

>> Sarah is actually receiving up to 20 orders some days, but on other days she receives only 2 or 3. Every so often, she finds herself falling behind by a day or two, but no more than that. The handful of customers she contacts to say "Your order will be a couple of days late, but I'll give you a 10 percent discount to thank you for your patience" mostly wind up buying even more items later on. So far, Sarah hasn't received a single complaint, nor has she had any orders canceled because of the occasional delay. The verdict? At least so far, she can do it! She can fill the orders on time, even as her side hustle is becoming more and more popular with each passing month.

>> One danger sign, though: What happens if Sarah's business continues to grow? Meeting her two-week turnaround all by herself, and still as a side business, may shift from "difficult" to "impossible"! At that point, Sarah needs to look at ways to either take her side hustle to the next level (see Chapter 15) or find some ways to slow the growth of her side hustle just to keep her customers happy — and herself sane!

>> At least right now, Sarah isn't exactly getting rich from her side hustle. But when she takes into account all her costs and revenues and balances them against her time spent, she's netting about $15 per hour. True, that's just about the same as a minimum-wage job, but at least she's not making only a couple dollars per hour or losing money. The verdict? Not really a big positive for Sarah's side hustle, but not a dealbreaker either.

>> Yeah, the business side of Sarah's side hustle is a total drag, but she has been able to keep up with all the tax and business filings, and her records look to be in good shape for income tax filings next month. The verdict? Well, not a lot of fun, but also not a dealbreaker.

>> For the most part, Sarah is having fun. She enjoys the artistry of designing and making jewelry. She has met a number of people and made a few new friends who share an interest in custom-made jewelry. When people ask Sarah what she does, she begins by mentioning her full-time job working at a local university but immediately adds "and I have a side business making custom jewelry." She honestly isn't trying to pitch her products to a potential customer; she truly enjoys the artistry of her side hustle and quickly (and proudly) tells almost anyone about her jewelry business. The verdict? Sarah absolutely *loves* what she's doing!

Sarah hits that one-year mark that she set for the end of her test-drive, and the path is crystal clear to her: Keep going!

Doing delivery services

Lori dove into the world of side hustles out of necessity, when her hours at a clothing store were cut in half at the start of the COVID-19 pandemic. Lori doesn't have any particular interests or hobbies that she's thinking about monetizing. More important, Lori needs to start side hustling *now* to try to make up her income shortfall from her hours being cut.

Fortunately for Lori, the gig economy exploded at the beginning of the pandemic as people hunkered down in their homes. Delivery services for groceries, pharmacy goods, and restaurant takeout meals became very popular, so Lori quickly signed up with Instacart.

REMEMBER

Even though the idea of a test-drive may seem silly for a gig-economy side hustle, Lori is still well advised to give her Instacart gig a test-drive.

Questions that Lori needs to answer

Lori needs to find out the following:

>> With Instacart, she needs to do the actual shopping, as well as delivering the goods. Truthfully, grocery shopping is one of those tasks that Lori doesn't really enjoy. But, hey, any port in a storm to try to make up her lost income, right?

>> How far will she find herself driving every day? Lori's car is starting to show its age. A few miles here and there wouldn't be a big deal, but a lot of miles could be a problem if she winds up needing any expensive repairs from overusing her car.

>> Lori knows that she'll be rated by customers, and her overall rating will factor into how much work she's given. She'll do her best, but how will people actually rate her, and what will that mean for her income?

Lori's test-drive success criteria

Lori's success criteria for her test-drive are pretty straightforward. At least for now, she's doing a side hustle out of necessity. So, as long as she's making enough money and she doesn't totally hate what she's doing, she'll keep going as long as she needs to.

The duration of Lori's side-hustle test-drive

Lori decides that by the end of two weeks she'll know enough to decide whether to continue working through Instacart or if she should consider other gig-economy side hustles, such as restaurant food delivery through Grubhub or DoorDash.

Is Lori having fun?

Fun? Ha! In Lori's case, "fun" isn't really a factor. A better way to evaluate her side-hustle test-drive is her second test-drive success criteria: As long as she doesn't totally hate what she's doing, she can keep going.

Where does Lori go from here?

Lori gets to the end of her two-week period. She didn't quite make up the difference of her lost income, but she came pretty close, and she's confident that she can pick up even more gigs in the weeks ahead to earn a little bit more money.

And although shopping and delivering groceries isn't exactly her dream job, after the first few days, she was able to adjust her frame of mind and started thinking, "It's decent money and even though the work isn't thrilling, it's not terrible."

The verdict? At least for now, keep going!

IN THIS CHAPTER

» **Unveiling your side hustle**

» **Watching your side-hustle calendar**

» **Watching for warning signs**

» **Facing up to side-hustle problems**

» **Playing side-hustle doctor**

Chapter **6**

Putting Your Side Hustle in High Gear

By this point, you're probably getting antsy. You came up with your side-hustle idea. You refined and added detail to that original side-hustle inspiration and made sure your personality was a good match for what you had in mind. You focused on all the nitty-gritty planning to dot your side hustle i's and cross your side hustle t's. You took your side hustle for a test-drive.

So, when can you launch your side hustle for real? Now! Do the side hustle!

Your Side Hustle Is Cleared for Takeoff

REMEMBER

Even though you've been test-driving your side hustle for a while, you need to formally transition from your test-drive to doing your side hustle for real. You need to

» Run down your checklist to make sure all your side-hustle ducks are in a row.

» Officially mark the date that you'll formally launch your side hustle.

» Publicize your side hustle's official launch.

Doing your preflight check

If you were a pilot about to take a plane up into the wild blue yonder, you would never fail to walk through your preflight checklist. Baggage? Stowed and secured. Navigation? All planned. Fuel quantity? Check. Flaps down? Check. Flight controls? Check.

You get the idea. While you're climbing to 10,000 feet or soaring over uninhabited desert, that's the wrong time to find out that you forgot to do something really important or that a key component of your plane is malfunctioning.

Treat your side hustle the same as you would an aircraft that you were flying. Thanks to all the thorough and diligent planning that you then validated during your test-drive, your side hustle *should* be "airworthy." Now make sure that it actually is!

Breanna is ready to formally launch her side hustle online boutique following a three-month test run. What does her "preflight" side-hustle checklist look like? How about:

>> Clothing and accessory vendors all performing as expected? Check.

>> All product layout and user navigation adjustments made to her Shopify storefront as a result of the three-month test run? Check.

>> All Shopify state sales tax settings correct? Check.

>> Shipping options and pricing in Shopify all correct? Check.

>> Social media ads designed and ready to run? Check.

>> Products for her grand opening sale all received and stashed in her spare bedroom? Check.

As long as each item on Breanna's checklist checks out okay, she's ready to go. Side-hustle wheels up!

The items that you include on your side hustle's preflight checklist will depend on what you'll be doing. In general, though, you'll build a checklist that takes into consideration the following:

>> The reliability of your suppliers (if you'll be buying products that you'll resell) or raw materials (if you'll be making brand-new products)

>> Any product inventory that you need to have on hand even before you throw open your doors

- Advertising and marketing channels, such as your social media ad accounts
- All the technology you'll be using, such as your website, storefront, and accounting systems

TIP

As you build your preflight checklist, ask yourself a single question, over and over: "What could go wrong?" Every time you come up with an answer such as "My website doesn't work" or "The pricing is wrong on my Shopify site" or "I can't get my Facebook ads to run," add that item to your checklist.

Marking the date

You already have at least a few getting-started dates for your side hustle in the record book:

- The date that the registration for your business as a limited liability company (LLC), S corporation, or some other legal structure came back to you (see Chapter 7)
- The date that the Internal Revenue Service (IRS) issued your employer identification number (EIN), or the equivalent in a country outside the United States
- The date when you "unofficially" started doing your side hustle by starting your test-drive

REMEMBER

For both ceremonial and practical business reasons, you should make note of the date that you *officially* start your side hustle.

On the ceremonial side, wouldn't it be great to someday look back on the anniversary of, say, March 20, 2034 or February 28, 2036 or some other date and be able to say "*That* was where it all began . . . and look what I've been able to accomplish in exactly three years from that date (or five years or whatever length of time has passed)!"

Yeah, marking an official start date for sentimental purposes of looking back may sound a little bit silly. But trust me: If you don't, someday you'll wish you had, especially if your side hustle becomes wildly successful, maybe even turning into a big-time business.

But you also have a practical reason to take note of when your side hustle kicked into high gear, for business reasons. You need to run your business like a business, which means digging into data for sales, products, the split between your various delivery and ridesharing gigs over time, and lots more interesting and important statistics and analytics.

Breanna is determined that even though her boutique is a side hustle alongside her day job, she'll run it like a real business. After all, she has aspirations of turning her side hustle into her full-time hustle not too far in the future. Her friends who have full-time online stores have told Breanna that they make their most critical business decisions "by the numbers" and pay close attention to how their businesses grow and change. They ask important questions along the lines of "How were my sales in my second three months in business versus my first three months?" or "How did I do, profit-wise, in the second half of my first year in business versus the first half?"

WARNING

To answer questions such as these, Breanna needs to know with absolute certainty what date she should count as the official start for her boutique. If she were to start counting from the date that she began her side hustle test run with limited inventory and limited social media marketing, she would get misleading results comparing some period of time where she was running her business in high gear versus an earlier period of time when she was only testing out her boutique.

Telling the world!

You can use the occasion of formally launching your side hustle to do whatever you can to call attention to your new business. You can let the world know about your new side hustle by

>> Putting the equivalent of a "Grand Opening!" banner on your website's or storefront's home page to let customers know that you're now headed for the bigtime

>> Creating a special video that you post on your website or on your YouTube channel (or both!) to celebrate and pump up the transition from your side hustle test-drive to "making it real"

>> Having a grand-opening sale for your products or special "going official" discounted pricing for your bartending gig or some other service-oriented side hustle

TIP

Even if your side hustle is a gig-economy job such as ridesharing or doing delivery services rather than starting a business, you should still make at least a little fuss to let your friends and family members know about your new venture. If they know what you're doing, they'll offer a few words of encouragement to help get you through any rough patches or slow periods.

Stick to the Plan, Stan!

WARNING

You swore that you would run your side hustle like a real business. But as your side hustle gets underway for real, you'll almost certainly need to fight the temptation to procrastinate or even ignore the dozens of mundane behind-the-scenes tasks that will pop up on a daily basis, such as the following:

>> **Recording business purchases that you make online or from a local office supply store:** Oh, that can wait — one of your main suppliers just emailed you that a whole bunch of new products are available, and going through all of them and ordering new inventory will take the rest of the evening. You'll do the manual entries for the boxes and packing materials and shipping supplies that you bought into QuickBooks, well, sometime later.

>> **Finalizing your next round of social media ads that you want to begin next Monday:** Come on, you're tired; you can work on them tomorrow.

>> **Sending out a couple dozen emails to influencers about your side hustle:** Maybe tomorrow, or the next day, or the day after that.

You spent a lot of time putting together a solid plan for your side hustle that included all the tedious-but-necessary supporting tasks. If you start procrastinating on record keeping and changing out your online ads or any one of a dozen other tasks, you run the risk of paying your vendors' invoices late or missing an important tax filing deadline. Do your best to cover all your side hustle bases every single day.

TIP

If you do miss a deadline to make entries into QuickBooks or reply to comments on your YouTube videos or perform some other task, get caught up as soon as you possibly can. Don't let a day or two of delay slide into a week or a month because "it's only my internal deadline — it's not important."

Alert! Alert!

If you did a good job with your side-hustle test-drive, you caught potential issues before they occurred or at least before they could cause too many problems.

You still need to be on guard and alert to problems that may surface as you kick your side hustle into high gear. In particular:

>> Keep a close eye on your techie stuff.

>> Watch your side hustle's supply chain.

>> Be on guard for abrupt social media marketing changes.

Paying attention to your technology

If your side hustle's online presence is built around simple, straightforward technology, you should be in pretty good shape for at least a couple years. Maybe you built a simple Squarespace or WordPress website or a Shopify storefront. Or you may be uploading your videos to a YouTube channel that you created. Unless something really crazy happens, your underlying technology for your side hustle should be very stable.

Suppose, though, that you settled on Shopify for your online storefront, but you also integrated a couple of additional Shopify apps to provide really cool capabilities for your side hustle:

>> Returnly (https://returnly.com) for enhanced product return processing

>> Wishlist Plus (https://apps.shopify.com/swym-relay) for advanced customer wish-list management

>> Buddha Mega Menu Navigation (https://apps.shopify.com/buddha-mega-menu) to change your site's navigation look and feel

>> Oberlo (https://www.oberlo.com) to connect your Shopify site with drop shippers

>> Upsell Product Add-Ons (https://apps.shopify.com/product-add-ons) to try to boost sales through cross-selling and *upselling* (basically, trying to get customers to buy additional or more expensive products while they're already looking at something on your site)

Speaking from experience as a long-time techie, integrating even a couple of products together can be a frustrating proposition — not necessarily at first, but down the road when one vendor makes a change that ripples into the integration with other products, causing something to "break." Eventually, vendors figure out what went wrong and patch the problem. But what happens to your side hustle in the meantime?

The more your side hustle is dependent on really cool tech, the greater the risk of something going wrong months or even years after you're up and running. Be prepared for your website or storefront to suddenly "break," and be as proactive as you can hunting down a solution.

TIP

You can counteract some of the tech integration problems for your side hustle by using packages of apps or plug-ins called *themes* rather than adding pieces to your storefront or website one by one. For example, Shopify's themes (`https://themes.shopify.com`) are a library of templates available for purchase where various apps are combined to provide various features. You can also choose a theme that's particularly suitable to selling various types of products, and then further customize your Shopify store using a software package called Shogun (`https://getshogun.com/learn/shopify-theme-customization`).

Having your backup supply chain on standby

You know that fantastic supplier you found for seasonal custom-made T-shirts for your store? That same supplier who helped you sell almost 100 Valentine's Day T-shirt's during your side-hustle test-drive?

Oh, you mean that same one-person supplier who suddenly went out of business because of personal or family reasons? Yeah, that one. So, now what?

REMEMBER

Even if your side-hustle test-drive went flawlessly, be prepared for suppliers to suddenly go out of business. If your side hustle is primarily providing services rather than products, you really don't have to worry about this problem. But if you're buying products that you resell, or buying raw materials that you then use to custom-make, say, jewelry or other fashion accessories, have backup suppliers on standby in case you need to play musical chairs with your supply chain.

Making sure you don't get blindsided by social media

Maybe you built the customer outreach portion of your side hustle all around social media marketing. You enrolled in several online courses, and watched about a hundred different videos on YouTube and Vimeo. You're pretty sure you're on top of how to create campaigns, do very precisely targeted online ads, analyze results, set your ad pricing, and all the rest of the social marketing game.

Think again.

You never know when one of the big social media players will change up its whole marketing environment, with devastating impact on everything you had planned.

A close friend — okay, my wife — has an online fashion boutique that she started as a side hustle. Her entire business plan was originally built around Facebook marketing, primarily through Facebook groups and pages. For about six months, she steadily increased her customer base and her overall audience by using Facebook ads, doing live show-and-tell videos for new product arrivals on Facebook Live, and similar tried-and-true social media marketing techniques. Then, in early 2018, Facebook suddenly announced that its users would "see more from friends, families, and groups and less from businesses, brands, and media" (www.falcon.io/insights-hub/industry-updates/social-media-updates/facebook-algorithm-change).

Many smaller businesses that built their customer reach models around Facebook — businesses such as my wife's — got slammed by the changes that Facebook made. Side hustlers who had painstakingly built groups for their businesses with 50,000 or more members used to go live on Facebook to unveil new products and regularly have 1,000 or more people watching. After Facebook's algorithm changed, the number of live viewers plummeted significantly. with dramatic drop-offs in sales.

I'm certainly not saying "Don't do social media advertising and marketing for your side hustle business." But be careful about putting all your eggs in any particular social media site's basket. If Facebook makes dramatic changes, what about Google Ads? What about using YouTube videos to advertise? Maybe you can make a shift to more targeted email marketing?

Check out *Social Media Marketing For Dummies* by Shiv Singh and Stephanie Diamond (Wiley) or *Social Media Marketing All-in-One For Dummies* by Michelle Krasniak, Jan Zimmerman, and Deborah Ng (Wiley) for all the ins and outs and do's and don'ts of social media marketing for your side hustle.

Bracing Yourself for Your First Side-Hustle Hiccups

You sailed through your side hustle's test-drive totally unscathed. Congratulations! No supplier problems, no angry customers, no Internet trolls ganging up to slam your videos or one-star your online course or your book. Whew!

WARNING

Guess what: Sooner or later, you're going to run into problems with your side hustle — maybe small problems, or maybe bigger ones, but problems nonetheless!

You know that scouting motto of "Be prepared"? Words of wisdom for your side hustle!

Mark is two months into his accounting side hustle, recording and publishing two videos a week. So far, so good. Then Mark posts a new video in which he makes a couple incorrect statements when discussing the impact of a new state sales-tax law on service-related side hustles.

Well, that did it. The trolls not only downvoted his video, but also posted comments like "This dude doesn't know what he's talking about," "I wouldn't take any advice from this guy," and "Don't listen to anything this person says."

Okay, pop-quiz time.

Should Mark:

A. Go head-to-head with the Internet trolls and blast them back with nasty comments to their comments.

B. Ignore the whole situation, quietly take down the video with the incorrect statements, and just record and publish his next one.

C. Double down on his incorrect statements and try to somehow spin what he said under the doctrine of "never apologize."

D. Address and correct his misstatements in his next video, admit that he made a mistake, and also refuse to engage with the trolls even when they go after him again on his next video.

E. Quit doing his side hustle because he made a mistake.

Hopefully you chose D. Mistakes happen. Sometimes those mistakes are customer-facing or audience-facing. If (or more likely, when) you make a mistake, own up to it and be professional. If the Internet trolls are after you, don't play their game. If you have an angry customer who's blasting you on social media because a product they ordered arrived broken or torn or otherwise defective, address the issue head-on and do your best to turn side-hustle lemons into lemonade.

A customer order never arrives? Replace it. A supplier doesn't deliver as promised? Try to resolve the situation, but be prepared to move on. Your website totally crashes, and you can't get it running again? Retrieve your backup copy (and make sure you're backing up all your systems!) and rebuild from that point.

If your side hustle is doing small software jobs through your listing on Fiverr, and if you quote someone a price based on 15 hours of work but you actually spend 30 hours on the job, take your lumps and try to do a better job estimating a fixed-price job the next time around.

Are you doing ridesharing gigs for Uber or Lyft? Quite possibly you'll wind up with an unruly, even argumentative passenger. Be ready! Be ready for unfair one-star reviews from jerky passengers, or even a passenger who *accidentally* gives you a one-star review.

Be prepared for the angry takeout delivery customer who is furious because you're delivering their dinner ten minutes past when they wanted their food to arrive or who blame you for the restaurant or the delivery service itself messing up the order.

REMEMBER

Be prepared! No matter what your side-hustle aspirations are, you *will* hit speed-bumps along the way, so make sure you have your head in the right place so you aren't tempted to quit when faced with a hiccup or two.

Doing Your Three-Month Checkup

You should be taking stock of your side hustle on an ongoing, almost constant basis. During the earliest stages of your side hustle, however, you have dozens, if not hundreds, of things on your mind. Most of the "taking stock" that you do will likely be in background mode. You may notice the biggest outliers — videos that aren't getting a lot of views, or products that aren't selling — but you're likely to gloss over many other aspects of your side hustle.

REMEMBER

At the three-month mark, do an end-to-end checkup for your side hustle. You need crystal-clear insight into the answers to questions such as the following:

>> How are sales going?

>> Are you getting enough bartending gigs?

>> How many views did you get for the video that you just dropped?

>> How about views for your earlier videos: Are people going back and watching them after just now discovering your YouTube channel?

>> Who are your best and most reliable suppliers?

>> Are you able to custom-make jewelry in the amount of time you allocated?

>> Are any of your custom-made items taking too long to make for the price that you're charging?

>> Are you able to stay on top of the record-keeping?

>> Have you filed tax and legal documents on time?

TIP

Also, take a look outside the borders of your side hustle. You're well past your side hustle test–drive now, so:

>> Do you still find your side hustle enjoyable?

>> Do you have enough free time for the fun things in your life?

>> How tired are you with three more months of side hustling behind you?

>> How stressed are you?

>> Is your side hustle causing any problems with your day job?

Give some honest thought to all of these questions. Take all the answers into consideration. Basically, at three months, you'll have three paths for your side hustle from this point forward:

>> Stay on course — no changes necessary.

>> Make some adjustments to your side hustle (see Chapter 14).

>> Pull the plug and stop doing your side hustle (see Chapter 14).

Chapter **7**

Running Your Side Hustle Like a Business

Your side hustle may be a side business, but it's still a business. Therefore, you need to manage your side hustle just as you would any business — just on a smaller scale.

You will need to:

» Decide what your side hustle's legal business structure should be.

» Most likely, choose a name for your side hustle.

» Set up the computer systems and other technology that you'll need.

» Make sure you have your legal i's dotted and t's crossed to stay out of trouble.

Choosing Your Side-Hustle Business Structure

You want to get as much benefit out of your side hustle as you can, while also minimizing your personal risk, right? Of course!

Start by establishing the legal business structure for your side hustle. In most cases, you'll want to legally separate yourself as an individual from your side hustle. You could, however, keep it simple, where you and your side hustle are one and the same.

In the United States, your main options for your side hustle's business structure are as follows:

>> Sole proprietorship

>> Partnership

>> Limited liability company (LLC)

>> S corporation

You could also establish your side hustle as some other legal structure, such as a limited liability partnership (LLP) or a "real" corporation, otherwise known as a C corporation. Usually, though, an LLP or a C corporation aren't good fits for side hustles.

Consult an attorney and/or accountant to find out which legal structure is best for you.

Sole proprietorship: The path of least resistance

Want to press Start on your side hustle and be up and running in the shortest time possible, with the least amount of hassle? Set up your side hustle as a *sole proprietorship.* Just as the term implies, you're the sole proprietor — in other words, the only owner — of your side hustle. In fact, you and your side hustle are one and the same when it comes to finances, taxes, and legal considerations.

According to the U.S. Small Business Administration (SBA):

> a sole proprietorship is the simplest and most common structure chosen to start a business. It is an unincorporated business owned and run by one individual with no distinction between the business and the owner. You are entitled to all profits and are responsible for all your business's debts, losses and liabilities.

You know what else is really convenient about a sole proprietorship? Let's go to the SBA again, because they have a great way of telling you some good news:

> No formal action is required to form a sole proprietorship. If you're the only owner, this status automatically comes from your business activities. In fact, you may already own one without knowing it. If you are a freelance graphic designer, for example, you are a sole proprietor.

Wow! The moment you started side hustling, if you didn't set up your business in some other form, you're already a sole proprietorship. No paperwork; no separate tax identification number; not even the need for a separate business name. No fuss, no muss. Now wasn't that easy?

So what's the catch?

Well, I'll quote three ominous words from that same SBA web page:

Unlimited

Personal

Liability

Uh-oh!

WARNING

Yep, you've got it: Because you and your sole proprietorship are one and the same, *you* are legally and financially responsible for anything that goes wrong with your side hustle. Suppose you do a little bit of software development on the side for clients that you find through Fiverr. Now suppose that you miss a really, really big problem in a software project for some company, and as a result of your mistake, your client winds up losing a lot of money. They could come after *you* for damages, which means that your savings and investments — even your house — could be at risk!

You can try to protect your sole proprietorship with various types of business insurance, such as general liability insurance and errors and omissions (E&O) insurance (see Chapter 10). However, you shouldn't rely solely on insurance to protect your personal assets from something going wrong in your side hustle, which means that either an LLC or an S corporation will likely be better for many types of side hustles.

So, what sort of side hustle fits with a sole proprietorship? If you're doing lifestyle blogging or videos where you discuss travel, cooking, or other seemingly "harmless" topics, you're probably pretty safe taking the easy path and sticking with a sole proprietorship for your side hustle.

What if you're doing gig-economy ridesharing or delivery services for your side hustle? Do you need to set up an LLC, or can you just stick with a sole proprietorship? You'll find opinions on both sides of the debate. Some people argue that as long as you have adequate business insurance, you don't need to go through the steps to set up an LLC; just get behind the wheel and — presto — you're underway. Others will tell you that you establish an extra layer of protection with an LLC in case you wind up in a serious automobile accident while doing your side hustle work. In my opinion, you should always err on the side of protecting your assets by doing that little bit of extra work to set up an LLC.

Partnership: Not going it alone

If you're about to enter the world of side hustles side-by-side with a partner, you could set up your business as a partnership — not just in name, but legally.

A partnership is a very straightforward way for two or more people to be in business together, whether for a side hustle or even a full-time business venture. The simplest form of a partnership is known as a *limited partnership,* where you have both

>> One *general partner* (the person running the business and making most of the decisions)

>> One or more *limited partners* (people sharing in the profits but with a lesser role in the business itself)

You and your partners would write up a formal partnership agreement in which you specify who the general partner will be, all profit-sharing percentage arrangements, and other terms that will govern how your side hustle will be managed and then what will happen at tax time.

You could think of a limited partnership as sort of a sole proprietorship except for more than one person. Your business taxes will be a bit more complex (see Chapter 10), but you can get a basic partnership up and running very easy.

So, what's the catch?

If you're the brains and energy behind your side hustle but you're partnering up with a close friend, you may set up your partnership with you as the general partner and your friend as a limited partner. As the general partner, you have the same unlimited *personal* liability as with a sole proprietorship, and the limited partner doesn't share in that risk.

Suppose you and two friends set up a side hustle to do website development and social media marketing. The three of you divide up the work and the profits, but you're the general partner. If one of your partners walks away from an assignment or makes a few big mistakes that don't get caught, *you're* the one on the hook with your personal assets and maybe even your home at risk.

All together now: No way!

TECHNICAL STUFF

You can form a partnership as a *limited liability partnership* (LLP) to limit *every* partner's liability, not just the limited partners. However, a better option for your side hustle might be an LLC. If you and one or more partners are going in together on a side hustle, consult with an attorney or accountant who can guide you to the right structure for your particular business: LLP, LLC, or S corporation.

Limited liability company: Playing it safe

Sole proprietorships and partnerships both come with a gigantic red flag: unlimited personal liability. Do you have any other options for setting up your side hustle without putting your personal assets at risk? Yes, you do.

A *limited liability company* is sort of a hybrid between a partnership and a corporation. Benefits of an LLC include

>> **Limited personal liability, as implied by the name:** In other words, you and your side hustle are totally separate legal entities as with a corporation side hustle.

>> **Flexibility in terms of the number of people involved:** You can set up an LLC regardless of how many people are involved in your side hustle — even if it's just you by yourself, which is known as a *single-member LLC* in legalese.

>> **Easier tax filing:** For a single-member LLC (just you in your side hustle), you can report your taxes on your personal tax return — just like with a sole proprietorship — instead of having to file separate forms with different filing deadlines that corporations and partnerships have to follow.

So, how do you set up an LLC for your side hustle? Every state has its own requirements, so check and then carefully follow the steps for your state. In general, though, you will

>> **Choose a business name (discussed later in this chapter).**

>> **Decide who will be the registered agent for your LLC.** A *registered agent* is the primary point of contact for "all things legal and important" for your side hustle. You can be your own registered agent, or you can hire an attorney or someone else to fill that role for your side hustle.

>> **Complete your state's official document to create an LLC.** The document is often called the *articles of organization* or the *certificate of formation* or something similar. Do a Google search for the name of your state and "LLC articles of organization" and you should see the correct link at or near the top of your search results. For example, in Arizona, you go to www.azcc.gov/docs/default-source/corps-files/forms/1010-articles-of-organization.pdf and find a form that you can then fill out online.

>> **File the articles of organization for your side hustle with the correct state government agency.** For example, in Arizona, the state's Corporation Commission handles LLC filings, as well as corporate filings. You'll find the correct agency name and address (or the details for filing online) either directly on the form itself or in accompanying instructions.

>> **Document your LLC's *operating agreement*, which includes all the specifics about financials and who is responsible for various tasks.** Your state may require you to file your LLC operating agreement, but even if you aren't required to file one, you should create an operating agreement as part of your overall business planning.

TIP

You may also have annual state filing requirements for your LLC. Take a look at www.corpnet.com/blog/annual-report-list-by-state and scroll down to "LLC Annual Report List by State" to see if you need to file an "annual franchise tax report" or a "annual registration" or "annual renewal" or some other document in the state where your LLC is registered.

S corporation: Straddling the corporate world

REMEMBER

An LLC (see the preceding section) is sort of a hybrid legal structure in between a C corporation and a sole proprietorship.

In the same spirit, an *S corporation* is a hybrid legal structure in between an LLC and a C corporation.

Unlike a C corporation, the revenue from an S corporation "passes through" to you rather than being counted — and taxed — separately. And whereas a C corporation could have thousands or even millions of shareholders, an S corporation is limited to no more than 100 shareholders, all of whom must be U.S. citizens. You'll find many other technical distinctions between C and S corporations, but you can think of an S corporation as a "small business corporation" (think "S for small business") that's perfect for a side hustle that you want to structure as a corporation rather than a single-person LLC.

TECHNICAL STUFF

Technically, comparing an LLC to an S corporation is an apples-to-oranges comparison. An LLC is a legal business structure, which is different from organizing a business as a corporation. An S corporation is a *tax classification* within the overall "family" of corporations (you'll also find B corporations and nonprofit corporations in that "family"). So, you would decide that your side hustle will be a corporation rather than an LLC, and then as you set up your corporation you elect the Subchapter S classification.

Why would you go down the S corporation path rather than set up your side hustle as an LLC? After all, with an S corporation, you need to file separate tax returns for your side-hustle income, even if that income "passes through" to your personal return (see Chapter 10).

If your side hustle is an S corporation, you do *not* pay self-employment taxes (Social Security and Medicare taxes). Instead, you can be your own employee and get paid a salary, just as you get paid a salary from your day job. You'll have to pay Social Security taxes (up to the IRS's annual limit for all your jobs) and Medicare taxes on your side-hustle salary, but the rest of your business profits aren't subject to self-employment taxes.

Whoa! That's pretty complicated! Is there a more straightforward way to decide whether an LLC or S corporation is better for your side hustle?

TIP

If you have big — I mean, *really* big! — plans for your side hustle, you should at least look into setting yourself up as an S corporation from the very beginning. Suppose you're starting a small tech consulting company on the side — small for now, but your business plan calls for growing and growing and then growing your side hustle even more until it's a "real" company with dozens of employees and plenty of clients all around the country, maybe even all around the world. You're probably better off heading down the S corporation path from the start to give you the freedom to issue stock rewards or other ownership stakes to your employees without having to restructure your company along the way.

Your Side Hustle by Any Other Name

If you decided that you'll just set up your side hustle as a sole proprietorship rather than an LLC, you don't need a business name. You and your side hustle are one and the same according to the rules of being a sole proprietorship. In most other cases, though, you should create a business name for your side hustle.

REMEMBER

If you structure your side hustle as an LLC or an S corporation, you *must* have a business name when you file with your state's corporation commission or other governmental agency to create your company.

Business names can get a little tricky. You need to find out if the name you want to use is "officially available" within your state. Depending on where you live and where you want to register your business, you'll conduct a search on an official government website to see if the name you want is available. For example, in Arizona, you need to check with both of the following:

>> The Arizona Corporation Commission for official business names

>> The Arizona Secretary of State for *trade names* (sometimes referred to as "doing business as" names)

As long as you don't find the name you want to use in either of those searches, you're *probably* in good shape to use that name for your side hustle's official business name.

Why "probably" in good shape? You have a little bit of a time lag between when you file for a business name and when you're actually granted the usage of that name. Suppose someone else filed to use the same name a few days before you did? Quite possibly, they'll be granted that name first, and then when your application is processed, the name that you thought was available is now being used by a different business.

Do you need to worry about business names in different states? Possibly. A business name that is *trademarked* in a different states is probably off limits, so don't even think about naming your side hustle "McDonald's Hamburgers" or "Pittsburgh IBM Software" or some other name that is the same as or incorporates a trademarked name. You also can create a trade name — a "doing business as" name — that is sort of your unofficial name in addition to your official registered business name.

For all these reasons, you really should consider retaining an attorney to help you take care of your business name. Otherwise, you may find yourself going back to the drawing board, which could mean that you'll run into delays getting your side hustle off the ground and underway.

Technology and Your Side Hustle

No matter what your side hustle is, you'll use technology frequently — maybe even on a daily basis. Even if your side hustle itself has nothing to do with the tech world, you'll need to keep track of your incoming money, make sure that your bills are paid, and pay your taxes. True, you could do a little bit of time traveling and take care of all those tasks manually with pen and paper. What do you think?

Nah!

Whether you do the tech work yourself or you find other people — maybe other side hustlers! — to help you out, you still should have an idea about technology, because some or maybe even all of the following will be necessary for your side hustle:

>> Your internal operational systems

>> Your website

>> Your storefront

>> Social media

Your technology behind the curtain

REMEMBER

Every side hustle — even gig-economy hustles such as ridesharing and delivery services — needs to have a couple of basic tech systems running things behind the curtain:

>> **A basic office package consisting of word processing, spreadsheet management, and software for graphics and presentations:** Microsoft Office has been the leader in this space for decades with Word, Excel, and PowerPoint. Many other small businesses make use of Google's version of these software packages — Google Docs, Google Sheets, and Google Drawings — that are part of its Google Workspace software suite.

>> **Accounting and finance software:** One example is QuickBooks. There's even a version of QuickBooks specifically for "part-time freelancers" called QuickBooks Self-Employed.

TIP

If you're doing only a little bit of uncomplicated side hustling — recording a couple of courses, or doing a little bit of ridesharing — you may be able to get away with doing your accounting and finance on Microsoft Excel or Google Sheets. But when your side hustle starts to grow, you should really look at a "real" accounting package.

TIP

You may also need tax-filing software if you decide to do your side-hustle taxes on your own instead of hiring an accountant. Chapter 10 discusses various tax software packages you may find useful.

Your side-hustle website

Websites have been around since the mid-1990s and quickly became an essential part of any business, large or small. If your side hustle is doing ridesharing or delivering packages, you probably don't need to build a website for your business. For almost any other kind of side hustle, though, you definitely need to be in the website game.

REMEMBER

You don't need to know anything about computer programming to build your side hustle website. Website-building sites such as Squarespace, Wix, and WordPress give you dozens or even hundreds of templates that you can use to drag and drop blocks for text, images, videos, audio clips, and all sorts of other artifacts to build your website. You can use the templates to quickly create and customize your menus, links among your pages, and other website navigation.

GOING BEYOND BASIC SOFTWARE FUNCTIONALITY

The more sophisticated your side-hustle business becomes, the more complex your computing infrastructure will become. You'll start to use applications for *customer relationship management* (CRM) — basically, managing the relationships with your customers (how's that for a statement of the obvious?). CRM software allows you to track all communications with customers and prospective customers, track and manage business leads, run advertising and marketing campaigns, and do other "customer-facing" activities that can help you grow your business.

Salesforce is a leading CRM company whose cloud-based software is used even in small businesses. However, you may find a scaled-down CRM package such as Keap or Microsoft Dynamics 365 CRM more suited to your side hustle.

The greater the number of applications you have, the more you'll find yourself taking data out of one application to put it into another. For example, you may want to send emails to everyone who signed up on your website to download information about a special program that you have coming up, and then track the responses through your CRM software. Manually copying all that data back and forth is not only tedious but also error-prone. You can use integration software such as Zapier to automate the exchange of information among your various systems, even when you have a lot of different software packages from many different companies.

If your side hustle stays on the smaller, less complex side, you won't have to worry about building a computing infrastructure that mimics that of a larger business. If, however, your side hustle starts to head for the big time, you should take a look at the next wave of integrating systems and advanced applications beyond where you start out for your side hustle.

Or you can always farm out your website development to someone else — even another side hustler who specializes in website development — and that person or company will create your website based on your overall requirements and maybe your high-level thoughts about the site's "look and feel."

Regardless of which approach you take — build it yourself or hire somebody — your website will be a critical element to the market-facing side of your side hustle.

Your storefront

If your side hustle is built around online selling and e-commerce, you'll likely need a storefront — basically a specialized website with built-in, extremely powerful capabilities for:

>> Listing and displaying your products for sale

>> Customers buying those products

>> Managing your inventory as customers buy products

>> Customers entering their payment and shipping information

>> Lots of other functions

If you've ever done any online shopping, you're familiar with the basic workings of storefront-type software that you may need for your side hustle.

You can use specialized software such as Shopify or the capabilities of general website-building software such as Squarespace or Wix to build your side hustle's storefront.

TIP

Plan and coordinate your overall website and storefront strategy as part of your business planning. You may not need both a "regular" website and a storefront. Depending on the nature of your business, you can likely combine these two related capabilities and keep your side-hustle life on the simple (or at least simpler) side.

Social media

Buckle up — time to take a ride on the social media roller coaster.

If you're like most people and you use various social media sites such as Facebook, Instagram, TikTok, or Twitter in your personal life, you have a head start in putting those social media platforms to work for your side hustle.

You'll need to do some or even all of the following:

>> Regularly post or tweet about what's going on in your side hustle, events out there in the world that are related to your side hustle's business, interesting things that you learned that are likely to catch someone's eye and draw attention to your side hustle . . . pretty much anything.

>> Gather as many followers, friends, connections, or whatever the term is on any given social media network.

>> Try to build a community for your side hustle using capabilities such as Facebook groups and pages or a YouTube channel that you can then use to help promote your side hustle.

>> Do paid advertising for your products or services — or just for the sake of awareness — targeting users who meet precise demographic criteria that you believe are most likely to be receptive to your messaging.

WARNING

Social media for side hustling is a hit-and-miss proposition. We've all heard of the teenager who has over a million followers on some social media platform and whose posts get tens of millions of views. "Why can't I do that?," you probably wondered a couple thousand times. You never know: Maybe you'll catch lightning in a bottle and turn into a social media celeb! If so, your side hustle is likely in for smooth sailing. But even if your social media results are more in line with the norm, you should still keep plugging away and working social media into your overall tech strategy.

Playing It Safe on the Legal Front

Quick quiz: Where you live, what are the rules and laws that relate to doing a business out of your home?

Aha! Bet you can't answer that question off the top of your head, right? Don't feel bad — not too many people can, including plenty of side hustlers who may be tiptoeing over the trouble line without even knowing it.

REMEMBER

You need to be aware of:

>> Your city's zoning laws

>> If you own or rent a house or condominium, any homeowner's association (HOA) *covenants* (rules) that impact home-based businesses in your neighborhood

>> If you rent an apartment, any rules issued by your apartment building or complex management company that may restrict or forbid a home-based business

You also need to know if you need to obtain and keep current any special licenses for your side hustle.

Welcome to the side-hustle zone

Most towns and cities divide their communities into several types of zones:

>> **Residential:** Where people live

>> **Commercial:** Where you'll find retail-type stores

>> **Industrial:** Where you'll find manufacturing and other plants

>> **Office:** Where you'll find — you've got it — office space

>> **Municipal:** Where government offices are found

TECHNICAL
STUFF

Some urban municipalities also have *mixed-use* zoning that combines multiple other zones into one — residential, commercial, and office all together, for example.

How does zoning apply to your side hustle?

>> Your side hustle is a business.

>> Three of the five zoning types — commercial, industrial, and office — are business-related.

>> You live in your house or apartment, which is likely found in an area that's zoned residential.

>> You need to run your side hustle — your business — out of your home, which means that you're operating a business in an area that is *not* zoned for business.

REMEMBER

So, do you have a problem? Not necessarily. The rules you'll find for most residential zoning allow you to operate a small business, provided that your business doesn't create any sort of nuisance (noise, traffic) or hazard to your neighbors. Basically, if you can run your business quietly without disturbing anyone in your neighborhood, you *should* be in good shape.

However, you still need to verify with absolute certainty that *your* side hustle is in the clear for you to operate in residential zoning. According to legal site Nolo.com (www.nolo.com/legal-encyclopedia/home-businesses-zoning-30080.html), some "affluent communities" have local zoning ordinances that prohibit *all* types of businesses.

Other residential zoning laws may allow "quiet" home-based businesses but don't allow you to have customers coming to your home. So, if you're baking pies, cookies, cinnamon rolls, and other goodies for your side hustle (yum!), you may not be able to essentially run a commercial bakery from your house, with customers coming and going. But doing videos about baking that you post on YouTube and then try to monetize? No problem.

What about home daycare? Doing pet sitting in your house where you bring dogs to stay overnight? Teaching yoga classes in your backyard on weekends? Maybe you're in the clear — or maybe not.

TIP

How do you know what you are and aren't allowed to do? Nobody is trying to hide the laws from you. Go online and find the zoning ordinances for your city. You may need to adjust your search terms because zoning ordinances go by different names in different places (for example, "codes" instead of "ordinances"), but try searching for the name of your city and your state along with "residential zoning ordinances" or "home-based business" plus your city and state.

Running a side hustle out of your home

Suppose you're in the clear in the eyes of your city when it comes to your home-based side hustle. You still may run into a roadblock in the form of your neighborhood's covenants, conditions, and restrictions (CC&Rs), as enforced by your HOA.

REMEMBER

Think of CC&Rs as "lower-level zoning" that applies to a particular residential development. For example, your city's residential zoning may place a limit on the number of household pets permitted in a single-family house — say, a maximum of five dogs, cats, rabbits, hamsters, or other small pets (no horses!). However, your development's CC&Rs may state that a maximum of *three* household pets is permitted in a house in your neighborhood.

A municipality's zoning would typically not deal with the permissible colors that a house could be painted or the types of vegetation and plants permitted in a house's front yard. Your HOA, however, could enforce provisions in your CC&Rs that require, for example, "earth tones only" or "no palm trees" or "no natural grass in a front or side yard."

What's that? You're not particularly interested in having some HOA tell you what color you can paint your house? You better read those CC&Rs — in fact, you really should read them *before* you move into a newly built house or buy an existing one. If you don't file for permission to do an addition or paint your house a permissible color or any one of the hundreds of other homeowner-type tasks, and if your HOA objects to something you did to your house, they can make you undo your addition or paint job or landscaping. If you refuse to comply, they can fine you or even place a lien on your house!

So what do HOAs and CC&Rs have to do with side hustles? As you can probably guess, you never know when a development may have extremely restrictive, even over-the-top restrictions on *any* home-based businesses. Minding your own business recording videos? You may be violating your development's CC&Rs, even if you're in full compliance with your city's residential zoning laws.

If you have a side hustle underway, read those CC&Rs before you move into a home. If you're just now thinking about a side hustle, check out your CC&Rs. Usually, a "quiet" side hustle won't be an issue, but make sure.

Considering the rules of your apartment complex

If you live in an apartment building or complex rather than a single-family house or condominium, you'll have the same potential issues with overly restrictive rules that could impact your ability to run your side hustle out of your apartment. In your case, however, instead of an HOA enforcing CC&Rs, you need to deal with your apartment lease terms and restrictions.

Read your lease carefully and be on the lookout for any restrictions that you think may affect your side hustle. Pay special attention to *callouts* in your lease — a reference to terms and rules contained in some other document rather than listing those rules and restrictions directly in your lease. Just because the words aren't right in front of you doesn't mean that you aren't impacted if some additional restrictions are included by reference.

License and side-hustle registration, please

Many side hustles in which you may be interested don't require any special licensing. Some, however, may require you to obtain a license from some local or state governmental agency.

For example, suppose your side hustle is cutting hair and providing other similar services. You'll likely need to apply for a *cosmetology license* to be able to go into business, even if you're providing your services as a side hustle rather than as a full-time business.

So, even if you're in the clear when it comes to your city's residential zoning and your neighborhood's CC&Rs, you still need to make sure that you have the all-clear from your state's board of cosmetology or whatever body governs the beauty business where you live.

REMEMBER

What about doing ridesharing for Lyft or Uber or delivering groceries or restaurant meals? Technically, you're driving for a business — your business — rather than doing personal driving. Do you need a commercial driver's license rather than a normal one? Many states issue taxi and livery driver's licenses for taxi drivers and chauffeurs. Will you need to get one of those special licenses?

Unfortunately, gig-economy driving is an ever-shifting combination of local and state rules along with the rules of the ridesharing and delivery companies themselves. For the most part, Uber, Lyft, Instacart, and many other ridesharing and delivery companies do not require you to have a commercial driver's license; your personal license is just fine.

TECHNICAL STUFF

Some states are cool with your doing all your side-hustle driving on a personal license, while others require special licenses. Arizona, where I live, allows gig-economy driving on your personal driver's license. New York City, however, requires you to have a special license from the city's Taxi and Limousine Commission (TLC) to do ridesharing.

Check with both the company for which you're thinking about doing any sort of side-hustle driving, as well as your local city and state. And be prepared for the laws and rules to change at any time!

Chapter **8**

Show Me the Money

E ven if your primary motivation for doing a side hustle isn't to make money, money will still be an important part of whatever you decide to do. Or, more accurately, *managing* money that comes in to, as well as goes out of, your side hustle will be critically important.

You need to have a good feel for the following:

» Some important do's and don'ts when it comes to the financial side of your side hustle

» How to set up your side hustle's budget

» How to adequately fund your side hustle with the money it will need to get underway and then keep going

» How to collect money that customers or clients are paying you and how to pay your suppliers and vendors

TIP

Taxes are also an important money-related topic for your side hustle — so important, in fact, that you'll find an entire chapter that covers side hustles and taxes (see Chapter 10).

Do's and Don'ts for Your Side-Hustle Finances

When you go to a party or a business event, you mingle with other people. You introduce yourself to people you don't know or you talk with a friend whom you haven't seen in a while, and you make sure to seek out the person throwing the party to tell them what a great time you're having. In a business setting, you seek out potential clients or customers and try to build a relationship. Mingling is an essential part of any social or professional encounter.

WARNING

When it comes to your side-hustle money, though, you need to follow one critically important rule: No mingling! Specifically, you should never

>> Entangle your personal money with your side-hustle finances.

>> Intertwine money from one side hustle with another side hustle.

TIP

You need to think of your side hustle as an *entity* — basically, "a thing" — that is every bit as legally separated from you as an individual as you are from a coworker or your cousin or your neighbor down the street.

Does your coworker write a check or do a cash app payment that withdraws money from *your* bank account? Of course not!

When your cousin fires up her phone's banking app to do a mobile deposit for a birthday check she received from her parents, does the money get deposited into *your* bank account? No way!

Can your neighbor decide that he's going to sell *your* stocks or withdraw money from *your* retirement fund, and pocket the proceeds? Definitely not!

You need to set up a separate business checking account, separate PayPal and Venmo business accounts, and separate accounts for anything money-related for your side hustle. And if you have more than one side hustle that are totally separate businesses, with different tax numbers from each other, you need to create and manage separate business accounts for *each* side hustle.

So, how do you actually get to use and spend your side-hustle money if you need to use banking and payment accounts that are separate from your personal ones? You *are* permitted to transfer money between your personal and business accounts — you just need to officially record money that you're transferring into your business and other money that you're pulling out from your business for bookkeeping purposes, rather than exchanging funds in a haphazard, carefree manner.

In fact, most big banks provide you with a single login that you can use to access *all* your accounts, both business and personal. The convenience of signing in only once is great! And even better: You can do online transfers among your various accounts when you need to put money into your side hustle, or when it's time to pull out a little bit of cash and spend it on yourself.

TIP

If you're in a hurry or if you simply make a mistake and intermingle your side hustle and personal money, or money from several of your side hustles with each other, just correct the problem as soon as you can and keep track of both your original mistaken transaction, as well as what you did to fix your error.

For example, suppose you have one side hustle through which you do a little bit of part-time software development and a totally different side hustle for weekend landscaping work. If you accidentally give a software client your PayPal business information for your landscaping gig and you wind up with a deposit in your landscaping bank account that should've gone to your software development bank account, write a check or do an online transfer of the money to get the money to the correct account as soon as you discover the error.

Chances are, for side hustle–size businesses, you'll never need to justify or explain either your original mistake or the transfer you made from one of your side hustles to the other. If, however, you do wind up getting audited and it's one of those audits where the Internal Revenue Service (IRS) wants receipts of literally everything that you did during a tax year, you'll have the details ready to go to track the flow of money into and out of each of your businesses.

Budgeting Basics for Side Hustles

You need to create and pay attention to a budget in your personal life:

>> How much money you make and when you get paid

>> How much you need to spend on housing, food, and other essentials

>> How much of your income needs to be spent on other living expenses that you may or may not be able to do without

>> How much money you should set aside for unpredictable expenses

>> The "leftover" money after you cover all your expenses that you can put into savings or investments

You'll also need to create a budget for your side hustle, and manage your business according to that budget. You need to

>> Predict your revenue, which can be tricky depending on what kind of side hustle you have going

>> Plan your expenses — both the expenses that you absolutely must incur, as well as those that can vary depending on what's going on in your side hustle

Forecasting your revenue

Maybe you have a full-time job with a regular salary that never varies from paycheck to paycheck. When you sit down to do your personal or family budget, you know that every two weeks (or whenever your paychecks show up in your bank account), you'll see a deposit of $2,000 or $4,000 or some other figure after all your taxes and other withholdings are deducted from your salary. You can always count on that deposit being made, without fail.

Or maybe your full-time job is a little more variable. Suppose your job qualifies for overtime pay whenever you work more than 40 hours a week. You know, then, that your paycheck comes with a "floor" — that is, you'll never see less than, say, $2,500 being deposited into your checking account. But some paychecks may be $500 higher, or maybe $1,000 higher. Pretty good, right?

Then again, you may have a job where your paycheck could be anywhere from a ton of money on the high end to absolutely nothing on the low end. Some sales jobs are like that, where you're paid solely on commissions — in other words, a percentage of what you sell. No sales? Sorry, no money this time around! Or, on the other, much better side of the spectrum, did you just sell $100,000 worth of products on which you receive a 30 percent commission? Then watch for a paycheck deposit of about $20,000, which would be your $30,000 *gross income* minus taxes and withholdings. Woo-hoo!

Your side-hustle revenue may fit any one of these three paycheck patterns:

>> Steady, maybe even guaranteed revenue

>> A revenue "floor" but also the potential for even more money in any given payment period

>> Revenue that could be anywhere from nothing to enough to pay cash for a new car (maybe even a really expensive car!)

Suppose you're doing gig-economy driving or delivery services for your side hustle, and you plan to work around the same amount of time every week. You know from your own research, your test-drive (see Chapter 5), and talking with others doing the same side hustle that you'll be busy almost every minute that you're logged in to the app, which means that you won't have to worry too much about downtime. So, if you're "on the clock" for 20 hours a week, you'll almost always be working the full 20 hours.

From your research, you know that you'll make around $15 per hour from your ridesharing or delivery services. Doing the math, that's $300 in revenue each week, or $1,200 per month. You can plug that $1,200 figure into your budget and feel pretty confident that you won't fall below that number when you start matching your revenue up against your expenses.

Or, if you want to take a look at the big picture, you can confidently plan on earning around $14,400 in the next year from your side hustle ($1,200 each month × 12 months). See the nearby sidebar for a slight complication, however.

QUICK: HOW MANY WEEKS ARE IN A MONTH?

Technically, you could be looking at more like $15,600 for your annual revenue forecast than $14,400. Why? One of the most frustrating things about budgeting is that a calendar month doesn't have an exact number of weeks (except for February, of course, but even then you have exactly four weeks in a month only three out of every four years because of leap year!).

If you start your budget on a weekly basis and then roll it up into a month, you would almost always use four weeks per month for your calculations. However, you actually have slightly *over* four weeks in a month.

So, to be as accurate as possible, you should do sort of "double-budgeting" from your weekly starting point: one for a monthly forecast, and a separate one for an annual forecast.

However, unless you're planning on not taking a vacation, or never taking a week off, you're pretty safe doing a week → month → annual single rollup, which in the case of the example ridesharing side hustle would give you a forecast of $14,400 in annual revenue. This way, you have four weeks of likely (or at least potential) downtime from your side hustle built into your revenue forecast. If you wind up working more than 48 weeks in the year, then that extra money will be a little bit of a bonus.

What about a side hustle that has less certainty about how much work you'll be doing? Suppose you're doing a little bit of technical writing for your side hustle. Each gig works out to $1,500 on average, based on your hourly rate of $50 and the typical amount of work that someone contracts you to do, which is 30 hours of work per project.

You could do one technical writing project each week, finding the 30 hours that you need on weekends and in the evenings. However, for budgeting and forecasting purposes, how many technical writing gigs you *could* do is only part of the calculations you need to do. A better question to ask is how many technical writing gigs you *will* actually get.

What's that? You don't have a crystal ball to look a year into the future and see how many projects you wound up doing? That's okay; nobody else who has to do this kind of budgeting, whether for a side hustle or for a much larger company, has a crystal ball either. So, you'll have to do what everyone else does: Play the odds and figure out a couple of different scenarios:

>> Your *realistic* best-case scenario

>> Your "most likely to occur" scenario

>> Your worst-case scenario

Theoretically, your best-case scenario would be that you could do one technical writing gig every week. After all, you have the time, right? Presuming you allocate 48 weeks to your side hustle (leaving a few weeks for vacations), you could forecast a best-case scenario of $72,000 in revenue ($1,500 per week × 48 weeks).

Will you get a technical-writing project every single week? Or do you really want to work an additional 30 hours every week, even if you *could* get an unbroken string of one project after another? The answers to both of those questions: Probably not!

So, what is a *realistic* number of projects that you could use to forecast your revenue? You do a little bit of research, and it looks like about three 30-hour projects every two months is what other technical writers are doing. Sure, you may have some projects that will take you longer; you also may have other projects where they won't pay your $50-per-hour rate, but you decide that $45 or even $40 per hour is okay on a one-time basis. But for budgeting purposes, you stick with $1,500 per project based on the $50 per hour and 30 hours figures that you've been using.

So, where does that leave you for your revenue forecast? Based on three projects every two months, or about 1½ projects per month, you're looking at $27,000 coming in from your side hustle: $1,500 per project × 1.5 projects per month × 12 months.

For forecasting purposes, you could play it safe and drop your three projects every two months down to two projects, which would then give you a "floor" of $18,000 for the next year in revenue, with a realistic upside resulting in your earlier $27,000 calculation.

TIP

Playing it safe with the lower end of forecasting will help you with "fits and starts" revenue — in other words, you have a burst of activity where you're busy almost every week for a little while, and then it's radio silence for the next month or two with absolutely no work at all.

So far, so good, right? But what about the side-hustle equivalent of revenue being anywhere between nothing and megabucks? Let's say your side hustle is developing courses that you'll post on Skillshare, Teachable, or Udemy. You set up a recording studio in your spare bedroom and over a three-month period, you record four different courses that cover a series of career-oriented topics for new college graduates. You price your first course at only $20 to try to get as many purchasers as possible, and each of your other three courses you price at $100.

What should your revenue forecast be as you start working on your budget? In theory, you could bring in hundreds of thousands of dollars from your courses, right? Each year, almost two million students graduate with a bachelor's degree in the United States. Let's see: 2,000,000 students × $320 if every one of those students purchases all four of your courses. . . .

Whoa! You *know* that you'll *never* have two million brand new college graduates buying every one of your courses! So, what's a realistic "high side" number for your revenue?

As a starting point, you could play the "one-tenth of one percent" game. If "only" one-tenth of one percent — so 0.1 percent — purchase your courses, what would that give you in revenue? Wait, before you do the math, consider one other reality: How many people among that 0.1 percent would buy all four of your courses? Better drop that down to, say, just the first and second course for planning purposes, which would be $120 revenue per person. Some people will only buy your first $20 course; others will buy two or three or maybe all four. But for now, just go with $120 in revenue.

So, now you have:

>> Two thousand people who buy your course (0.1 percent × 2,000,000 college graduates)

>> A revenue of $120 per person

>> An upside revenue of $240,000

Not bad! Sure, you spent around 400 long, long hours into the deep, dark night, week after week for three months, recording and editing your courses. But, hey, if you can make $240,000 *in the first year alone* from those courses, that would've been time well spent!

WARNING

But what happens if you build it and *nobody* comes? Not one single new college graduate purchases any of your courses? Maybe nobody ever finds your courses; or maybe they browse the descriptions but decide they don't want to spend $20 for the first one, let alone $100 each for the others. The reason that nobody buys any of your courses isn't important for budgeting and forecasting purposes; the simple fact that you don't sell any of your courses is *the* single relevant data point.

Let's see, that would mean your side hustle revenue works out to, well, nothing!

"Nothing" is definitely your worst-case scenario, but is that a *realistic* worst-case scenario? Probably not. Because you're uploading your courses to one or more of the big-time learning platforms, you'll probably sell at least *some* courses, simply because those platforms get a ton of traffic. At this point, though, you're basically throwing darts at the wall to come up with a number — in other words, you're guessing.

You could presume that only 50 people will purchase any of your courses. You can use that same $120 per person figure ($20 for your first course and $100 for an additional one), and that would give you a low range, worst-case scenario of $6,000 in revenue for the next year — far different from your "Woo-hoo!" upper-range figure of $240,000!

So, what's a realistic number? Honestly, you just don't know until you try. If you've already published a couple of courses, you can use your historical sales numbers and revenue figures as the foundation to forecast revenue for new courses. However:

>> If you're just starting out your side hustle, you don't have any prior course data of your own to go by.

>> You could try to find *comps* (comparable data, to use the common real-estate term) from other side hustlers' courses, but such data is difficult to find. And even if you do get some stats, you have no idea if their figures will be comparable to yours.

>> Markets and interests change over time — sometimes very frequently — and for all you know, your courses are already out of style even before you get them published, or shortly afterward.

>> As much as you don't want to consider this possibility, you need to: Your courses may not be very good and may receive pretty bad ratings and reviews from early purchasers, which sort of kills any future interest from others.

Basically, with many side hustles, especially those involving online content, whether they're paid courses or free (with ads and affiliate links), you are taking the proverbial shot in the dark as you head down this particular path. Maybe you'll hit it big; maybe you'll wind up with a big fat nothing for all your efforts; or maybe you'll find the sweet spot where you'll earn a fair bit of revenue for your efforts.

But will you make any money? The answer to that question comes from the second part of your budgeting: the expense side.

THE SORT-OF-STEADY PAYCHECK

If your side hustle is something like college teaching where you get paid a part-time salary as a W2 employee, you have a lot of predictability to your income. Still, you need to account for periods where you won't receive any income, at least from that gig.

For example, suppose you sign a contract to teach two undergraduate classes in the upcoming fall semester, and you'll be paid $4,500 per class. The college issues paychecks every two weeks, and the payroll calendar is set up as follows:

- Nine paychecks during the fall semester

- Nine paychecks during the spring semester

- One paycheck during the winter holiday break after the fall semester but before the spring semester starts

- One paycheck immediately following the spring semester, but before summer school starts

- Six paychecks during the summer

(continued)

(continued)

Regular full-time faculty members get paid year-round, even if they aren't teaching during the summer, or they can choose to receive their salaries only during the 20 weeks of the academic year.

But for you and any other side-hustle instructors doing part-time teaching, your teaching money is paid in full during the semester that you're teaching. So, you'll receive your $9,000 ($4,500 per class × 2 classes) in equal increments during each of the nine fall semester paychecks — $1,000 in gross income per paycheck, before taxes and any other withholdings are deducted.

But you will *not* receive any money over the winter holidays during that one pay period, because you aren't teaching. And if you only sign up to teach one class during the following spring semester, you'll receive a gross payment of $500 ($4,500 ÷ by 9 pay periods) every two weeks.

So, on the one hand, side hustles like teaching, where you receive a fixed, predetermined salary are the *most* predictable when it comes to budgeting and forecasting your revenue. On the other hand, though, that predictability only lasts for a relatively short period of time (such as one academic semester) before you need to "reset" your calculations, possibly based on different underlying data, such as teaching only a different number of classes. And you also need to account for down periods where, even though you know with certainty that your revenue will continue for a while, you may have a week or two, or a month or two, where you won't receive any side-hustle income until you start back up again.

Separating your gross revenue from your net revenue for budgeting purposes

Here's a brainteaser: When is your side-hustle revenue less than your side-hustle revenue?

If this question makes no sense at all, how about if I expand on it just a little bit: When is your *net* side-hustle revenue less than your *gross* side-hustle revenue?

The answer: Very often, depending on the nature of your side hustle and how you reach your customers or clients.

Suppose you list your website development services on Fiverr, and you have a decent amount of business for your side hustle. Fiverr will take 20 percent of the *gross* amount of the fees you earn for each job you do. So, if you bill a client $500 for a web development job, Fiverr will keep $100 and you'll receive $400, or 80 percent of the amount paid.

REMEMBER

When you do your revenue budgeting, make sure to account for any platform fees through Fiverr, Thumbtack, or any other marketplace platform where you list your services. Ideally, you should plan for both the *gross* revenue, as well as your *net* revenue after taxes. But for the "money that you will actually receive" category, go by the net proceeds, after any platform fees.

Likewise, if you're doing courses on Udemy, or writing a book and using a literary agent, make sure that you're crystal clear on how much in fees will be paid so you don't count your revenue chickens that will never hatch!

Planning your expenses

If you thought your *revenue* picture was all over the map, wait until you get a look at the expense side!

Depending on what sort of side hustle you're doing, some or all of the following expense categories may apply to you.

Raw materials

If your side hustle involves making items that you'll resell, you'll need to buy raw materials that you'll use to make your products.

Sarah makes custom jewelry for her side hustle that she sells on her website. She doesn't just materialize that custom jewelry out of nowhere, of course. She buys metals (copper, silver, bronze, gold) and stones (emeralds, rubies, sapphires) that she uses to make her jewelry.

Sarah needs to account for raw materials when she starts budgeting for her expenses. In some ways, Sarah has a straight-line relationship between her revenue and her raw materials expenses when it comes to forecasting: The more jewelry she sells, the more raw materials she needs. Sarah can use this sales-to-materials equivalence to help forecast her raw materials costs.

On the other hand, unless Sarah's business model is "You order, then I buy the materials and make your jewelry," she'll need to *preemptively* order various metals and stones even before she knows for sure exactly what items will be ordered. Sarah doesn't want to order too much raw materials — especially gold, silver, and expensive stones that will cost her a fair bit of money — but at the same time, she doesn't want to always have to wait weeks or months after an item is ordered until she finally can make and ship the item. So, Sarah's revenue forecast will definitely be a consideration when she's doing her raw materials budget.

TECHNICAL STUFF

Raw materials are a little bit tricky when it comes to your taxes (see Chapter 10). You'll enter most of your expenses as just that: expenses. Raw materials, however, typically fall under a category known as *cost of goods sold* (COGS), which is exactly what it sounds like: your direct costs for items that you sell. If you're buying premade jewelry or clothing or almost anything else that you'll just resell rather than make, your COGS will be your wholesale costs from your suppliers. If you're doing what Sarah is doing for her side hustle — buying raw materials that you then use to make finished items — your COGS will be the materials that you use to make your ready-for-sale goods.

TIP

Confused? Don't be — and in fact, for *budgeting* purposes, you should forget all about tax distinctions between COGS and your other expenses. Both categories may be different for tax purposes, but when it comes to budgeting, you have a key similarity that outweighs tax form differences: You're spending money as part of your side hustle that you need to factor into your overall financial plans.

What if you aren't making any items as part of your side hustle? Most likely you won't have any raw materials expenses to budget for. Doing ridesharing or package delivery for a gig-economy side hustle? No raw materials. Providing software development or technical writing or similar services? No raw materials. Nice and easy!

Tools of the trade

What if you're providing services for your side hustle and you need to buy materials — just not materials that you use to create items? You would categorize such items as *tools of the trade* for whatever your side hustle is.

For example, Cindy does weekend bartending gigs for her side hustle. She doesn't have any raw materials relevant to her bartending — her clients supply their own drinks and mixers, drinking glasses, cocktail napkins, and all the rest of the items needed for their parties. All Cindy has to do is show up, set up, and then the party guests can drink up!

Cindy still spends a little bit of money on just-in-case items, though, such as a couple of corkscrews and fancy wine bottle openers in case she shows up and her client can't find theirs or the one she's using breaks. She also keeps a couple packages of cocktail napkins, a few boxes of toothpicks, and other assorted bartending supplies in the trunk of her car in case she needs them. For Cindy's bartending gig, these items are all her tools of the bartending trade that she needs to budget for. She'll probably only spend a little bit of money on these items, but she still needs to take them into consideration.

Cindy's "bartending soulmate" Miguel is doing videos for his side hustle. Miguel also has tools of the trade to budget for: video equipment, video-editing software, and other techie tools that he needs to make his videos.

REMEMBER

Other than ridesharing and similar gig-economy delivery-type side hustles, you'll probably have a few tools of the trade for your side hustle: the things that you need to buy to get yourself set up.

Outside services

Are you planning on having an accountant do your tax returns? That should cost you around $1,000 per year, give or take, depending on how complex your side hustle is.

Did you set up your side hustle as an S corporation? Does your attorney takes care of your various state-level Corporation Commission filings every year? Your attorney will probably charge you around $500 to take care of that paperwork for you.

Are you paying someone a couple hundred dollars a month to do your online search engine optimization (SEO) to try to move your side hustle's listing up higher in Google's search results? Are you paying an outside public relations firm $500 a month to send out press releases about your side hustle consulting business?

Many side hustles make use of outside providers for accounting, legal, technical, marketing, and other services. As your business plans took shape, you decided what tasks you would take care of yourself and what ones you would farm out to someone else. Anything that some other person or company is doing will fall under the "outside services" bucket for your budgeting.

Tech expenses

If you're doing Uber or Lyft ridesharing, or delivering meals for DoorDash, you shouldn't have to worry about tech-related expenses, but almost every other side hustler will need to budget for computer hardware, software, website development and hosting, and other techie stuff.

WARNING

Make sure you don't double-count some of your tech expenses as you're budgeting. If you already accounted for someone to do SEO as an outside service, even though search engines are definitely techie, don't duplicate your SEO expenses also under "tech expenses."

Marketing and advertising

Stop me if you heard this before, but if you're ridesharing, shopping and delivering groceries, or picking up and delivering restaurant meals, you almost certainly won't have any marketing and advertising expenses, and won't need to budget for those categories.

You may still not have any marketing and advertising expenses to budget for even with other side hustles — but you might. Advertising and marketing can range from flat fees that you pay to list your services on a website to hundreds or even thousands of dollars paid to an outside public relations firm. And don't forget social-media marketing — running ads on Facebook or Instagram or doing Google Ads.

REMEMBER

As with your tech expense budgeting and forecasting, make sure not to double-count expenses that may fit into more than one category. If you're paying someone to do your social-media advertising or you've hired a public relations firm, and you've already counted those projected expenses under "outside services," don't double-count them under "marketing and advertising."

Expenses for keeping your side hustle safe and legal

You'll need to budget for some or all of the following, depending on which items apply to your side hustle:

>> **Basic business liability insurance:** Covers claims against your side hustle, such as someone getting hurt while on your property, or your accidentally hurting someone physically in the course of doing your work.

>> **Errors and omissions (E&O) insurance:** Protects you if you make an error or omit "something important" from what you deliver to a client, or otherwise make a big-time mistake that a client claims causes harm to their business. You'll need this insurance if you're performing any type of professional services — software development, consulting, technical writing, accounting, and so on.

>> **Licenses:** This category includes general licenses, such as paying for a *transaction privilege tax* (TPT) license to be able to sell products and collect sales tax, or an industry-specific license for doing certain types of services (a good example would be a cosmetology license that you need to cut hair, do nails, and provide other appearance-related services, even as a side hustle).

Vehicle and transportation expenses

Vehicle and transportation expenses can be tricky for side-hustle budgeting purposes.

Suppose you're doing ridesharing through Uber and Lyft. You couldn't provide ridesharing if you didn't have a car, right? But unless you specifically purchased a car so you could do ridesharing or other gig-economy delivery services, you're using your own car that you already have. If you weren't doing ridesharing or delivery services, you would still have a car, and you might still have a car payment if you haven't yet paid off your car. So, do you really have to budget for your car if you already have one?

REMEMBER

The answer to that all-important question: maybe not your car itself, but you will have *incremental* expenses related to your car-based side hustle. Specifically:

>> You'll need more gasoline to drive for your side hustle than if you weren't doing ridesharing or delivery services.

>> You'll need to do routine maintenance (such as oil changes or new tires) more often than if you weren't using your car for your side hustle, simply because you're putting way more miles on your car than you otherwise would.

>> You *might* need significant repairs, or even need to buy a new car, sooner than you otherwise would because you're wearing out your car through ridesharing.

REMEMBER

When it comes to budgeting for vehicle and transportation expenses for your side hustle, focus on the difference between the amount of driving you would be doing outside of your side hustle versus the amount of driving you'll now be doing because of your side hustle.

Real estate and property

If you're doing a side hustle out of your house or apartment, you shouldn't have any real-estate or property expenses related to your side hustle. Even if you're taking a home office deduction (see Chapter 10), you really don't have any *incremental* real-estate costs associated with your side hustle. You're using a spare bedroom that you already have or some other area of your house that already exists and just dedicating that space to your side hustle.

If you have any sort of physical location for your side hustle, however, then you will have real estate–related expenses to budget for. Suppose Brittany's online boutique or Sarah's custom jewelry business go so well that they decide to open up small stores in a local strip mall. Now each of them needs to account for rent, utilities, property taxes, and other property-related expenses.

When else might real-estate expenses come into play for your side hustle? Oh, yeah, when real estate *is* your side hustle! If you're leasing out a second home, or listing your vacation property on Airbnb or Vrbo, you'll be planning and budgeting for real-estate revenue but also for the associated real-estate expenses.

Travel expenses

Depending on your side hustle, you might have some out-of-town travel for your business that you need to budget for. If you're running a retail type of side hustle, you may find yourself traveling to various retail shows where suppliers show off their latest goods. For example, lots of online retailers — including plenty of side hustlers — go to MAGIC (www.magicfashionevents.com) in Las Vegas, New York, Nashville, or some other location to check out "the largest selection of trend-driven and young contemporary apparel, footwear, and accessories in the industry" (according to the MAGIC website).

If you need to do any traveling for your side hustle, work those costs into your budget.

Funding Your Side Hustle

Side-hustle revenue? Good stuff!

Side-hustle expenses? Well, not necessarily "bad stuff," but you do have to ask yourself: Where will you get the money to start your side hustle and keep it running?

Eventually, you want to get to the point where your side-hustle expenses are easily covered by your revenue and you're also stashing away some of that hard-earned cash for your own use. But what about the time frame until your revenue starts flowing? How do you get the money that you need — or do you even need any money to get going?

You have three primary sources of funding for your side hustle:

>> Your own money

>> Borrowed money

>> Invested money from outsiders

For your side hustle, any one or more — maybe even all three — of these sources could be relevant.

Using your own money

You may need only a little bit of money to get going with your side hustle. Suppose you're packaging and selling courses on platforms such as Teachable or Udemy or posting videos onto YouTube.

Good news: You need a webcam, maybe a backdrop and lighting if you're going to be recording yourself live (versus narrating slides or talking into your computer), some video-editing software, a high-quality microphone — probably $1,500 or less in total.

Even better news: You may already have a webcam, a microphone, and the video-editing software, which means that you might only have to spend a couple hundred dollars before you're off and running.

REMEMBER

If you only need a little bit of money — and especially if you only need a *very* little bit of money — for your side hustle, your best course of action is to fund it yourself.

Even if you need more than a little bit of money, you can always dip into your own savings and investments for the funding that you need instead of borrowing money or going to an outside investor.

WARNING

Keep in mind, though, that if you tap your savings or investments for your side hustle, you could end up losing some or all of that money if your side hustle flops.

In fact, you could use this warning as a litmus test as you hit the final stages of your planning and start looking at the numbers on both the revenue and expense side. Look at your side hustle as if someone else were planning to do it, and ask yourself: "Would I invest *my* money in this business?"

If your answer is "Yes," then by all means, consider using your own money as needed to get your side hustle up and running. If, however, you answer that question with a "No" — or if you're just not sure — then you may need to go back to the drawing board and take a fresh look at your side hustle plans from the very beginning.

Borrowing money for your side hustle

You can borrow money for your side hustle from a variety of sources:

>> Friends or family members

>> Banks or other financial institutions

>> So-called "alternative lenders"

>> Special borrowing programs offered during extraordinary times

Hitting up your friends and relatives

WARNING

Your friends and family members may represent an easy source of funding for a loan, but you need to really give this idea a second thought, and a third thought, and a fourth. . . .

Nothing says "hard feelings" like borrowing money from someone close to you and not being able to pay back that money. Unless you have a friend or relative who is just rolling in money and wouldn't be affected in the least if your side hustle flopped and you can't pay them back, look elsewhere for a business loan first.

Borrowing from the banks

Many banks and some credit unions provide loans to small businesses — including side hustles — that are backed by the Small Business Administration (SBA). The SBA is a U.S. governmental agency that encourages financial institutions to offer commercial loans by insuring those loans in case you don't pay back part or all of the loan.

The SBA offers a variety of loan programs for small businesses, ranging from its flagship SBA 7(a) program to so-called "SBA microloans" that are issued through nonprofit community-based lenders. Check out the latest information about the SBA loan programs (www.sba.gov/loanprograms) that are offered to see what ones may be best for your side hustle. Then, when you decide on a specific type of SBA loan, you need to find a lender — a bank or credit union — that actually lends you the money.

TIP

The first place to check is the place where you usually do your banking. But be sure to check out other banks and credit unions as well to compare rates, loan terms, and other details.

Funding from alternative lenders

In recent years, the concept of peer-to-peer lending has caught on. Companies such as Funding Circle and Upstart provide you with the opportunity to apply for and receive a small business loan that you can use to fund your side hustle.

TIP

On the other side of the peer-to-peer lending equation, you can usually invest in pools of funding that the companies use to lend out to other small businesses and side hustles. So, if your side hustle hits the big time, you can always "pay it forward" by helping other side hustlers get their businesses off the ground.

Once-in-a-lifetime (you hope!) lending programs

When the COVID-19 pandemic hit in early 2020, governments all around the world scrambled to help out businesses large and small. In the United States, the Coronavirus Aid, Relief, and Economic Security (CARES) Act offered a variety of programs for individuals and businesses. One of these programs was the Payroll Protection Program (PPP).

The SBA took on the PPP alongside its other lending programs. Small businesses could apply for special loans that would cover their payroll and some of their business operating expenses so businesses could keep their employees on the payroll instead of having to lay them off, even if their revenues were heavily impacted by the pandemic. Then businesses that received PPP funding could apply for loan forgiveness, which turned those loans into free money that didn't need to be paid back.

REMEMBER

The PPP program has ended, but as your side hustle grows, you should always keep an eye out for special lending programs that come into existence because of unusual circumstances. Back in 2008 and afterward, during the Great Recession, all sorts of special lending programs and stimulus spending were available for businesses to help them through those tough times.

If you're doing food delivery or weekend bartending or creating videos, chances are, you won't find any special lending programs that would apply to your business. But you never know, so keep your eyes open.

Bringing in outside investors

What's that? You hate the idea of borrowing money from anybody, even banks or financial institutions? But you don't have enough money right now for all the investment that you need to get your side hustle going, according to all the startup expenses that you calculated you'll need?

You can always seek an investor for your side hustle — someone who will provide money for your business that isn't a loan, and that you don't have to pay back. So, what's the catch?

An investor is a part-owner of that business. Basically, you "sell" or trade some portion of your *equity* (ownership stake) in your side hustle in exchange for the money that you receive.

Suppose you have pretty big ambitions for a major online retail business. You want to hire some highly skilled web developers to build the slickest website with *virtual reality* (VR) features to have customers feel like they're actually shopping in a store. You want to have a ton of inventory, and you need to lease a separate facility to be your warehouse and shipping facility. You need to hire a couple of part-time workers because you plan to keep your day job for another two years to qualify for the pension that you worked so long to qualify for.

What's your total price tag just to get off the ground? Close to $100,000!

So, you reach out to someone you know who once got investment funding for her startup, and she connects you with an *angel investor* (someone who typically invests in businesses as they're just getting started). Angel investors usually provide funding in exchange for about a 20 percent to 25 percent ownership stake in the business. If your side hustle hits the big time, and presuming you never add any other investors, you'll own 75 percent to 80 percent of your business, but your angel investor will own the balance and be entitled to that portion of the money that you make.

In contrast, if you borrow money from a bank, after you pay back that loan, they have no claim on your business at all. So, which is better: borrowing money, or getting funding from an investor who you don't pay back but for whom you've given up some of your ownership? The debt-versus-equity decision is part of the big-time finance decisions that large companies go through all the time, and you won't find an easy answer that fits all circumstances. Consult a trusted financial advisor who is experienced in small business funding to explore your various options for *your* side hustle.

Side-hustle investors come in two flavors:

>> **Passive investors,** who put money into your business and may provide advice here and there, but otherwise don't have an active role in running your business

>> **Active investors,** who not only put money into your business, but also take on some portion of helping to run your business — basically, becoming your partner in an operational sense

WARNING

If you decide to accept money from an investor who will become your business partner, be *very* careful to make sure that the two of you (or more than two of you, if you'll have multiple investors) are compatible. Check out Chapter 13 for more information.

Money Coming and Going

After your side hustle is underway, money will be coming in on a regular basis, and money will also be going out. How will you take care of both incoming and outgoing payments?

Collecting payments

REMEMBER

You want to automate your incoming payments as much as you possibly can. If you were side hustling back when I started, long ago in the 20th century (!), most of your incoming payments would have been via paper checks, either handed to you in person or mailed to you. How quaint!

These days, you can automate almost all your incoming payments through one or more of the following:

>> Direct deposits into your business bank account, through the automated clearing house (ACH) system

>> Direct payments into a cash app system such as PayPal Goods and Services (G&S) or Venmo for Business

>> On-the-spot credit-card payments at places such as arts-and-crafts fairs or pop-up retail locations through a plug-in device for your phone or tablet

Suppose your side hustle is writing books, doing online video courses, and otherwise creating content that people pay for. When you get your accounts set up with your publisher or literary agent, or with a learning platform such as Udemy, you'll provide your business checking account number and routing number to the place that will periodically send you money. When payment time arrives — presto! — your royalties or other payments travel electronically into your bank account. All done!

WARNING

Make sure that for cash apps such as PayPal and Venmo, you use their business versions for your side hustle rather than their personal versions such as PayPal Friends and Family. PayPal, for example, offers PayPal Purchase Protection to protect buyers and sellers in the case of disputes.

TIP

Even if someone pays you by an old-fashioned physical check, you can still automate the deposit process a great deal. Most large and even midsize banks and credit unions offer mobile deposits via your phone, so you can sort-of-automate the check-deposit process without having to run to the bank.

Paying your bills

Just as you want to automate your incoming side-hustle money as much as possible, you should do the same for your outgoing payments. Make use of:

>> ACH payments directly from your bank account into a supplier's account

>> PayPal Goods and Services, Venmo for Business, or other business cash apps

>> Online bill-paying services from your bank for both recurring and one-time payments directly from your bank account without having to write a physical check

TIP

Most bank bill pay services offer two forms of payment: directly into some other company's bank account (so basically like an ACH account-to-account payment) or by printing a physical check that the bank mails to the recipient, so you still can avoid having to personally write checks.

WHAT ABOUT PAYING EMPLOYEES?

If you've taken your side hustle to the big time and you have employees you need to pay, check into using a payroll service such as APS Payroll or Paychex. Some payroll providers advertise that they specialize in small businesses, so also check out Gusto or the online payroll component of QuickBooks.

Chapter **9**

Keeping Track for You and Everyone Else

Between your side hustle and your day job, you're running fast and furious. Time is scarce, and you're juggling a lot of balls on a daily basis. Just like a crowded hospital emergency room where the staff needs to quickly examine and then prioritize a flood of patients — a process called *triage* — your mind is looking at everything that you have on your plate and yelling, "Triage!"

So, do you really want to add to your to-do list with a bunch of tedious record-keeping tasks? Well, you may not *want* to, but you have to!

REMEMBER

It doesn't matter if your side hustle is doing ridesharing for Uber or Lyft or doing delivery service gigs, or if you're recording and then trying to monetize a whole bunch of videos, or if you've created a "mini-business" like an online clothing and accessories boutique that has its own supply chain and where you're stashing inventory in your spare bedroom. Keeping careful track of *everything* related to your side hustle is essential!

That old saying "a stitch in time saves nine" means that you have a choice: a little bit of time now versus a whole lot of time down the road. So, grit your teeth and accept that your side hustle comes with a side order of record-keeping. By organizing your side hustle's record keeping from the start and doing your best to avoid playing catchup, you'll find yourself in pretty good shape.

Accessing Your Side Hustle's Foundational and Tax Documents

Starting and running any business — even a side hustle — is sort of like joining the Army. You need to fill out forms, *lots* of forms!

Depending on the specifics of your side hustle, you will likely:

>> Formally structure your business as a limited liability company (LLC), an S corporation, or a sole proprietorship (see Chapter 7).

>> Apply for an employer identification number (EIN) for your business.

>> Open a business checking account.

>> Maybe also open a business savings account.

>> Apply for a business credit card.

>> Apply for a general business liability insurance policy and maybe specialized business insurance such as errors and omissions (E&O).

>> Set up various business payment apps such as PayPal Goods and Services, Venmo for Business, and Block (formerly known as Square).

With every piece of the getting-underway puzzle comes documents, *lots* of documents.

You need to keep all your side hustle's foundational documents readily at hand. If you have physical paper copies, keep your originals in a safe-deposit box or a home safe, and also keep copies in well-organized file folders. If you have electronic copies, keep those files on your laptop and also safely stored in the cloud (for example, on a site like Dropbox).

Quickly pulling information from documents

TIP

Make sure you can get to documents quickly, because you may need to frequently access information from one or more documents.

Ali does a variety of tech consulting work on the side, in addition to his day job as a software tester. Every client asks him for the same information before he gets started on a job:

>> His tax identification number, which in Ali's case is his EIN

>> The routing and account numbers for his business checking account for the client to electronically transmit payments for Ali's work

Unlike his Social Security number (SSN), Ali doesn't know his EIN by heart. And he doesn't know his business banking information by heart, either. But he doesn't have to! With a few clicks on his laptop, Ali can bring up the documents that he needs and copy the applicable information onto the W-9 form for his EIN and the client's online payment form. All done. Now on to the side-hustle work itself!

Have another helping of documents

Your foundational documents are usually only the beginning. More documents related to those originals are on the way!

TECHNICAL STUFF

If you organize your side hustle as an S corporation, you have some pretty hefty document filing requirements every year. The filing requirements will vary depending on where you live, even in the United States. Why? Your state — not the federal government — governs corporations.

For example, I live in Arizona, and one of my side hustles is organized as an S corporation. Every year, I need to file documents with the Arizona Corporation Commission related to the "annual meeting of shareholders and the board of directors." I'm also required to file an annual report with the Corporation Commission. The paperwork never stops!

TIP

But you know what? I personally hate paperwork, even electronic paperwork. So, I have a corporate attorney act as a *statutory agent* who files those forms on my behalf. But I also have to file paperwork and pay an invoice related to my attorney filling this role. No matter where you live, you need to be aware of all *ongoing* document filing requirements for your S corporation, LLC, or sole proprietorship, as well as shortcuts you can take to ease your paperwork burden.

Regardless of what you do personally and what tasks you farm out to an attorney or accountant or someone else, *you* are the one responsible for organizing and managing all the documents related to your side hustle.

Keeping Track of Everything

Do you need to buy materials or products from a supplier for your side hustle? If so, you will

>> Place an order.

>> Pay for what you purchased — maybe half now, and then half when the goods arrive.

>> Receive an email informing you that your order has been received, when your order is ready for shipment, when your order has been shipped, and perhaps also when your supplier has been informed by the shipping company that they delivered your order.

Every single activity you do for your side hustle, and probably at every significant stage of each of those activities, will generate some sort of record that you need to track and manage.

Some of those records will automatically find their way into your record-keeping system. Other records will be managed in sort of a catching-up-later manner. You're responsible for staying on top of both of these "incoming information" models.

Your official side-hustle records

Depending on the nature of your side hustle, you'll need to keep track of many, most, or perhaps even all of the following:

>> Products that you purchase, either that you'll use yourself for your side hustle or for resale

>> Materials that you purchase that you'll use to make products that you'll sell

>> Services that others provide for your side hustle, such as building a website, designing a logo, or doing your business taxes

>> Products that you sell to others, regardless of whether you made those products yourself or you're reselling something that you bought from a supplier

>> Products or materials that you return because they're defective or (if permitted by a supplier) because you no longer need them

>> Services that you provide to others

>> Defective products returned to you by customers

>> Online content that you create

For each item in the preceding list, you need to further separate out your records into:

>> The details of the transaction itself, including (but not limited to) the following:

● How many different products

● How many of each product

● The amount of time you spend performing a service

● The amount of time someone spends performing a service for you

>> The financials associated with the transaction

In some cases, the transaction details and the financials flow from a supplier to you, or from you to a customer, in some standardized form such as a purchase order or an invoice that can be read into whatever financial system you're using for your side hustle (see "Side-hustle record-keeping tools and tech," later in this chapter). In these situations, when you hook up your financial system to both inbound and outbound transactions, you're all set.

In other situations, however, those transaction details and financials do *not* automatically get loaded into your system, even if they're done online rather than on old-fashioned paper. Maybe you've had an appliance repairperson come to your home to fix your refrigerator, and when the repairperson is finished working, they:

>> Fill out an invoice on their iPad.

>> Hand you the iPad for you to sign off on the work.

>> Process your credit card on the iPad.

For *them*, both the details of the transaction itself (parts used, amount of time spent, and so on) and the financials (the amount you paid) will be automatically transmitted into their financial system. But what about you? Chances are, you'll receive, via email, a PDF that is, essentially, little more than an image in terms of being able to access the transaction and financial details in an automated manner.

Many of the transactions you do for your side hustle will likely be communicated to you in the form of a "flat" PDF that can't automatically feed the data into your financial system, at least easily. For the repairperson coming to your home and emailing you an invoice in PDF form, that's not a big deal. Chances are, you'll just stuff that invoice into an email folder called "Home Repairs" and rarely, if ever, look at that email again.

But for your side hustle? You *need* that data! You have a couple of choices:

>> Use some sort of "PDF scraping" software such as Astera (www.astera.com/type/blog/pdf-scraping) or Wondershare (https://pdf.wondershare.com/how-to-extract-data-from-pdf-form.html) to try to extract transaction and financial data from the "flat" PDF file and then have that extracted data available for you to load into your system.

>> Take a look at each PDF as it comes in and manually enter the data into your financial system.

The first option could work, but you need to keep a close eye on the automated data feeds to make sure that your software doesn't "hiccup" because of a strangely formatted PDF.

The second option is the "easiest" because you don't need to build and monitor any automated interfaces. However, as you can probably guess, you need to spend the time actually doing the manual entry into your own system. If you have a lot of files flying in and out, that's a lot of manual entry for which you need to make time (see the next section).

Your backup and catchup plan

Okay, you're running a hundred miles an hour between your side hustle, your day job, and your life in general. Who has time to make a bunch of entries into your financial system?

TIP

For a couple of my own side hustles, I use what you could call a "backup and catchup" model for incoming transaction and financial details that arrive in PDF or other non-automated form. I have several email folders where I forward all incoming emails with the attached documents. Every week or so, I go through all new messages in those folders (with *new* meaning "since the last time I went in and cleaned up everything") and do the manual entries for those transactions into my own systems.

Then, until the next time I get my official systems caught up, if I need to check out the details of a transaction that hasn't yet been officially processed, I know to take a look at the email folders and grab the information I need from there.

What happens, though, if I go to Staples or Costco or any other physical store and buy something in person? True, I'll have the credit-card transaction record with the total amount of a purchase. But suppose I bought 10 or 15 different items at a time? If I had made that purchase online, I would have a PDF of the transaction, but not in person.

TIP

No problem, thanks to my cellphone camera. I take a quick picture of the itemized receipt that lists all products and all prices, and then email that photo to myself the same as if it were a PDF from an online transaction. That message then goes into a "backup and catchup" email folder alongside its PDF siblings. When it's time to go through the email folder and get caught up, the in-person side-hustle transactions are right there with the online ones.

WARNING

You probably see one big potential flaw in the "backup and catchup" plan, right? Procrastination! Hey, I'm as likely as anyone to say, "No, not today — I'm exhausted. I'll get all the transactions transferred over tomorrow." And then tomorrow, I'll say — tell me if you've heard this before — "No, not today — I'm exhausted. I'll get all the transactions transferred over tomorrow." Before you know it, it's "lather, rinse, repeat" time, and the email folders are getting bigger and bigger, with more and more PDFs and images to transfer when I finally steel myself to just do it already!

There's your secret: Just do it. You can't procrastinate forever. You have tax filings to do, and the last thing you want to do is wait an entire year to transfer a whole lot of financial information and put all the numbers into the correct tax categories. Besides, all that data can be pretty useful in helping you understand how well your side hustle is, or isn't, doing (see "Digging Into Your Side Hustle's Analytics," later in this chapter).

Side-hustle record-keeping tools and tech

What systems and technology should you use for your side-hustle record-keeping?

As much of a pain as "raw" PDFs are when it comes to extracting transaction and financial details, those PDFs do comprise the core of your side hustle's business records. You need to keep them safe and every bit as accessible as your side hustle's foundational documents.

REMEMBER

Follow a two-tier model for all your business documents — not just PDFs, but Microsoft Office files (Word, Excel, PowerPoint) and other file formats. First, store those documents in well-organized folders on your computer. Additionally, store every document in some sort of cloud storage facility such as Dropbox, iCloud, or any one of dozens of other cloud-storage facilities.

From a financial transaction perspective, you have a couple options:

>> If your side hustle has relatively low activity, you can keep things simple by using a spreadsheet program such as Microsoft Excel or Google Sheets to keep track of money coming into and going out of your business.

>> If your side hustle has dozens or even hundreds of transactions each month, you're better off using a small-business accounting and finance program such as QuickBooks as the backbone of your business.

If you're using a program such as QuickBooks, you can keep your accounting up to date through automated feeds from financial systems such as:

>> Your business checking and savings accounts

>> Your business credit cards

>> Payment apps such as PayPal and Venmo

WARNING

Every so often, an automated feed may not connect properly, requiring you to reauthorize the connection by resetting the password, issuing and entering a one-time authorization code, or something along those lines. Yeah, it can be a pain, but most likely, you won't have to patch up an automated feed too often. So, think of these occasional glitches as minor tech hiccups, and try not to get too frustrated.

Digging Into Your Side Hustle's Analytics

No matter what your side hustle is, you'll frequently be asking questions about your finances and activities. If you're doing a gig-economy side hustle, your questions will be fairly straightforward, and — with good record-keeping — be fairly easy to answer. If your side hustle is a mini-business such as boutique or a hair salon or helping people do local moves, you'll have even more questions, and your record-keeping ducks will need to be even more in a row.

Rhianna doesn't have a full-time salaried job. Instead, she divides her time among five different gig-economy side hustles:

>> Ridesharing for Uber

>> Ridesharing for Lyft

>> Delivery services for Uber Eats

>> Delivery services for Instacart

>> In-home pet-sitting through Rover

In any given week, Rhianna may do more ridesharing but less of the food delivery and pet sitting, or more food delivery but less ridesharing and pet sitting, or more pet sitting and ridesharing but less food delivery. . ..

You get the idea. Building your full-time "job" out of a side-hustle portfolio as Rhianna is doing tends to be unpredictable at times. But because this collection of side hustles is — at least for now — the only way that Rhianna is earning money to pay her rent, make her car payment, and cover her other monthly expenses, she needs to have some idea of what her side-hustle activity has been in the past, as well as what her side-hustle activity looks like right now.

Good news for Rhianna: Each of those gig-economy companies provides its contractors with reports about their earnings and activity.

But in Rhianna's case, she needs more insight than just what she can get from each of the companies through which she does her gigs. Figure 9-1 shows how Rhianna can take these "raw inputs" and mash them all together to give her a comprehensive picture of her activity in any given time period, past or present, to help her make critical decisions about her side-hustle activity.

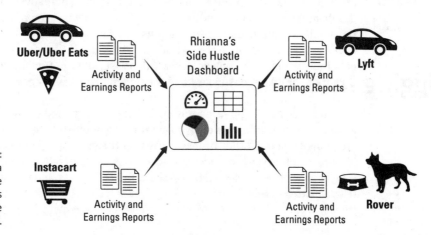

FIGURE 9-1: Creating a comprehensive set of analytics across multiple side hustles.

By turning rudimentary record-keeping into an integrated set of data from *all* her side hustles, Rhianna can now dig into the numbers across her entire portfolio and see:

>> How the proportion of her side-hustle income coming from ridesharing has trended over the past three months, as well as the proportion of her income from Uber versus Lyft during that time

>> How the proportion of her side-hustle *time* coming from ridesharing has trended, along with any important trends in her earnings per hour from ridesharing

>> How much her overall tips have been, week over week, from all her side hustles; what the ratio of base earnings to tips has been; and how that number is trending

Armed with these insights, Rhianna can not only see what has happened and what is happening right now, but also make key decisions about what she should do for her side hustles:

>> Should she slow down on the Instacart activity and do more Uber Eats, because she's making better money and receiving better tips there?

>> Should she shift more of her ridesharing to Lyft rather than Uber?

>> If she has a three-week in-home pet-sitting job coming up for a family who will be vacationing in Europe, how much other side-hustle activity can she squeeze in during those three weeks, and which ones should she do to make the most money in the available time she'll have?

TECHNICAL STUFF

From Rhianna's perspective as a consumer of data-driven insights about her side hustles, all she wants is "one-stop shopping" for key reports and analytics that are built from data coming from Uber, Lyft, Instacart, and Rover. Underneath that dashboard comprised of reports and graphs and maybe even advanced visualizations will be data coming from various providers, in various formats. Someone needs to merge and integrate all that data together. If Rhianna wants to dabble in data integration, more power to her. Otherwise, she can find a techie on Fiverr or Upwork to build her dashboard and the underlying data integration for her.

Side hustlers in the gig-economy realm need reports and analytics, just as Rhianna does. Other side hustlers who are running online boutiques or salons, or who are doing yoga and other fitness classes on the side, or who are custom-making jewelry or other fashion accessories that they then sell wholesale to retailers (maybe even other side-hustle retailers!) need reports and analytics even more than Rhianna does.

REMEMBER

Reports and analytics all come from data, and data comes from good record-keeping. Remember this important equation: The better your record-keeping, the more insightful your reporting and analytics will be, and the better you'll be able to manage and grow your side hustle. Or, reversing and condensing that equation: Your ability to manage and grow your side hustle starts with good record-keeping.

Taking Those Old Records Off the Shelf

You walk down to get your mail one afternoon, open your mailbox, and there it is: that dreaded "Greetings from the Internal Revenue Service" letter! You're being audited! Or, more specifically, your side-hustle business is being audited.

Or you find a letter from your state's Corporation Commission, and they "have some questions" and "need some information" from you about the legal structure and operations of your side hustle.

Or perhaps you've been unable to resolve a dispute with one of your suppliers from whom you ordered and paid for hundreds or even thousands of dollars' worth of merchandise that turned out to be defective, and they're refusing to honor their quality guarantee and issue you a refund. Now you have to take them to court, and your attorney needs copies of all correspondence and receipts related to not only this particular transaction, but other purchases you made from this supplier as well.

How about one more? You used to have a side hustle going where you recorded videos about various health and wellness topics. After getting a big promotion at your day job, however, you stopped doing your videos because you didn't have enough time anymore and were doing a lot of business travel. One evening, in your hotel room after dinner, you do a little bit of web browsing and stumble across somebody else's health and wellness channel on YouTube and guess what you see? An entire series of videos that are nearly identical to your old ones — like someone watched your videos, copied down everything you said, and just recorded their own versions of your old ones. The attorney who you contact asks you to provide your original time-stamped recordings along with a whole lot of other materials.

REMEMBER

You never know when you'll need to retrieve computer files, legal documents, lists, banking records, emails, direct messages — you name it! — from what you thought was the distant past. You may be focused on the here and now with your side-hustle records, but at any point, for a variety of reasons, you need to dig into your side-hustle archives.

How long should you keep your side hustle records?

A famous ad campaign proclaimed, "A diamond is forever." You can say the same thing about your side hustle: "Record-keeping is forever!"

WARNING

Don't plan to maintain your records only for the least amount of time you may read in a news article, in some blog post, or even on an official governmental agency's website.

How long should you keep the tax records and receipts for your side hustle? If you're in the United States, according to the IRS's guide for small businesses and self-employed individuals (www.irs.gov/businesses/small-businesses-self-employed/how-long-should-i-keep-records), the answer to that question *starts off* with a simple, straightforward "Keep records for 3 years." Easy, right?

Sorry. If your eyes land on "3 years," but you don't read any further, you may find yourself with big problems! That same sentence continues on to say ". . . if situations (4), (5), and (6) below do not apply to you." So, what are "situations (4), (5), and (6)"?

>> Situation (4) reads "Keep records for 6 years if you do not report income that you should report, and it is more than 25% of the gross income shown on your return." Wow, that's confusing! But you're going to correctly report all your income from your side hustle, so no worries there, right?

>> Situation (5) reads "Keep records indefinitely if you do not file a return." Once again, no problems because you've filed your tax returns every year.

>> Situation (6) reads "Keep records indefinitely if you file a fraudulent return." Wow, that sounds ominous! But you're definitely *not* going to file a fraudulent tax return — ever! — so once again, nothing to worry about.

But what happens if:

>> You somehow mistakenly don't include some of your side-hustle income on your tax return as described in the IRS's situation (4), which triggers an audit, and now you need to document all your revenue and business expenses?

>> Even though you did file a return — situation (5) — somehow the IRS didn't process it or lost your return, and now they're claiming you didn't file a tax return 5 years ago?

>> You find yourself accused of filing a fraudulent tax return related to your side hustle as described in the IRS's situation (6) and you definitely need to document and prove all your business revenues and expenses?

REMEMBER

Keep all your side hustle business records — forever!

Even beyond taxes, you never know when you may need to produce legal documents related to your side hustle. You don't even need to be in trouble. Suppose at the beginning of the COVID-19 pandemic, you went to apply for a business loan for your gardening and landscaping side hustle under the Paycheck Protection Program (PPP) provisions of the Coronavirus Aid, Relief, and Economic Security (CARES) Act. Even though you were still doing your day job, you had grown your side hustle to the point where you had four part-time employees.

You had to fill out a lot of forms online, but for the sake of your side hustle in light of all the economic uncertainty, you definitely wanted to get that PPP loan. Part of the PPP application requirements was to provide a copy of all documents related to your business's legal formation as an LLC or S corporation.

What's that you say? You don't know where those documents are? In fact, you're not sure that you even have those documents anymore? Well, time to make a phone call — or ten phone calls — to your state's Corporation Commission or some other governmental agency to see if they can provide you with photocopies of the documents you filed a long time ago. And given the rush for PPP loans right after the CARES Act was passed, you and a couple thousand of your closest friends were all flooding the overworked folks at some governmental agency for documents that you should've had at your fingertips! And all the while, you're racing the deadline to apply for that much-needed money from a PPP loan. Will you somehow get the important paperwork that you need in time to file your loan application before the deadline?

In case you might think that this scenario is an exaggeration for purposes of this chapter, nope — it's a 100 percent true example from someone I know.

Record-keeping for your real-estate side hustle

If you've ever owned and then sold a home, you had to figure out your profit or loss during the time that you owned that property in order to correctly calculate the tax impact of that sale transaction. Say you sold a home for $500,000, and for the sake of this example, presume that you either purchased the home for cash or you paid off the mortgage a few years ago. Because you don't owe a bank or finance company anything from the sale to clear a mortgage, you'll receive $500,000 from the transaction, minus any closing costs such as state transfer taxes or brokerage fees to the real-estate agent who sold your home. To keep the example simple, assume your closing costs are an even $10,000, which means you'll pocket $490,000 (your $500,000 sales price minus the $10,000 in closing costs that are taken directly out of the proceeds).

You do *not* owe income taxes on $490,000! You only owe taxes on your *gain* from the transaction. If you purchased the home for $300,000, you would owe taxes on your $190,000 gain ($490,000 minus your $300,000 purchase price).

As they say in the infomercials: But wait! There's more!

Suppose that while you owned your home, you actually spent $40,000 building an addition when you first bought the home and $15,000 on a new air-conditioning system seven years ago when your original one broke down and couldn't be repaired. That $55,000 ($40,000 plus $15,000) actually gets added to the *cost basis* of your home. So, you'll really owe taxes on the difference between your proceeds (still $490,000) and your cost basis, which is

>> Your $300,000 purchase price

>> The $55,000 in improvements that you're legally allowed to add to your basis

So, now you'll pay taxes on a gain of $135,000 — not $190,000. In other words, you'll owe less in taxes than if you didn't include the qualified improvements.

Well, how did you know for certain that years earlier you had spent exactly $40,000 building an addition to your home, or that you had spent $15,000 on a new air-conditioning system? Maybe that $40,000 addition wasn't paid through a single check, but rather on dozens of credit-card transactions to Home Depot or Ace Hardware, and several checks over a period of two years to various building contractors. No problem! You wrote down all those amounts and transaction dates on a page labeled "Home Improvements" in a notebook, or you made entries onto a spreadsheet by the same name on your computer. And then, if the IRS were to come calling, how do you prove you actually spent what you claimed? You saved all the receipts: physically on paper or as images in cloud storage or both.

Now at this point, you may be thinking "Wait a minute! I thought I was reading *Side Hustles For Dummies*, not *Real Estate Investment For Dummies* (Wiley) or some other book about buying and selling a home! What's the story here?"

Substitute the phrase *side-hustle real-estate investment* for *home* in this scenario. Aha!

If you buy a second house for an investment that you lease out for a number of years until you sell that property, or if you periodically rent a vacation house on Airbnb or Vrbo, you *will* put money — maybe even a lot of money! — into that property while you own it. When you finally sell that property that you've been using for a side-hustle real-estate investment, you want to pay as little in taxes as possible. All along the way, you've been offsetting your rental income with allowable expenses when you file your income taxes each year; you need to do the same when you sell the property, which means you want to make sure that you accurately adjust your cost basis.

In the spirit of the song "All About That Bass" when it comes to real-estate side hustles, it's "all about the records." Keep them handy, because you'll need them!

And make sure that you hang on to those records long after you've sold a property, pocketed or reinvested your proceeds, and gone happily on your way. In the United States, the IRS tells you the following (www.irs.gov/businesses/small-businesses-self-employed/how-long-should-i-keep-records):

> keep records relating to property until the period of limitations expires for the year in which you dispose of the property. You must keep these records to figure any depreciation, amortization, or depletion deduction and to figure the gain or loss when you sell or otherwise dispose of the property.

But on that same web page, the IRS also advises — make that "warns" — you that you may need to hang on to *all* tax records *indefinitely* if you need to prove that you didn't file a fraudulent return or if they somehow lost your return, as discussed earlier in this chapter. So, just keep your real-estate side-hustle records, including all receipts, indefinitely.

Even beyond tax-related reasons, play "real-estate record pack rat" and keep your records handy. Don't believe me? Then believe the IRS when they tell you (www.irs.gov/businesses/small-businesses-self-employed/how-long-should-i-keep-records):

> When your records are no longer needed for tax purposes, do not discard them until you check to see if you have to keep them longer for other purposes. For example, your insurance company or creditors may require you to keep them longer than the IRS does.

REMEMBER

Your real-estate side-hustle records are important even after you've sold a property for more than just external reasons, such as an IRS audit or your insurance company belatedly asking for documentation to support a claim that you filed several years earlier. Suppose that after a few years away from the real-estate side-hustle game, you're itching to jump back in and buy a new property. You know you'll be dropping a lot more cash on the property than just the original purchase price. In fact, you're thinking about doing much the same as you did on the property that you sold a couple of years ago:

>> Buying new appliances

>> Installing new carpeting

>> Installing an alarm system

>> Repairing a couple of leaky faucets

And the list goes on and on! (If you've owned a home, and especially if you've ever owned rental property, you know that spending money is unavoidable.)

But how much did the alarm system in your previous investment property cost? Was it $1,000? $1,500? Wait a minute: Wasn't the alarm system itself free with a two-year monitoring contract? Or was it a three-year contract? And how much did all those kitchen appliances cost again? A total of $5,000, right? Or was it $7,000?

Sure, you could start calling around to different appliance stores and alarm companies and flooring companies to get prices — and you probably will anyway. But you want to have some idea of the overall price range for your improvements and repairs before you start pricing things out.

Oh, yeah, one more thing: This whole real-estate investment stuff is a side hustle, not your main hustle. You have a day job where you're working 50, sometimes 60 hours a week. In fact, part of the reason you're thinking about jumping back into real-estate side hustles is that you're bone-tired all the time from your job, and you have an eye on maybe turning this real-estate side hustle into your full-time moneymaking business in the next couple of years.

Wouldn't it be great if you had the answers to "How much did those kitchen appliances cost last time?" and "How much was the carpeting, and for how many rooms?" right at your fingertips?

TIP

You would — make that *should* — if you kept the detailed records from your real-estate side hustle handy even after you sold off your last investment property.

IN THIS CHAPTER

» **Surveying income-tax basics for your side hustle**

» **Avoiding temptation that can lead to tax trouble**

» **Following all the tax-filing rules**

» **Sending important tax documents to others**

» **Collecting and filing sales taxes**

Chapter **10**

Pay Up: Side Hustles and Taxes

E ven if you're doing your side hustle on your own rather than with a partner or with the assistance of employees, plenty of other people want to share in your success — specifically, your friends and family.

Guess who else wants to share in your success? The tax people.

And unlike your friends and family, who share in your success by offering you encouragement and celebrating your accomplishments, the tax people want something from you. Actually, they want two things from you:

» Lots of documents and forms

» Money

Like it or not, you'll need to deal with all sorts of tax-related matters for your side hustle. Some of the tax stuff is pretty easy to understand, while other tax-related requirements and rules can get tricky. So, buckle up!

Income Taxes and Your Side Hustle: The Basics

You won't find a one-size-fits-all playbook or checklist for your taxes. Your tax-filing requirements will vary depending on:

>> The legal organization you set up for your side hustle

>> What type of business you're doing for your side hustle

>> Where you live and work

Filing requirements based on your side hustle's legal organization

If you organized your side hustle as a sole proprietorship or a single-member limited liability company (LLC), I have good news for you: Your U.S. federal tax filings for your business will be just another section of your personal taxes on your Form 1040. You don't have to file any separate returns, at least at the federal level. You will, however, need to file an additional form — a Schedule C — that is basically an attachment to the rest of your personal tax return (see "Keeping the feds happy," later in this chapter).

What if you set up your side hustle as an S corporation or a partnership? Or what if you set up an LLC with a partner? Great news . . . if you enjoy more paperwork. In addition to your personal tax return, you'll need to file a *separate* return, not just an additional form attached to your personal tax return. Depending on how you structured your business, you need to file either:

>> Form 1065 if your side hustle is organized as a partnership or a multi-member LLC

>> Form 1120-S if your side hustle is organized as an S corporation

TECHNICAL STUFF

Don't worry, your Form 1040 for your personal tax return won't feel left out if your side hustle financials show up on either a Form 1065 or a Form 1120-S. Technically, you don't pay taxes on either S corporation or partnership income — at least not directly. If you used either of those legal structures for your side hustle, your business income (or loss) will *pass through* to your Form 1040, where you'll mash all those details together with income from your day job, your personal deductions, and the rest of your personal tax stuff. You use an IRS form called a K-1 to carry your side hustle corporate or partnership finances over to your personal return. (You'll have slightly different versions of a K-1 depending on whether your side hustle is an S corporation, a partnership, or a multi-member LLC.)

The more complicated your side hustle's legal structure is, the more complex your tax filing requirements will be — basically, you have a straight-line relationship up the complexity ladder. But I step you through the highlights in the "Filing Your Side-Hustle Income Taxes" section later in this chapter.

TECHNICAL STUFF

Here's a little bit of good news: If your side hustle is one of those where you're paid as a part-time employee rather than as an independent contractor — say, teaching a class or two at the local community college — then you'll receive an IRS Form W-2 for each tax year, the same as you get from your full-time employer. In that case, all you need to do for your taxes is treat your side hustle just like it's another job and add your side hustle income to your regular income.

Tax rules and forms depending on your specific side hustle

If your side hustle is service-oriented and you aren't dealing with any physical inventory, your tax returns won't be all that complicated, even if you did set yourself up as an S corporation or a partnership. If, however, you're running an online store where you need to keep track of your cost of goods sold (see Chapter 8) and the value of your inventory, then not only is your overall side hustle record-keeping more complicated, but your taxes may turn into a head-scratcher, too.

TIP

Remember this simple equation: The more physical items you have that play any sort of a role in your side hustle, the more complicated your taxes will be. If you're buying goods to resell, or if you need to purchase shelving and containers to hold products, then your taxes will be more complicated than if you're recording and uploading videos, or doing software work, or doing ridesharing for Uber or Lyft.

Everyone wants a piece of the tax action

If you live in the United States, you're well aware of the Internal Revenue Service (IRS). If you live outside the United States, then you need to file tax returns with the equivalent of the IRS in your country.

You don't only have to pay up and file returns with the feds, however. Your state and maybe even your city want their cut of your side-hustle profits, and you'll need to file the proper returns along with writing the checks or doing the electronic funds transfers to pay the taxes that you'll owe.

As complicated as the federal side of taxes can be, in many cases the state and local side is even more complicated. Why?

>> If you're doing your side hustle in Arizona, you'll file different state tax return forms than if you're side hustling in Pennsylvania or California or any other state.

>> Some states just wants a copy of your federal return, but others have their own sets of forms. And to complicate matters even further, many states allow different deductions for expenses than the feds do, meaning that the net income from your side hustle for tax purposes may be different for the IRS than it is for the state where you live.

>> Some cities get in on the act also, and you have to file yet another set of tax returns — and shell out even more money — to the city where you live and where you're side hustling. Or maybe you're getting hit at the county level rather than the city level. Sometimes those local taxes are only on W-2 wages (basically, the money you make from your day job), but in other cases, they're full-blown tax returns that apply to side hustles.

Decision time

You have two paths you can take when it comes to your side-hustle taxes and filing your returns:

>> Do it yourself.

>> Hire an accountant.

Even if you decide that you want to do your own taxes, you don't have to study up on a ton of tax laws that are always changing or do a whole lot of calculations by hand. All the big tax-filing programs such as Credit Karma Taxes, TaxSlayer, TurboTax, and many others will step you through not only your personal taxes but also basic small-business taxes that would apply to your side hustle, no matter how you set up your business (sole proprietorship, partnership, S corporation), even if your side hustle is just another part-time job with a regular old W-2.

TIP

And speaking of small-business taxes: You don't need to be an expert in taxes for your side hustle. After all, you have dozens or even hundreds of other tasks to take care of or decisions to make. However, you should still have a basic idea of the big picture, tax-wise, for your side hustle. Beyond the basics I cover in this chapter, you can also check out *Small Business Taxes For Dummies*, 3rd Edition, by Eric Tyson (Wiley).

REMEMBER

Even if you made the command decision to hire an accountant to file the tax returns related to your side hustle, you still need to pay attention to some key points and beware of a few big-time traps that could really trip up you and your side hustle. Specifically:

» Avoid the temptation to use your side hustle to "get creative" with your tax returns.

» Be aware that if your side hustle crosses state lines, your tax picture could get murky and complicated.

» Remember that tax laws change frequently and can be tricky.

» Be sure to correct any tax-related mistakes that you make.

Staying Legal and Staying Honest

Maybe you've read or heard someone saying something along the lines of "I deduct all kinds of expenses through my home business — it's great!"

WARNING

If that person's statement really meant "I *legally* deduct all kinds of *allowable* expenses through my home business," then no problem. If, however, the statement actually meant "I sneak in all kinds of personal expenses and deduct them through my home business" then that person may be in for all sorts of tax and legal problems. And if you follow in their footsteps and start playing shady tax games with your side hustle, *you* could wind up in a lot of trouble.

Business deductions for your side hustle

Suppose your side hustle is an online retail site, where you buy clothing items from wholesalers that you then list and sell. While you're buying clothing items for your business, why not buy some for yourself that you can "hide" among your business purchases? Then you can deduct all that clothing, and basically get your jeans and shirts and shoes at a 30 percent or 35 percent discount because you'll owe less in federal and state taxes.

Don't do it!

Maybe you do a little bit of traveling for your side hustle, and you deduct all those travel-related expenses. You know what? Why not deduct the costs of your next family vacation as well? You already have a bunch of legitimate tax deductions for airfare, hotels, meals, and other travel expenses, so who would ever know if you added a few more travel expenses that really shouldn't be on your side hustle's tax return?

Don't do it!

Suppose you send a lot of packages to your customers via FedEx, UPS, and the U.S. Postal Service (USPS). Everything that you spend on packing materials and shipping costs is deductible. Why not also include the cost of shipping about a dozen packages to your out-of-town friends and family members for the holidays?

Don't do it!

REMEMBER

Even if you're not swayed by the morality and ethics of cheating the government by lying — yeah, I said lying! — on your tax returns, how about a practical reason to be honest when it comes to your side hustle's taxes? If you get caught, you'll be in big trouble! At best, you'll owe money — maybe a lot of money! — for back taxes, interest, and (most likely) penalties. At worst, the government could decide to criminally charge you with tax fraud. Even if you escape being convicted, you'll have to spend a ton of money on attorneys' fees.

Will the government really come after you for claiming $100 in shipping expenses that you shouldn't have, or for "only" $2,000 in personal travel that you inaccurately claimed as a legitimate business expense? Maybe not — but do you really want to take the chance?

Taking your side hustle across state lines

Even if you're determined to be 100 percent honest when it comes to your business taxes, you still need to be aware of several complications that could affect you, depending on what you do for your side hustle.

How would you like to be treated like a professional athlete? Well, maybe you can't dunk a basketball or hit a 100-mile-per-hour fastball or score a game-winning field goal. But you can pay taxes to a bunch of different states just like the pros!

TECHNICAL STUFF

The so-called *jock tax*, sometimes referred to as the Michael Jordan Rule after the legendary basketball player, came into existence in the early 1990s. Jordan's Chicago Bulls defeated the Los Angeles Lakers in 1991 to win the National Basketball Association (NBA) title. According to legend, the folks in California decided to get a little bit of revenge by declaring that because Jordan "worked part-time" in California — that is, he played professional basketball games each season in the state — technically he should owe *California* state taxes on the portion of his income earned there.

Before long, many states had versions of California's law governing out-of-state athletes playing professional games within their borders, and those pro athletes found themselves (or, more accurately, found their accountants) filing tax returns in a bunch of different states each year.

So, what does all this jock tax stuff have to do with side hustles? If your side hustle is, say, doing some consulting work that involves travel to a different state, you could find yourself subject to the same paying-some-other-state tax laws as Michael Jordan or almost every other professional athlete. Even though my personal experience with the non-athlete's equivalent of the jock tax came from my full-time consulting days rather than from one of my side hustles, I've seen and dealt with this complicated tax picture first-hand.

TECHNICAL STUFF

If your side hustle doesn't cross state lines, then (in the spirit of where the so-called jock tax began) "no harm, no foul." In other words, you won't be impacted at all. But just be aware that if your side hustle grows to the point where you do wind up "working" in another state, you need to check up on any nonresident tax rules that may apply to you. Even if your home state has a *reciprocal agreement* with another state to help their residents avoid out-of-state taxes, very often the reciprocal agreements only apply to regular salaried wages, not self-employment income — which is where your side-hustle income usually sits.

Now for your next side-hustle tax trick . . .

Your full-time employer sends you a W-2 tax form that shows you how much you earned in salaries, bonuses, and other taxable income. You then use the numbers from that W-2, or give the form to your accountant, as the foundation for the income portions of your personal tax return. If you had more than one job during the year, you'll have multiple W-2s that you combine onto the "Wages, Salaries, Tips, etc." line near the top of your tax return.

What about your side-hustle income? Unless your side hustle is something like part-time teaching, where you'll receive a W-2 because you're technically an employee of a university or community college, you won't receive any W-2s for your side-hustle income. Instead, you *may* receive a Form 1099-MISC and/or a Form 1099-NEC.

TECHNICAL STUFF

The IRS added the 1099-NEC in 2020, splitting out many side-hustle payments from those that previously were reported on the 1099-MISC onto this new form. "NEC" stands for *nonemployee compensation*, which means exactly that: compensation paid by a company or an individual to someone who is *not* an employee, but rather an independent contractor. If you pay rent or make attorney payments for your side hustle, you still use the 1099-MISC to report those payments.

Beginning in 2018 and thanks to tax-law changes in the United States called the Tax Cuts and Jobs Act, some nonemployee compensation and other income got even more complicated when it came to tax season. This time, however, the complications were actually *good* for tax filers, including many side hustlers.

In the past, if you earned $50,000 from your side hustle after deducting all your expenses, you would be taxed on that full $50,000 in addition to your full-time salary, interest, dividends, and all the usual taxable items in any given tax year. Now, thanks to the 2018 tax law, you're allowed to deduct up to 20 percent of your side-hustle income before you start figuring out your taxes. So, that $50,000 that used to be fully taxable gets magically changed into $40,000 by deducting $10,000 (20 percent) before you do your tax calculations.

TECHNICAL STUFF

The Tax Cuts and Jobs Act (TCJA) is actually more complex than the simple math shown here. First, your side hustle needs to be structured as one of the following *pass-through* entities:

>> A sole proprietorship

>> A partnership

>> An S corporation

>> A limited liability company (LLC)

Well, guess what? Take a look at Chapter 7 and your options for setting up the legal structure of your side hustle. Let's see: a sole proprietorship . . . a partnership . . . an S corporation . . . an LLC. Four for four! So, in almost all cases, your side hustle will have passed the first test to take advantage of that wonderful 20 percent deduction.

TECHNICAL STUFF

Then you're allowed to take the 20 percent deduction on what the IRS calls *qualified business income* (QBI). QBI is actual income from your small business operations. So, you wouldn't include dividends, capital gains, or other non-operations income. Most likely, though, a small business that is your side hustle wouldn't really have any of those other income streams anyway, so you should be in good shape.

The TCJA law has a lot of other technicalities that you really don't need to worry about, because either your tax software or your accountant will take care of walking through the complications and rules for you.

WARNING

You should, however, know that this bonus 20 percent deduction on pass-through qualified business income may not last forever. Lots of folks aren't too happy about businesses getting a lot of tax breaks that became effective in the United States in 2018, even small businesses — including side hustles. Tax laws change frequently, so don't be surprised to see the TCJA 20 percent deduction going away at some point in the future. Take advantage of those extra tax savings while you can!

Uh-oh — you goofed!

Your side hustle taxes can get really complicated. Even though you try to be as accurate as possible, sometimes you make a mistake.

WARNING

If your side hustle is set up as either an S corporation (where you file a Form 1120-S) or a partnership (where you file a Form 1065), your filing deadline is *not* the same as the normal April 15 due date for your personal taxes. You actually need to get all your separate side hustle business tax filings done a whole month earlier, on March 15 of each year. Even if you file for an automatic extension as you can do for your personal taxes, you don't have until October 15 to belatedly get your S corporation or partnership taxes done. You need to take care of those extended filings by September 15 of each year.

So, did you forget to file your side-hustle business taxes on time back in March? And did you also forget to file an extension? Or did you forget to include some of your side-hustle income or accidentally enter the wrong number for an expense? Maybe you made a mistake the other way around: you double-counted some of your side hustle income or forgot to include some legitimate business expenses, and wound up paying more in taxes than you actually should have.

REMEMBER

If you discover after you filed a tax return that you made a mistake, file an amended return as soon as you can. If you'll owe more in taxes than you actually paid, the sooner you file the amended return, the less you'll have to pay in interest and penalties.

Likewise, if you forgot to file a return by a deadline, get that form in as soon as you can to cut down on the amount you'll have to pay in interest and penalties — not to mention avoiding potential legal issues for not filing your taxes.

Filing Your Side-Hustle Income Taxes

Nobody really enjoys filing taxes and paying up, but there's no escaping it, so you might as well get going for your side hustle. You'll need to file

>> Federal taxes

>> State taxes

>> Maybe even local taxes

Keeping the feds happy

REMEMBER

If you organized your side hustle as a sole proprietorship or single-member LLC, you attach a Schedule C (see Figure 10-1) to your personal tax return and your Form 1040. Schedule C includes all the tax information for your side hustle for the previous year. You can download the current Schedule C at `www.irs.gov/pub/irs-pdf/f1040sc.pdf`.

Enter the business activity code that applies to your business.

Provide a brief description of your business activity.

Enter your SSN.

SCHEDULE C (Form 1040)	**Profit or Loss From Business** (Sole Proprietorship)	OMB No. 1545-0074
Department of the Treasury Internal Revenue Service (99)	▶ Go to *www.irs.gov/ScheduleC* for instructions and the latest information. ▶ Attach to Form 1040, 1040-SR, 1040-NR, or 1041; partnerships must generally file Form 1065.	20**21** Attachment Sequence No. **09**

Name of proprietor — Social security number (SSN)

A Principal business or profession, including product or service (see instructions) — B Enter code from instructions ▶

C Business name. If no separate business name, leave blank. — D Employer ID number (EIN) (see instr.)

E Business address (including suite or room no.) ▶
   City, town or post office, state, and ZIP code

F Accounting method: (1) ☐ Cash (2) ☐ Accrual (3) ☐ Other (specify) ▶

G Did you "materially participate" in the operation of this business during 2021? If "No," see instructions for limit on losses ☐ Yes ☐ No

H If you started or acquired this business during 2021, check here ▶ ☐

I Did you make any payments in 2021 that would require you to file Form(s) 1099? See instructions ☐ Yes ☐ No

J If "Yes," did you or will you file required Form(s) 1099? ☐ Yes ☐ No

Part I   Income

1	Gross receipts or sales. See instructions for line 1 and check the box if this income was reported to you on Form W-2 and the "Statutory employee" box on that form was checked ▶ ☐	1
2	Returns and allowances	2
3	Subtract line 2 from line 1	3
4	Cost of goods sold (from line 42)	4
5	**Gross profit.** Subtract line 4 from line 3	5

FIGURE 10-1: Use a Schedule C to file your side-hustle taxes for a sole proprietorship or single-member LLC.

Select Yes if you were actively actively involved in your business, even if you lost money.

Enter your EIN.

If you filed for and obtained an employee identification number (EIN) for your side hustle, you need to show *both* your personal Social Security number (SSN) and your EIN on your Schedule C (refer to Figure 10-1). The IRS separates your tax return into various forms, schedules, and attachments before it does its processing, so this way it can keep track of not only your side hustle (via your EIN) but which individual is actually running that side-hustle business.

You also need to enter what your side-hustle business is (for example, online retail or book editing) onto your Schedule C, along with a standard *business activity code* that identifies your business (refer to Figure 10-1). The IRS can periodically change those business activity codes, so make sure that you always check each year to make sure you're using the correct code. You can find them at `www.irs.gov/pub/irs-pdf/i1040sc.pdf`.

WARNING

Line G on Schedule C (refer to Figure 10-1) asks, "Did you 'materially participate' in the operation of this business during [the tax year]?" Basically, the IRS is asking you: "Is this a real business, or are you just trying to take a bunch of deductions?" You don't want to lie, but you really want to check the "Yes" box to indicate that you're actively involved in your business, even if you wound up losing money. If you have any doubts about whether your side hustle qualifies as "material participation," check with an accountant!

What if you set your side hustle up as an S corporation? You have to file a separate tax return, right? Figure 10-2 shows Form 1120-S, which you need to file if you organized your side hustle as an S corporation. You can download the form at www.irs.gov/pub/irs-pdf/f1120s.pdf.

FIGURE 10-2:
Use Form 1120-S
to file your
side-hustle
taxes for an
S corporation.

Form **1120-S**	**U.S. Income Tax Return for an S Corporation**	OMB No. 1545-0123
Department of the Treasury Internal Revenue Service	▶ Do not file this form unless the corporation has filed or is attaching Form 2553 to elect to be an S corporation. ▶ Go to *www.irs.gov/Form1120S* for instructions and the latest information.	20**21**

| For calendar year 2021 or tax year beginning | , 2021, ending | , 20 |

A S election effective date		Name		D Employer identification number
B Business activity code number (see instructions)	TYPE OR PRINT	Number, street, and room or suite no. If a P.O. box, see instructions.		E Date incorporated
		City or town, state or province, country, and ZIP or foreign postal code		F Total assets (see instructions) $
C Check if Sch. M-3 attached ☐				

G Is the corporation electing to be an S corporation beginning with this tax year? See instructions. ☐ Yes ☐ No
H Check if: **(1)** ☐ Final return **(2)** ☐ Name change **(3)** ☐ Address change **(4)** ☐ Amended return **(5)** ☐ S election termination
I Enter the number of shareholders who were shareholders during any part of the tax year . . . . ▶
J Check if corporation: **(1)** ☐ Aggregated activities for section 465 at-risk purposes **(2)** ☐ Grouped activities for section 469 passive activity purposes
Caution: Include **only** trade or business income and expenses on lines 1a through 21. See the instructions for more information.

Income	1a	Gross receipts or sales	1a		
	b	Returns and allowances	1b		
	c	Balance. Subtract line 1b from line 1a		1c	
	2	Cost of goods sold (attach Form 1125-A)		2	
	3	Gross profit. Subtract line 2 from line 1c		3	
	4	Net gain (loss) from Form 4797, line 17 (attach Form 4797)		4	
	5	Other income (loss) (see instructions—attach statement)		5	
	6	**Total income (loss)**. Add lines 3 through 5 . . . . ▶		6	

Suppose you sold $10,000 worth of products last year, and you spent $2,000 to buy those products. You'll do the simple math on your 1120-S to come up with $8,000 of total income. Easy, right?

Notice, though, that on Form 1120-S, you enter your side hustle's EIN, but not your personal SSN. You also don't *directly* pay taxes when you file a Form 1120-S. Instead, that information needs to get attached to your personal return. But how does the IRS know that the Form 1120-S is for you, when your SSN isn't anywhere on your business tax return?

Figure 10-3 shows a Schedule K-1 that your side-hustle business will issue to you as an individual. Yeah, that sounds a bit formal for a side hustle, but that's how the IRS keeps all the money stuff straight. Notice that the Schedule K-1 has *both* your side-hustle EIN *and* the rest of your side-hustle basic information (company name, business address, and so on), as well as your personal SSN and your personal information. You can download Schedule K-1 at `www.irs.gov/pub/irs-pdf/f1065sk1.pdf`.

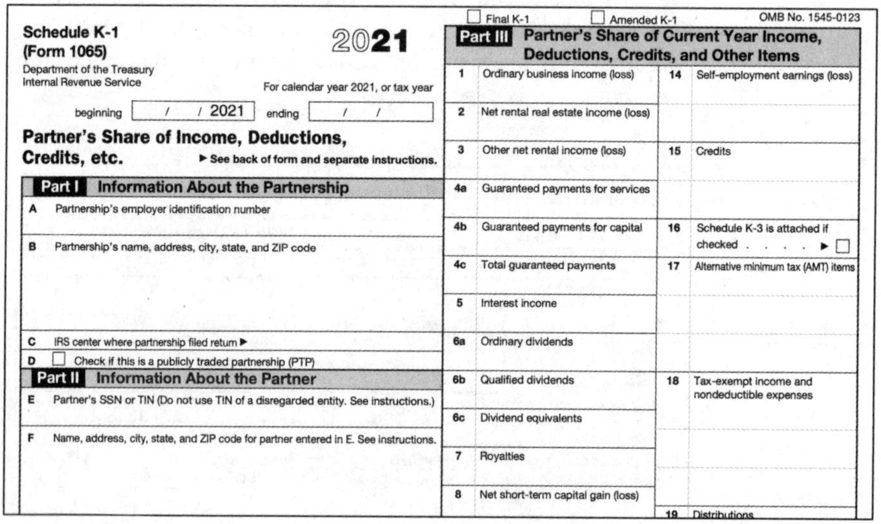

Schedule K-1 (Form 1065)
2021
Department of the Treasury
Internal Revenue Service
For calendar year 2021, or tax year
beginning / / 2021 ending / /
Partner's Share of Income, Deductions, Credits, etc.
▶ See back of form and separate instructions.

Final K-1 | Amended K-1 | OMB No. 1545-0123

Part I Information About the Partnership

A Partnership's employer identification number

B Partnership's name, address, city, state, and ZIP code

C IRS center where partnership filed return ▶

D ☐ Check if this is a publicly traded partnership (PTP)

Part II Information About the Partner

E Partner's SSN or TIN (Do not use TIN of a disregarded entity. See instructions.)

F Name, address, city, state, and ZIP code for partner entered in E. See instructions.

Part III Partner's Share of Current Year Income, Deductions, Credits, and Other Items

1 Ordinary business income (loss)
2 Net rental real estate income (loss)
3 Other net rental income (loss)
4a Guaranteed payments for services
4b Guaranteed payments for capital
4c Total guaranteed payments
5 Interest income
6a Ordinary dividends
6b Qualified dividends
6c Dividend equivalents
7 Royalties
8 Net short-term capital gain (loss)
14 Self-employment earnings (loss)
15 Credits
16 Schedule K-3 is attached if checked . . . . ▶ ☐
17 Alternative minimum tax (AMT) items
18 Tax-exempt income and nondeductible expenses
19 Distributions

FIGURE 10-3: Use a Schedule K-1 to link your side hustle business tax return with your personal tax return.

Suppose you file your business taxes on March 15. When you file your personal taxes a month later, you'll attach Schedule K-1 to the rest of your personal tax return and enter your net business income onto a Schedule E on your personal tax return (see Figure 10-4) to make sure that you do your tax calculations correctly. You can download Schedule E at `www.irs.gov/pub/irs-pdf/f1040se.pdf`.

Your Schedule E will contain your personal SSN (refer to Figure 10-4), which the IRS uses to link all this tax data to you personally. You also indicate the official business name of your side hustle and that you set your business up as an S corporation, along with your side hustle's EIN (refer to Figure 10-4). Presto! The IRS now has all your side-hustle S corporation information and your personal information, all linked together, including your business income (refer to Figure 10-4), which you pull from your Schedule K-1 (refer to Figure 10-3).

Enter the name of your business in the first column
and the letter S in the second column.

Enter your EIN here.

Enter your SSN here.

| Schedule E (Form 1040) 2021 | Attachment Sequence No. **13** | Page **2** |

Name(s) shown on return. Do not enter name and social security number if shown on other side.

Your social security number

Caution: The IRS compares amounts reported on your tax return with amounts shown on Schedule(s) K-1.

Part II **Income or Loss From Partnerships and S Corporations** — **Note:** If you report a loss, receive a distribution, dispose of stock, or receive a loan repayment from an S corporation, you **must** check the box in column **(e)** on line 28 and attach the required basis computation. If you report a loss from an at-risk activity for which **any** amount is **not** at risk, you **must** check the box in column **(f)** on line 28 and attach **Form 6198.** See instructions.

27 Are you reporting any loss not allowed in a prior year due to the at-risk or basis limitations, a prior year unallowed loss from a passive activity (if that loss was not reported on Form 8582), or unreimbursed partnership expenses? If you answered "Yes," see instructions before completing this section . . . . ☐ **Yes** ☐ **No**

28	(a) Name	(b) Enter P for partnership; S for S corporation	(c) Check if foreign partnership	(d) Employer identification number	(e) Check if basis computation is required	(f) Check if any amount is not at risk
A			☐		☐	☐
B			☐		☐	☐
C			☐		☐	☐
D			☐		☐	☐

	Passive Income and Loss		Nonpassive Income and Loss		
	(g) Passive loss allowed (attach **Form 8582** if required)	(h) Passive income from **Schedule K-1**	(i) Nonpassive loss allowed (see **Schedule K-1**)	(j) Section 179 expense deduction from **Form 4562**	(k) Nonpassive income from **Schedule K-1**
A					
B					
C					
D					
29a	Totals				
b	Totals				

30	Add columns (h) and (k) of line 29a.	30	
31	Add columns (g), (i), and (j) of line 29b.	31	( )
32	**Total partnership and S corporation income or (loss).** Combine lines 30 and 31	32	

Part III **Income or Loss From Estates and Trusts**

33	(a) Name	(b) Employer identification number

Enter your business income here.

FIGURE 10-4: Transfer your side-hustle income information from your Schedule K-1 onto a Schedule E for your tax calculations.

WARNING

If your side hustle is organized as an S corporation, you will *not* receive 1099-MISC or 1099-NEC forms from businesses that provide you with your side-hustle income! The IRS rules state that 1099s do not need to be sent to S corporations. So, you can't calculate your side-hustle business revenue by just adding up all the amounts on 1099s that you receive at the end of the year, the same as you do for your W-2s and personal 1099s (interest, dividends, royalties, and so on) for your personal taxes. So, how do you know how much money you took in? Through your business records, of course! See Chapter 9 for the inside scoop on keeping track of *everything* that goes on in your business, including your income and expenses.

If you and one or more partners legally organized your business as a partnership, you'll file Form 1065 (shown in Figure 10-5). You can download Form 1065 at www.irs.gov/pub/irs-pdf/f1065.pdf.

Enter the number of people in the partnership here.

Form 1065 — U.S. Return of Partnership Income — OMB No. 1545-0123 — 2021

Form **1065**
Department of the Treasury
Internal Revenue Service

U.S. Return of Partnership Income

For calendar year 2021, or tax year beginning _____ , 2021, ending _____ , 20 ____

▶ Go to *www.irs.gov/Form1065* for instructions and the latest information.

OMB No. 1545-0123

2021

A Principal business activity

B Principal product or service

C Business code number

Type or Print

Name of partnership

Number, street, and room or suite no. If a P.O. box, see instructions.

City or town, state or province, country, and ZIP or foreign postal code

D Employer identification number

E Date business started

F Total assets (see instructions)
$

G Check applicable boxes: (1) ☐ Initial return (2) ☐ Final return (3) ☐ Name change (4) ☐ Address change (5) ☐ Amended return
H Check accounting method: (1) ☐ Cash (2) ☐ Accrual (3) ☐ Other (specify) ▶ _____
I Number of Schedules K-1. Attach one for each person who was a partner at any time during the tax year ▶ _____
J Check if Schedules C and M-3 are attached . . . . ▶ ☐
K Check if partnership: (1) ☐ Aggregated activities for section 465 at-risk purposes (2) ☐ Grouped activities for section 469 passive activity purposes
Caution: Include **only** trade or business income and expenses on lines 1a through 22 below. See instructions for more information.

Income	1a	Gross receipts or sales	1a	
	b	Returns and allowances	1b	
	c	Balance. Subtract line 1b from line 1a	1c	
	2	Cost of goods sold (attach Form 1125-A)	2	
	3	Gross profit. Subtract line 2 from line 1c	3	
	4	Ordinary income (loss) from other partnerships, estates, and trusts (attach statement)	4	
	5	Net farm profit (loss) (attach Schedule F (Form 1040))	5	

FIGURE 10-5:
Use Form 1065 to file your taxes if you organized as a partnership.

Suppose you and one other person went in together on a side hustle. You would enter the number 2 on the line that says, "Number of Schedules K-1. Attach one for each person who was a partner at any time during the tax year" (refer to Figure 10-5). Just like your K-1 from an S corporation, you would receive a K-1 from your partnership — and so would your one partner in this case, because you indicated on the form that two K-1s were attached, meaning that your side hustle is made up of two partners.

Your state wants their cut, too

REMEMBER

Even if you live in a state that doesn't have a personal income tax, you probably have to file business taxes for your side hustle. After all, your side hustle may be a *small* business, but it's still a business!

Every state has its own laws and peculiarities. If you do your own taxes, your tax software will step you through your state filings after you're done with your federal returns. If you hand all your tax-filing stuff over to an accountant, they'll take care of the state side for you as well — including any cross-state filing requirements that may apply (see "Taking your side hustle across state lines," earlier in this chapter).

Keeping your tax money local

REMEMBER

If you live in a city that requires you to file a local income-tax return, you *may* owe money on your side-hustle income. Some cities, though, only tax wages — basically, your salary — so if you're running a business for your side hustle rather than receiving a W-2 for, say, teaching college courses on the side, you may not owe any additional taxes or have to worry about filing a return. Check with your accountant or make sure that your tax software takes care of figuring out your city taxes as well.

Calculating and Filing Estimated Income Taxes

If you only make a little bit of money from your side hustle, you may not have to worry about filing quarterly estimated tax returns and making quarterly payments. If, however, your side hustle is bringing in a fair bit of money, then you definitely need to at least take a look at whether you need to do estimated tax filings.

TECHNICAL STUFF

The IRS has a lot of complicated rules based on last year's taxes owed; how much in federal taxes were withheld from your paycheck; the percentage of your eventual final tax bill that you paid through paycheck withholdings, credits, and estimated taxes . . . your head may be spinning here. Check with your accountant or put your accounting software to work to figure out if you need to make quarterly estimated tax payments for your side hustle.

If you do need to file estimated returns and make payments, pay attention to the filing deadlines, which are:

>> April 15 for your first quarterly payment

>> June 15 (only *two* months after your previous payment, not *three* months) for your second quarterly payment

>> September 15 for your third quarterly payment

>> January 15 of the following year (*four* months later) for your fourth and final quarterly payment

The standard "15th day of the month" could also shift a few days later if the 15th day of a month in which a payment is due falls on a weekend or holiday (see the sidebar "I'm late, I'm late for a very important tax date").

I'M LATE, I'M LATE FOR A VERY IMPORTANT TAX DATE

The IRS and state tax authorities regularly change the due dates for tax returns. If the normal "15th day of a month" — whether March for corporate or partnership filings, April for your personal taxes, or later in the year as the deadline following an extension — falls on a weekend or a holiday, your deadline may be a little bit later. Say that March 15 in some year falls on a Saturday, and normally your S corporation tax filing for your side hustle is due on that date. The IRS will change the due date to March 18 — the next regular business day, so the following Monday.

You'll find the same policy of "business days only" for your estimated tax filings (see "Calculating and Filing Estimated Taxes," later in this chapter). You may commonly find the January 15 date for your final estimated tax payment for the previous year falling not only on a Saturday, but also right before the Martin Luther King federal holiday the following Monday. In this case, your fourth-quarter estimated taxes won't be due until Tuesday, January 18. Take a look at the due date on each form that you file to see if you have an extra couple of days to finish up your taxes.

You may also find delayed deadlines in extraordinary circumstances. In 2020, as the COVID-19 pandemic took hold, the IRS postponed all its tax-filing dates from the normal March and April dates to that summer, with corresponding delays in the deadlines for filing after receiving an extension. Again, just pay attention to due dates and you'll be in good shape.

Tracking and Reporting Payments You Made to Others

If you make certain types and amounts of payments to other businesses for your side hustle, you need to do even more tax filing. Yay! (Or would that be "Groan"?)

Just as you receive 1099 forms for some of your side-hustle income (unless your side hustle is an S corporation; see "Keeping the feds happy," earlier in this chapter), you'll need to send 1099 forms to other businesses to which you pay money.

REMEMBER

If you pay $600 or more to another business that's a sole proprietorship, partnership, or LLC, you need to send *them* a 1099 form. The IRS has lots of other rules about who you do and don't send a 1099 form to, so double-check with your accountant if you're not sure.

And if you enjoy the additional tax paperwork from sending 1099 forms, you'll *really* appreciate that you have to file yet another form: the 1096. Will this tax paperwork ever end?

Don't worry — the 1096 and 1099 forms are pretty easy to take care of. First, the 1096 (see Figure 10-6). You can see Form 1096 at www.irs.gov/pub/irs-pdf/f1096.pdf, but note that the version available online is for informational purposes only — you can't file this version with the IRS.

Select ONE of these boxes.

Do Not Staple	6969					
Form **1096**		**Annual Summary and Transmittal of U.S. Information Returns**			OMB No. 1545-0108	
Department of the Treasury Internal Revenue Service					2022	

FILER'S name

Street address (including room or suite number)

City or town, state or province, country, and ZIP or foreign postal code

Name of person to contact	Telephone number	**For Official Use Only**
Email address	Fax number	

1 Employer identification number	2 Social security number	3 Total number of forms	4 Federal income tax withheld	5 Total amount reported with this Form 1096
			$	$

6 Enter an "X" in only one box below to indicate the type of form being filed.

W-2G 32	1097-BTC 50	1098 61	1098-C 78	1098-E 84	1098-F 03	1098-Q 74	1098-T 83	1099-A 80	1099-B 79	1099-C 85	1099-CAP 73	1099-DIV 91	1099-G 86	1099-INT 92	1099-K 10	1099-LS 16
☐	☐	☐	☐	☐	☐	☐	☐	☐	☐	☐	☐	☐	☐	☐	☐	☐

1099-LTC 93	1099-MISC 95	1099-NEC 71	1099-OID 96	1099-PATR 97	1099-Q 31	1099-QA 1A	1099-R 98	1099-S 75	1099-SA 94	1099-SB 43	3921 25	3922 26	5498 28	5498-ESA 72	5498-QA 2A	5498-SA 27
☐	☐	☐	☐	☐	☐	☐	☐	☐	☐	☐	☐	☐	☐	☐	☐	☐

Return this entire page to the Internal Revenue Service. Photocopies are not acceptable.
Send this form, with the copies of the form checked in box 6, to the IRS in a flat mailer (not folded).

Under penalties of perjury, I declare that I have examined this return and accompanying documents and, to the best of my knowledge and belief, they are true, correct, and complete.

Signature ▶   Title ▶   Date ▶

Instructions

Future developments. For the latest information about developments related to Form 1096, such as legislation enacted after it was published, go to www.irs.gov/Form1096.

Enter the filer's name, address (including room, suite, or other unit number), and taxpayer identification number (TIN) in the spaces provided on the form. The name, address, and TIN of the filer on this form must be the same as those you enter in the upper left area of

FIGURE 10-6:
File Form 1096 to help the IRS keep track of who your side hustle paid money to.

Think of Form 1096 as sort of an envelope for your 1099 forms. Most likely, you'll be sending 1099-NECs for nonemployee compensation. On Figure 10-6, the IRS tells you that you need to check one *and only one* box to indicate which of the many different types of 1099s you're sending, as well as some other IRS forms that most likely won't apply to your side hustle.

TIP

If you had to issue *both* 1099-NEC and 1099-MISC forms, you need to fill out and submit *two* different 1096s — one for your 1099-NECs, and the other for your 1099-MISCs. If you're only sending one kind of form, you'll only need to submit one Form 1096.

Figure 10-7 shows Form 1099-NEC, which you fill out to send to some other business that you paid for, say, website development help. Notice that you need to include your *taxpayer identification number* (TIN), which is your EIN (if you have one) or your SSN, as well as the TIN of the business that you paid. You can download Form 1099-NEC at www.irs.gov/pub/irs-pdf/f1099nec.pdf.

Enter your EIN or SSN here.   Enter the recipient's EIN or SSN here.

FIGURE 10-7:
File Form 1099-NEC to tell the IRS who you paid money to for your side hustle.

How do you know which TIN to enter for some other company? When you get set up to do business with them, you ask them to fill out a Form W-9 (see Figure 10-8), through which they tell you their TIN for the 1099-NEC form that you'll eventually file.

TIP

Likewise, when you get set up to do business with people who will be paying *you*, you'll need to fill out a Form W-9. You don't file the W-9 with the IRS; instead, you send the completed W-9 to the other company so that when they issue you a 1099-NEC at the end of the year, they have your tax information ready to go. You can download Form W-9 at www.irs.gov/pub/irs-pdf/fw9.pdf.

REMEMBER

The IRS deadline for submitting Form 1096 and all your Form 1099-NECs is January 31 of the following year. You file the forms with the IRS, and you *also* send a copy of the 1099-NEC to every other business that you paid and for which you filed information with the IRS.

Form W-9
(Rev. October 2018)
Department of the Treasury
Internal Revenue Service

**Request for Taxpayer
Identification Number and Certification**

▶ Go to *www.irs.gov/FormW9* for instructions and the latest information.

**Give Form to the
requester. Do not
send to the IRS.**

1 Name (as shown on your income tax return). Name is required on this line; do not leave this line blank.

2 Business name/disregarded entity name, if different from above

3 Check appropriate box for federal tax classification of the person whose name is entered on line 1. Check only **one** of the following seven boxes.

☐ Individual/sole proprietor or single-member LLC   ☐ C Corporation   ☐ S Corporation   ☐ Partnership   ☐ Trust/estate

☐ Limited liability company. Enter the tax classification (C=C corporation, S=S corporation, P=Partnership) ▶ _____

Note: Check the appropriate box in the line above for the tax classification of the single-member owner. Do not check LLC if the LLC is classified as a single-member LLC that is disregarded from the owner unless the owner of the LLC is another LLC that is **not** disregarded from the owner for U.S. federal tax purposes. Otherwise, a single-member LLC that is disregarded from the owner should check the appropriate box for the tax classification of its owner.

☐ Other (see instructions) ▶

4 Exemptions (codes apply only to certain entities, not individuals; see instructions on page 3):

Exempt payee code (if any) _____

Exemption from FATCA reporting code (if any) _____

(Applies to accounts maintained outside the U.S.)

5 Address (number, street, and apt. or suite no.) See instructions.

6 City, state, and ZIP code

Requester's name and address (optional)

7 List account number(s) here (optional)

Print or type.
See Specific Instructions on page 3.

Part I   Taxpayer Identification Number (TIN)

Enter your TIN in the appropriate box. The TIN provided must match the name given on line 1 to avoid backup withholding. For individuals, this is generally your social security number (SSN). However, for a resident alien, sole proprietor, or disregarded entity, see the instructions for Part I, later. For other entities, it is your employer identification number (EIN). If you do not have a number, see *How to get a TIN*, later.

Note: If the account is in more than one name, see the instructions for line 1. Also see *What Name and Number To Give the Requester* for guidelines on whose number to enter.

Social security number

☐☐☐ – ☐☐ – ☐☐☐☐

or

Employer identification number

☐☐ – ☐☐☐☐☐☐☐

Part II   Certification

Under penalties of perjury, I certify that:

1. The number shown on this form is my correct taxpayer identification number (or I am waiting for a number to be issued to me); and
2. I am not subject to backup withholding because: (a) I am exempt from backup withholding, or (b) I have not been notified by the Internal Revenue Service (IRS) that I am subject to backup withholding as a result of a failure to report all interest or dividends, or (c) the IRS has notified me that I am no longer subject to backup withholding; and
3. I am a U.S. citizen or other U.S. person (defined below); and
4. The FATCA code(s) entered on this form (if any) indicating that I am exempt from FATCA reporting is correct.

FIGURE 10-8:
Form W-9 is where you their share tax identification numbers and details with people who hire you (or get that information from people you hire).

Sales Taxes and Your Side Hustle

Income taxes aren't the only type of taxes you need to worry about for your side hustle. You *may* need to collect and submit sales taxes as well.

⚠ **WARNING**

If you thought income taxes were complicated with different forms depending on your business structure and all the various filing dates, then you'll *really* cringe at sales taxes:

>> You may have to collect and submit sales taxes not only to your state, but also your county and city.

>> You may have to collect and submit sales taxes to *other* states beyond where you live.

>> You may have to collect and submit sales taxes for products that you sell in person, but not online. Or you may have to submit sales taxes for *every* product that you sell.

>> If someone who lives in another state buys something from you in person, you may or may not have to collect sales tax, depending on your state's laws.

>> You may have to only worry about sales taxes for *products* that you sell, or you may also have to deal with sales taxes for *services* if you live somewhere that charges sales taxes on, say, consulting or doing software development.

You also need to file for a sales tax license or permit. You may need to file for a sales tax license or permit from your city or county. Sometimes a sales tax license is referred to as a *transaction privilege tax* (TPT) — basically, you're being taxed for the "privilege" of being able to conduct business transactions.

If you were to examine a hundred side hustles from all around the country, you could have a hundred different circumstances when it comes to side hustle sales taxes, with no two businesses having identical situations.

TIP

What should you do about sales taxes for your side hustle? Check with an accountant, even if you plan on doing your side-hustle income taxes yourself. If you're subject to sales taxes, make sure you know what you do and don't have to tax, along with how you file your returns — and how frequently. Also, be prepared for the sales-tax rules to change every so often, because state, county, and local jurisdictions are always looking for ways to bring in more tax revenue.

3
Mastering the Side-Hustle Game

Chapter **11**

Avoiding Conflicts with Your Day Job

Congratulations! You did it! World's best cup of coffee!

Wait: That's the movie *Elf.* How about this instead:

Congratulations! You did it! Big-time side-hustle success!

You're making money. You have satisfied customers. You just finished your plans for the next stage of whatever your side hustle happens to be. Life is good!

How would you like the company where you work full-time to suddenly cause your entire side-hustle universe to come crashing down? To prevent you from continuing with your on-the-side activities? To force you to write them a check — maybe a very large check — and turn over some or even all of the money that you've made thus far from your side hustle to them?

What's that? You really wouldn't like all that to happen? Well, I don't blame you — nobody would!

That's why you need to be very, very careful to keep what you're doing with your side hustle out of trouble when it comes to your full-time employer. This chapter shows you how.

Trouble Ahead, Trouble Behind: Navigating Issues with Your Employer

Josh works for a Silicon Valley software firm, while his brother Jeremy works for a state government in the eastern part of the United States. Another brother, John, works for one of the largest fast-food chains, while their sister Julie is employed by a midsize university in Texas. Finally, another sister, Rachel (their parents ran out of names beginning with J), works in the corporate headquarters of a department store chain.

Josh is an artificial intelligence researcher working on self-driving vehicles, Jeremy is an accountant, John is a tech project manager, Julie is a tenure-track college professor, and Rachel is a software developer.

So far, other than having the same parents, Josh, Jeremy, John, Julie, and Rachel don't seem to have a lot in common, at least professionally. Actually, though, they do — just not within the realm of their respective full-time jobs.

Each of the five has their own online side hustle going. Each of the five also decided to save a little money and, instead of buying separate computers for their side-hustle businesses, they all built their respective websites or online storefronts using their work computers. They all still do online advertising, accounting, and manage their social media presences on those same computers from their full-time jobs.

And all five are now in trouble.

WARNING

The first rule of the side-hustle business when it comes to your day job is to *never* use your work computer to do *anything* with your side hustle.

Josh, Jeremy, John, Julie, and Rachel only have themselves to blame. If they had carefully read their respective employment agreements, they would've seen the crystal clear rules spelling out what they could and couldn't do with their computers or any other resources belonging to their employers.

So, what's the big deal? Does using your company computer during off hours for a little bit of side business really do any harm?

The short answer is "It doesn't matter — that's what the employment agreement states," but the more thorough response requires digging into the outer edges of the sometimes precarious relationship between employer and employee. Beyond the wording of your employment agreement, you need to be aware of three over-arching potential points of contention when it comes to doing a side hustle along-side full-time employment:

>> Noncompete clauses

>> Conflicts of interest

>> Conflicts of commitment

Noncompete clauses

WARNING

Almost every employment agreement in the professional realm contains some form of noncompete clause.

This clause, as you may infer from its name, prohibits you as an individual from competing with your employer. You're bound by a noncompete clause for the duration of your employment, in any form: as a sole proprietor working on your own, in a partnership, or setting up shop in a corporate structure such as an S corporation. (I cover side-hustle business structures in Chapter 7.) A noncompete clause also typically prohibits you from competing with your full-time employer as the employee of another business.

TECHNICAL STUFF

Many companies try to extend noncompete restrictions past the term of your employment with them if you quit or even if you're laid off. Typical durations of noncompete clauses are either six months or one year after your last day of employment. Often, though, if you were given a severance package as part of leaving a company, either voluntarily or involuntarily, a noncompete clause could run even up to several years. So, even future side hustles that you're not doing right now could be impacted by the noncompete restrictions of your current employer. Be careful!

Here's an example: Avi went to work for one of the big-time tech consulting firms right out of college and has worked there for the past five years. He works extra-long hours, deals with a pretty high stress level, and lately has been thinking about doing something — anything — else.

One day, Avi heard about an analytics strategy consulting engagement that's on the radar of the firm's business development team. Unlike the yearlong projects with teams of two dozen or more consultants that Avi has worked on thus far during his time there, this strategy engagement is projected to be about three months in duration and require only two consultants. Ideally, if the firm wins this engagement and delivers a solid analytics strategy, the client would then hire them for a longer development effort with about ten consultants racking up the billable hours.

Avi has an idea: Janet, a friend of his at the firm, is also thinking about quitting to do something different. Avi focuses on data work, while Janet has a master's degree in quantitative analytics. What a perfect team for this strategy engagement!

Avi knows that his employer isn't going to propose either Janet or himself — or the two of them together as a team — for this engagement, because they're both in the middle of another longer project at a different client. Avi approaches Janet and pitches her the idea of the two of them going after this analytics strategy engagement outside of their full-time employment. The word on the street is that this prospective client is pretty flexible with consulting agreements and doesn't absolutely need to have the strategy completed within three calendar months. So, Avi and Janet could work about 15 to 20 hours each week, in the evenings and on weekends, doing this company's analytics strategy as a side hustle while still meeting their full-time project obligations. Down the road, maybe they'll quit and set up shop together as a small boutique consulting firm. But for now, they'll stay squarely within the side-hustle universe.

Penalty flag!

Avi's naïve thinking is that as long as he and Janet continue to work on their full-time projects, "no harm, no foul" when it comes to doing side work. Ah, to be that innocent! The truth is that Avi intends to violate the *noncompete clause* with his current employer, which is an absolute no-no! And worse, he's pulling Janet into the abyss and is about to get her in big trouble as well!

Conflicts of interest

Many people confuse a *conflict of interest* with a noncompete clause. In a very general sense, violating a noncompete is a conflict of interest with your current employer: Your interests in what you want to do as part of a side hustle conflict with the interests of your employer, who may be going after the same work.

More precisely, though, conflicts of interest come into play with contracting and procurement. Using the example from the preceding section, let's say Avi realizes that going after that analytics strategy engagement on the side was a nonstarter because of his noncompete. Instead, he and Janet start a little side business to buy computer subsystems wholesale and then sell ready-to-use personal computers to businesses. Avi's employer only does "pure" consulting and doesn't sell or resell hardware, so he and Janet are in the clear when it comes to the noncompete clauses in their employment agreements.

Now Avi hears that the consulting firm plans to upgrade all the laptops used by their consultants, as well as internal staff (accounting, recruiting, marketing, and so on). Avi has a great idea: He can put in a bid for his employer's computer purchase, and they can become the first customer — a big customer — for his side hustle.

Another penalty flag!

Avi's interests for his side hustle are in conflict with those of his employer, even if he doesn't immediately realize the problem. His interests include *making* money; his company's interests include *saving* money. Even though Avi is a relatively low-level consultant, he represents his employer in many different ways: through client work, by adhering to data privacy standards, and dozens of other less-noticeable ways, including doing what he can to save his company money.

In Avi's case, the financial and contracting conflict of interest may not be quite as apparent because his consulting firm is a private enterprise. Suppose, though, that Avi worked for a state or local government or a public state university. If he tried to sell computer equipment to his government employer as a side hustle, he would be in a position where he could conceivably influence the government procurement process to the detriment of the public and to his own private benefit.

REMEMBER

The bottom line: Especially in a governmental setting but also with private-sector employers, an employee trying to "sell into" that employer as part of a side hustle is almost certain to be engaged in a conflict of interest.

Conflicts of commitment

When you see the definitions for *noncompete* and *conflict of commitment*, you can easily see how your side hustle can run afoul of your full-time job. A *conflict of commitment* is fuzzier and murkier than its sibling side-hustle traps. Often, an employer doesn't explicitly specify the terms of a conflict of commitment.

REMEMBER

In fact, explicit language regarding conflicts of commitment are typically found in university settings. Still, you should be aware of the principles of a conflict of commitment regardless of where you work, because employers sometimes try to invoke the spirit of a conflict of commitment even if their employment agreements don't explicitly include the phrase.

GETTING INTO TROUBLE BY TRYING TO STAY OUT OF TROUBLE

I started my first side hustle — a consulting business — while I was a U.S. Air Force officer. Back in the early '80s, not a lot of people were familiar with personal computers (PCs), which were just coming onto the market. The lack of PC-knowledgeable computer professionals was a problem for thousands of organizations just starting to work with PCs.

When I began my consulting side hustle, I partnered with a local computer store in Colorado Springs. Customers would buy PCs from them, and if a customer needed custom software developed, I was one of the outside consultants they would use to deliver those services.

One day about a year after my side hustle was underway, the computer store contacted me and said that one of the Air Force organizations in Colorado Springs was looking for someone to help them develop some PC-based applications. Being an Air Force officer myself and technically an employee of the U.S. government and the U.S. Air Force, I immediately recognized the conflict of interest. How could I work from the outside, contracting back to my full-time employer and making extra money, even for a different organization within the Air Force than the organization where I worked? Of course, I couldn't!

I told the computer store to let its Air Force customer know that I was unable to do the requested work because it would be a conflict of commitment because the Air Force was my full-time employer. I thought that was the end of it.

Oh, I was so wrong.

I was assigned to the only branch within the Air Force Space Command that had computer programmers in the early '80s. A couple days later, I got called into our colonel's office, something that occurred, well, never. The colonel was my boss's boss's boss, so this was a big deal for all the wrong reasons. The colonel demanded to know why in the world I had refused to help another Air Force organization that requested some sort of programming assistance and justified my refusal by claiming that I had a conflict of interest. "Just what kind of officer and team player are you anyway, Lieutenant Simon?" Yeah, those are words a junior officer really wants to hear — not!

I finally was able to get the full story across — that this other Air Force organization hadn't contacted me in my capacity as an Air Force officer (which would've been pretty strange anyway, directly contacting a lieutenant in some other organization rather than going through proper channels), but instead through a local computer store in the capacity of my outside consulting work. I would be glad to help out this other Air Force organization as part of my job, if the colonel wanted me to, but I was fully aware that I couldn't "double-dip" and make money from the Air Force both as an employee and as an outside contractor.

Even though I talked my way out of trouble, the unfortunate by-product of the whole event was having a glaring spotlight shined on my side hustle for my colonel. I was allowed to do outside work, as long as I didn't have a conflict of commitment (see the next section), but Air Force officers in general are expected to be "all in" on their military careers. Officers who had side hustles going typically kept them low-key and out of the line of sight of their commanding officers. In my case, I was most likely getting out of the Air Force after fulfilling my four-year commitment, so I wasn't particularly concerned about the longer-term career impacts. Still, the military can make your life pretty unpleasant if they want to, even in the shorter term, if your commanding officer isn't happy with something you're doing.

Fortunately, the whole matter evaporated and never surfaced again. But there you go: Even striving to be on the right side of the whole conflict-of-interest picture can still cause some big-time complications with your full-time employer.

A conflict of commitment comes into play when you, as an employee, neglect or somehow fall short of meeting your primary job responsibilities because something you're doing outside the scope of your job — such as a side hustle — is interfering with your job. Stated another way, from your employer's perspective: "We're paying you to do your job, but your little side hustle there is interfering with your ability to do your job, so we have a problem!"

You can't really argue with the premise that if an employer such as a university is paying an employee — say, a faculty member — to teach classes, grade tests and assignments, attend faculty meetings, hold office hours, and whatever else comes with being a member of a university faculty, the university has every right to expect that the instructor's primary commitment is to fully meeting those job requirements. If you were a student, would you want one of your teachers to regularly cancel class to go do outside consulting work or to get paid to speak at conferences? (Well, maybe if it were a 7 a.m. class you wouldn't mind, once in a while. . . .) Or what if you need help understanding course material, but your teacher is always off doing outside consulting and never actually holds office hours?

WARNING

From a side-hustle perspective, the conflict-of-commitment waters become murky if your employer requires activities and an in-person presence above and beyond what is "reasonable" for your job.

Suppose you're a college professor, and you're assigned four classes each semester. Each class is held twice a week and lasts for an hour and fifteen minutes. Fortunately, all your classes are on Tuesdays and Thursdays, which means you have no classes Mondays, Wednesdays, or Fridays. You also need to hold office hours, so you schedule one hour on Tuesday and Thursday every week.

Once every semester, you need to attend a department faculty meeting, which is usually held on Fridays. Your presence is also requested in the occasional meeting about improving student success or helping to revise the department's curriculum. Of course, you attend each of these meetings. In fact, you fully meet every assignment that is part of your job.

So, what about Mondays, Wednesdays, and Fridays when you *don't* have any university meetings to attend? Are you totally on your own for outside consulting? For recording YouTube videos about sports card collecting or some other hobby? To run an online business? Well, maybe.

WARNING

Every university may have its own conflict-of-commitment policies, and you need to be fully aware of just what does and doesn't apply to you. Your employment agreement holds part of the answer, but only part (see "Dodging Employer Tricks and Traps," later in this chapter).

If you're not a university instructor, does the whole conflict-of-commitment business apply to you? Absolutely! Consider each of the following:

>> Mike works full-time as a cashier at one of the big-box retailers. He's studying computer programming at the nearby community college, and he also started a side hustle where people connect with him via Fiverr for small software jobs. One of his clients texts Mike one day, in a panic, while Mike is at work, to let him know that their website's shopping cart is now calculating sales tax incorrectly. Worse, it's the middle of the holiday season, and the client is making a lot of sales, so the tax calculation problem needs to be fixed immediately. Mike turns off the "Open" light above his checkout lane, sneaks into the back, and steps his client through diagnosing and fixing the problem.

>> Kylie works full-time at the same big-box retailer where Mike works, but she's responsible for stocking shelves in the toy section. Just like Mike, Kylie has a side hustle — hers is a small online clothing boutique. Kylie receives several text messages from her best customers that her website suddenly "looks funny," with text and graphics all messed up. It's the middle of the holiday shopping season, and the last thing Kylie wants is for prospective customers to come to her website and be turned off by an unprofessional appearance. Kylie always has her iPad at work, so she slips into the back of the stockroom (just as Mike is hurrying back to his checkout lane!) to see what's going on with her side hustle's website.

>> Raul, who processes auto insurance claims, began working at home in early 2020, as the COVID-19 pandemic really took hold. The management at his employer has always been skeptical of the whole work-at-home model, so they required every employee to install keystroke-monitoring software. This way, they figure, if Raul and other employees are tempted to slack off because they're not in the office and instead check sports scores or hang out on social media, the keystroke-monitoring software will catch them. Raul typically spends about half of his workday actively processing claims, and his department's policies call for him to spend the rest of his time reviewing past claims and working through a list of other work-related tasks.

Raul has his own side hustle going: He makes hobby-related videos that he posts on his YouTube channel. Raul is a smart guy — smart enough not to use his work computer to record videos for his side hustle. He also wonders if a company that requires employees to install keystroke-monitoring software may also be sneaky enough to check up on him through his work computer's camera and microphone. So, Raul has his own computer on the other side of the house, and once or twice a day when he isn't actively working on an insurance claim, he sneaks away for 15 minutes to record a short blurb or edit one of the videos he's already recorded but hasn't yet uploaded.

Even though you may think that Mike, Kylie, and Raul are staying on the proper side of running their side hustles and avoiding problems with their employers, each of them has a conflict of commitment. Even if they can sneak away for a few minutes here and there without anyone noticing, and even if they can make up any missed work by working just a little bit faster after doing whatever needed to be done for their side hustle, they're all on the wrong side of the conflict-of-commitment equation.

WARNING

Can an employer act unfairly when it comes to potential conflicts of commitment for their employees? Of course. But at the same time, employers are the ones who set the rules for their companies. Whether your full-time job is in retail or academia or any other setting, it's your responsibility to:

>> Know exactly what your employer's commitment requirements are for being in a particular place, or performing various tasks, or any other aspects of your job.

>> Fully comply with your employer's policies to avoid even getting *close* to a conflict of commitment between your side hustle and your full-time job.

BALANCING COMMITMENTS BETWEEN A SIDE HUSTLE AND THE U.S. AIR FORCE

Even though my first side hustle doing computer consulting got me in hot water once with my colonel (see the sidebar "Getting into trouble by trying to stay out of trouble," earlier in this chapter), I always managed to stay in the clear when it came to any potential conflict of commitment between my side hustle and being an Air Force officer.

Back in the early '80s, the office where I worked didn't have a separate development system for our software. Instead, we were given time on the operational computer several days a week, for about four hours each session. However, our scheduled computer time was almost always in the middle of the night: 1 to 5 a.m. and 3 to 7 a.m. were the most popular shifts. The only good news about the always-in-the-dark schedule was that on days when we had post-midnight computer time, our duty day would begin with that shift and then end eight or nine hours later. So, if you had computer time beginning at 1 a.m., you were done for the day at 9 or 10 that morning, and the rest of the day was yours.

From a lack-of-sleep perspective, these shifts were excruciating, and we did everything we could to write our software correctly the first time so we wouldn't have to make too many additional middle-of-the-night trips before we could check off a particular programming assignment as completed.

From a side-hustle perspective, however, this erratic computer time schedule was absolutely perfect!

I scheduled sales calls, client meetings, training sessions, and other aspects of my side hustle for late mornings or afternoons on days when I knew I would have computer time beginning at zero dark thirty that morning. This way, I stayed in the clear when it came to any conflicts of commitment between my Air Force duties and my side hustle. I could have a daylight meeting with a current or prospective client with a clear conscience. I was off duty — I wasn't sneaking away from our Air Force office (which technically would've made me absent without leave — the dreaded AWOL!), but rather working around my regular "oddball" schedule to have my side-hustle cake and eat it, too!

Knowing Which Outside Activities Are Approved

If you're concerned about staying on the right side of the conflict fence with your full-time employer, the good news is that employers often help their employees out by specifying what they are and aren't allowed to do outside of work — in other words, as a side hustle. The bad news, however, is that sometimes employers can be, shall we say, unfair and overbearing and unjust and, well, you get the idea.

Let's say Julie, the college professor from earlier in this chapter, never ran afoul of her university by using her work computer for a side hustle. Instead, she wants to take advantage of the highly flexible schedule that typically comes with academia and do a little extra teaching on the side. In fact, another university where Julie previously taught recently contacted her and asked if she would teach an online course or two for them, in addition to her full-time teaching schedule at her current university. She wouldn't have to do any teaching in person, and she could do all her grading and other tasks for these outside classes on her own time, including weekends — whatever worked for her.

Sounds like a great plan, right? Julie teaches a couple extra classes to help out her previous university while she fully meets her teaching and other commitments where she now works. And she makes a little extra money. Everybody wins!

Julie's full-time university also offers online classes that, like those from her previous university, are available to anyone around the world. So, technically, Julie's current university and her former one are competitors — at least that's how Julie's employer sees it. Their annual faculty employment agreement, which Julie and every other professor must sign, specify that while faculty members can do consulting and speaking and similar work, they're prohibited from classroom teaching — either on campus or online — at any other university without first receiving permission from the university administration. Wow!

REMEMBER

Is Julie's current university being too harsh and too restrictive in what they will and won't allow Julie to do as her academic side hustle? Perhaps — or perhaps not. The key point here isn't the fairness, or lack thereof, of this university's policies on outside teaching, but rather the fact that they clearly specified this restriction as part of their faculty employment agreement. Consequently, Julie *must* follow these rules. If Julie really wants to teach those online classes for her former university, she can request permission — as specified in her employment agreement. Maybe the administration of her current university will give her permission, or maybe they won't.

What if Julie wants to do consulting rather than teach? Or do a paid speaking gig at an industry conference? Her employment agreement explicitly referenced teaching at another university *but nothing else*, so she's in the clear, right?

Not so fast.

Julie's university also has another trick up its sleeve when it comes to the outside activities (side hustles) of their faculty and staff. Every university employee is required to submit a form for each outside activity to request approval. A consulting assignment? Submit the form and wait for approval. Speaking at a conference? Once again, submit the form and wait for approval.

And it gets even better (with "better" actually meaning "worse"). Julie's university caps the number of hours any faculty member or other employee is permitted to spend on outside activities during the academic year. Specifically, Julie's faculty employment agreement specifies a maximum of 300 outside hours during the academic year.

That's right: Even if Julie wanted to work every evening and every weekend day, from late August through mid-May, on some side hustle, and even if Julie fully met every one of her teaching and other academic obligations, she would be in violation of university policies and probably wind up in trouble — maybe even denied tenure or possibly even not have her teaching contract renewed.

Again, the operative question here isn't fairness or unfairness, but rather full-time employers being in a position where they set the rules that can impact your side hustle — and your being required to follow those rules. So you may as well know what the rules are!

Suppose that Julie's side hustle wasn't related in the slightest to her academic work. Instead of consulting and speaking, she wrote novels, or ran an online retail business, or bought fixer-upper houses to remodel and flip. Could her university place restrictions on any of those activities? Perhaps, but now you're into more of a gray area.

TIP

If your employment agreement wherever you work doesn't specifically prohibit you from certain activities, or doesn't explicitly cap the number of hours you spend on some side hustle totally unrelated to your full-time job, you have a lot more latitude and freedom with what you can do on your own time. You may still eventually find yourself in conflict with your employer, but you have avenues to protect your side-hustle work if you think they're overreaching and being unfair (see "The employer strikes back" later in this chapter).

REMEMBER

The world of academia is far from the only business realm where employers may specify what employees are and aren't permitted to do for side hustles. Do you work for a retailer? Your employer may let you do all sorts of activities on the side — just not run your own online retailer that they consider to be competing with them. Or maybe you work for a clothing retailer, and they *do* permit their employees to do an online retail side hustle — just not for clothing. If you want to sell packaged meals or vitamins or home décor, no problem — just not clothing.

Making Sure You Don't Use Your Employer's Resources for Your Side Hustle

In the old days, the classic example of misappropriating — okay, make that stealing — your employer's resources was taking home office supplies: pens and pencils, printer paper, paper clips, maybe a red stapler. . . .

These days, with computer technology so pervasive in almost every company on the face of the earth, the concept of misappropriating your employer's resources is not only broader, but perhaps even a bit fuzzier. You need to be especially aware of the following types of company resources and keep them far, far away from your side hustle:

>> Computers

>> Company Wi-Fi networks

>> Audio/video resources

>> Official company work hours

>> Your company's location

Computers

Earlier in this chapter, I explain how an entire family of side hustlers — Josh, Jeremy, John, Julie, and Rachel — improperly used their work computers for their various side hustles. And now each one of them is in trouble.

"Oh, come on," you may be thinking. "If I use my work laptop for a couple minutes to fix my side hustle's website, or to answer an email or other message from one of my customers, or to place an order with one of my suppliers, what's the real harm? It's not like I'm stealing some physical item that the company paid for, like office supplies."

If you're tempted to dismissively shake your head at the "morality factor" of using your company's computer for your own side-hustle business, maybe you'll be persuaded by a couple of more tangible, more personally impactful considerations:

>> **You may lose your job.** You may not see any real impact or harm from borrowing a few computer cycles and a little bit of laptop storage here and there, but your company sets the rules. Whether you agree with their rules or not, you still signed your employment agreement. They may exact all sorts of penalties, up to and including firing you *for cause* (meaning you're being terminated for doing something wrong, as opposed to being caught up in some overall layoff or workforce reduction that has nothing to do with your actions or job performance).

>> **Your company could force you to hand over to them some or even all of your income from your side hustle because you made money while using their resources.** Sending you a nasty "Hand over the money!" letter or even suing you in court is usually on the outer extremes of penalties a company may try to impose for unauthorized usage of their computers. But why take the chance?

Just buy your own computer! If you don't have all the cash you need to buy one, take out a small business loan or find some other way to get the dough and stay out of trouble with your employer. (I cover business loans and other financial aspects of side hustles in Chapter 8.)

Maybe this whole separate-computer stuff seems like a no-brainer. But I can tell you from personal experience that I've offered side-hustle advice to almost a dozen people who already had some sort of outside activity underway separate from their full-time jobs, but who *weren't* using separate computers. My advice: Pull the plug immediately before your employer stakes a claim to your side-hustle intellectual property and even your income.

Company Wi-Fi networks

You're so clever! You think you found a loophole in the whole "don't use your company's computer" restriction for your side hustle.

Your cellphone may as well be a personal computer. You have your own computer at home that you use for your side-hustle work, and you're smart enough not to bring that computer with you to your full-time job. So, if you need to spend a minute or two during your workday doing some small task for your side hustle, even while you're at the office or some other location for your full-time job, just do it on your phone!

TRAVELING LIGHT? NOT ME!

During the years that I was a consulting executive, heading up national or global practices, I spent most of my time traveling for business. Sometimes I drove; often I flew. But whether I hit the road in a car or the skies in a plane, I almost always carried not one, but two and sometimes three laptop computers with me.

The first computer was the one issued to me by my full-time employer. I used it for everything related to my day job. Makes sense, right?

The second computer was my personal laptop. For a while it was a bulky Windows PC, but eventually I switched to a much lighter and smaller Apple MacBook Air. I often spent evenings and sometimes weekends doing side hustle–related work in my hotel room. Everything I did for any of my side hustles — writing, speaking at outside seminars or conferences, you name it — was done on this personal laptop, *never* on my employer's laptop.

And sometimes, a third laptop made the trip with me. Some consulting customers issued outside consultants client-provided laptops to connect to the client networks or to have access to tightly controlled, sensitive company data.

If I traveled by car, two or even three laptops wasn't a big deal. Flying, though — that was a different story. Going through security, lugging a couple different laptop bags with me and making sure that I didn't accidentally leave one of them behind somewhere in the airport or at the rental car counter. . . .. But no matter what, I was — and still am — always incredibly careful to make sure that I didn't any of my side-hustle work on a computer belonging to an employer. And if that meant, well, whatever the opposite of traveling light is, then that's what I did and still do.

Wait, what's that? You configured your phone to automatically connect to your office Wi-Fi? And you just received and then answered a text from a client or supplier or business partner? Too bad. You may as well have done so from your work computer, because you just made unauthorized usage of your employer's resources — in this case, their Wi-Fi network.

Come on! Would a company really be so petty to cause you grief because you answered a text over their network? Maybe not. Many companies are pretty lax about nonwork Wi-Fi usage while at work. Want to check Facebook for a minute or two during a break? No problem. Want to see if you have any new responses to the Evite you posted for your spouse's surprise birthday party? That's cool!

So, what about answering a side hustle–related text, or spending 5 minutes to fix a client's Shopify cart or WordPress site or anything else along those lines?

The response you probably don't want to hear is "It all depends," but that's the best answer for this question. If your employer doesn't have any issues with you and your coworkers doing your own side hustles — as long as you fully meet your job tasks — then chances are, those occasional communications blips over their Wi-Fi network will mean nothing.

If, however, your employer is less accommodating to outside work, or if they decide to "go after you" for *any* reason, then they'll do a hard target search for anything they can use against you — including sending or receiving a little bit of your side-hustle communications traffic onto their network.

TIP

Get in the habit of turning off your phone's Wi-Fi when you get to work. Or don't ever connect in the first place. Or set your phone to forget that network and never reconnect after you start a side hustle. Even if you're aware enough to stridently avoid sending messages or checking client websites or doing anything else related to your side hustle, you have no control over someone texting or messaging you. You may be ignoring these incoming communiqués, but if your phone is connected to your company's Wi-Fi, the messages are still traveling to your phone via your employer's network. If you're on a cellular connection, though, those messages aren't hitting your company's Wi-Fi, and you go a long way toward protecting yourself — and your side-hustle business.

Audio/video resources

Sean, Arun, and Cheryl all have the same great idea: Each of them wants to create a YouTube channel and series of videos that they can then monetize into a side hustle. Sean's videos will be about basic statistics; Arun's videos will be about real estate investing in the 2020s; and Cheryl's will be a series of health and wellness tips.

Sean works in the human resources (HR) organization of a large retailer. A recording studio is in the back corner of where the HR folks sit. Internal training videos are created in that in-house studio to save money on using expensive outside studio resources. Even better, the recording studio is set up for individual self-usage without needing a videographer.

Arun is a non-PhD instructor in the college of business at a university. The business school has an in-house studio that is very similar to the one in Sean's company. Faculty use this self-service recording studio to record lectures for online lectures.

Cheryl works in the medical data analysis department of a large hospital, that also has a self-service recording studio for medical-related instructional videos.

That shared great idea? Use their respective employers' self-service recording studios — during off-hours, of course — to create the videos for their side hustles. The studios are all top-quality: green-screen capabilities, marks on the floor for where to stand, software to split-record stand-up speaking with slides in the background, you name it!

TECHNICAL STUFF

Of course, none of the three will do the actual video editing there. They'll save the videos onto a jump drive and then use editing software on their home PCs to get the final videos into YouTube-ready quality.

On second thought, maybe this isn't such a great idea after all. In fact, this idea is on par with using a company computer and a Wi-Fi connection: foolish and dangerous!

Just because Cheryl or Arun or Sean intends to do their videos in the evenings or on weekends, when nobody else would otherwise be using the recording studios, doesn't shift this plan into the "good idea zone." The recording studios and every piece of technology in each one of them are property of the respective employers, and absolutely should not be used for some employee's side hustle or making a birthday video for a family member or anything else nonwork related.

Maybe Arun can just sneak into the recording studio on the weekend — after all, would anyone even know? Ha! Stealth is impossible here. Arun needs to swipe his access card to get into the business school building on weekends and then also to access and enter the recording studio. They'll know!

True, the quality of videos from these semiprofessional, self-service recording studios is better than any of them can do with a webcam and some area at home. And when it comes to online video-based side hustles, quality is paramount!

WARNING

Don't do it! The same warnings for company computers and Wi-Fi networks apply to other employer assets such as a video-recording studio. Suppose your relationship with your employer turns contentious, even adversarial. Do you really want to give them ammunition to come after your side-hustle business? To maybe shut you down? To perhaps force you to hand over your hard-earned side-hustle income to them? Nah, I didn't think so.

Company time

Maybe your job is incredibly flexible when it comes to official work hours. In the past 20 years or so, more and more companies have shifted toward a philosophy — and written company policy — of focusing more on your actual work than the way in which you do that work. As long as you achieve your assigned tasks, and meet or exceed your assigned goals, you're in good shape.

If you're a morning person, you can start working very early — maybe even five or ten minutes after you roll out of bed, if you're working from home — and be done by early or midafternoon. Or maybe you're pretty much useless early in the morning, but you pick up steam and become more productive as the day rolls on. Start working around 9:30 or 10 a.m. or even later? And continue until 7 or 8 p.m.? Sure, no problem.

Other companies adhere to a *core hours* policy. Every employee needs to be in the office, or "on the clock" working from home, between, say, 10 a.m. and 3 p.m., with a half-hour allocated for lunch. That gives you four and a half hours. How you make up the other three and a half hours each day, well, that's up to you. Mornings but not later afternoons? Sure. Later afternoons and even evenings but not mornings? No problem. Switch it up from day to day? Yeah, why not.

If your full-time employer has at least some degree of flexibility to your working hours, you're in good shape when it comes to allocating time to your side hustle and avoiding the dangers of doing side work during company hours. Just be careful and aware of when you are and aren't on the clock.

If, however, your company is more traditional with their work hours, you still need to be careful — just more careful. You'll know with 100 percent certainty, day after day, that from, say, 8:30 a.m. to 5 p.m. you absolutely need to stay clear of your side hustle — no exceptions.

REMEMBER

A *conflict of commitment* occurs when your company can make the argument that your side hustle is interfering with your ability to meet your full-time job's requirements. Doing something — anything — for your side hustle during official company hours opens the door to being accused of having a conflict of commitment. Don't do it!

Company premises

You make sure that your cellphone isn't connected to your company's Wi-Fi network. You never use your work computer for side-hustle business. You set your phone's alarm to remind you exactly when you're on and off the clock. So far, so good.

MAKING SURE EVERYBODY YOU EMPLOY FOLLOWS THE SAME RULES

WARNING

Even if you're extra-cautious about avoiding any whiff of conflict with your employer, what about your partners or employees or anyone else involved in your side hustle? Suppose your spouse isn't an "official" participant in whatever your side hustle is but helps answer emails and texts. Is your spouse accidentally exposing your side hustle to unnecessary risk by using a work computer or sending texts on company time or any of the other no-nos?

Not only you, but every single person who has any involvement at all in your side hustle needs to be fully aware of every little "gotcha" that can create difficulties for you.

But suppose when you're officially done for the workday, you just know that it's been a busy day in side-hustle land. You're still sitting in your office, and you thumb your phone over to your emails and then your texts. Wow! You have a whole lot of "PLEASE CONTACT ME IMMEDIATELY!"–themed communications, from suppliers and customers alike. Better get cracking, right?

WARNING

You just stepped onto the highway to the side-hustle danger zone. Not using your work computer? Check. Phone not connected to the company Wi-Fi network? Check. Off the clock? Check. Doing personal business while you're still at work? Uh-oh!

To be fair, many — maybe even most — companies would turn a blind eye toward your answering some of your own side-hustle emails or texts while you're still at work, especially if you're off the clock. But why take the chance? Wait another five minutes, maybe ten minutes, until you're out of the building, away from the parking garage or parking lot, and totally off company premises. In most cases, you'll still be fine. But if you ever wind up in an adversarial relationship with your employer — whether over your side hustle or just in general — why give them ammunition that could cause you grief?

Dodging Employer Tricks and Traps

In a perfect world, you and your employer would be perfectly transparent and act in good faith when it comes to outside work such as side hustles. Your employment agreement would clearly spell out what you are and aren't permitted to do. Any uncertainty would be addressed promptly and fairly. The overarching philosophy at play would be this: As long as you're meeting or exceeding your goals at work and continually performing at a high level, then what you do on the side is your own business — literally. Your employer wouldn't be casting a wary eye on what your side hustle is, or lay traps to potentially siphon off some or even all of your hard-earned proceeds.

Alas, it isn't a perfect world, is it?

Side-hustle awareness begins even before you start a job

You need to be fully aware and informed of every possible complication for your side hustle *before* you accept a new job. Or, if you don't have any side hustles at the moment but you're thinking about starting one, you need to check out exactly what you signed up for to stay out of trouble.

For most jobs, you receive a formal offer letter that spells out your salary, your starting date, and other aspects of the position being offered to you. You would think that everything you need to know that might impact your side hustle would be found in that offer letter, right? Think again! Here's the start of a typical offer letter:

> Dear Tyler,
>
> On behalf of the management at ABCDEF Corporation, I am pleased to offer you a full-time position as a Shift Manager I, starting February 29, 2024.

So far, nothing to worry about. But somewhere about halfway down the page, suppose you see the language shown here:

> Dear Tyler,
>
> On behalf of the management at ABCDEF Corporation, I am pleased to offer you a full-time position as a Shift Manager I, starting February 29, 2024.
>
> . . .
>
> By accepting this position, you agree to comply with all rules and regulations of ABCDEF Corporation. All rules and regulations with which you must fully comply and which will govern the terms of your employment can be found in the ABCDEF Corporation Employee Manual on our company website at https://we-gotcha-now.com.

Technically, your prospective employer isn't hiding anything. They're telling you that not only are you bound by the company's employee manual, but exactly where to find every sentence of that employee manual with which you must fully comply.

If you don't read that employee manual, you may well be walking into a trap — even if your employer isn't actually out to get you.

So, what's in that employee manual that can give you side-hustle heartburn? Say you do click the link in your emailed offer letter and get redirected to the company's online employee manual. Here's the start of what you may find there:

ABCDEF Corporation Employee Manual

Table of Contents

Section 001   Introduction

Section 002   ABCDEF Corporation Overview

Section 003   Required Professional Behavior

Section 004   Dress Code

Two things about this manual should jump out at you. First, the first four sections are probably going to be some pretty uneventful — maybe even boring — reading. Required professional behavior? Dress code? Yeah, you'll get around to reading this stuff later on, maybe the weekend before you start your new job.

But also, notice that the actual *text* of the manual's introduction — the company overview, the professional behavior guidelines, and the dress code — aren't actually in front of you. In fact, what you have are even more hyperlinks to take you to even more web pages to find all this information. Hmm, you may be thinking: Maybe the company is trying to hide something, or at least make it a little difficult and tedious for someone contemplating a job offer to do a deep dive into the terms of the job?

You're on to something here. Here's where side-hustle troubles can become front and center:

ABCDEF Corporation Employee Manual

Table of Contents

Section 001   Introduction

Section 002   ABCDEF Corporation Overview

The details of any restrictions are not only still a few hyperlinks away from being unveiled, but the problematic employee manual clauses are way, way down the list. Would you even read that far down the employee manual, to Section 122, before you accepted a job? Maybe — but probably not, unless your side-hustle awareness radar is blipping away.

REMEMBER

If you're aware enough to know what to look for, you can now decide exactly what this potential new employer will and won't permit for any side hustle you have going at the moment. Or, if you're already working at some place and are thinking about a side hustle, you have a comprehensive inventory of potential restrictions laid out right in front of you. To borrow from an old '70s song that was also redone in the early '90s: "Do this, don't do that, can't you read the employee manual?"

You already took a trip through the conflict of interest, conflict of commitment, and noncompete danger zone earlier in this chapter. Now, get ready for something that's *really* scary: rules about intellectual property rights! Boo!

Notice that Section 125 in Figure 11-4 is labeled "Assignment of Intellectual Property to ABCDEF Corporation." Wondering what that means? Okay, get ready: Your full-time employer wants ownership of any *intellectual property* you create.

**TECHNICAL
STUFF**

An intellectual-property assignment clause may read along these lines: "Upon acceptance of this job offer, you hereby assign to ABCDEF Corporation all right, title, and interest in intellectual property created or invented by you in which ABCDEF Corporation claims an ownership interest under its Intellectual Property Policy."

Wait a minute! Wouldn't an intellectual-property assignment clause apply only to something that you create or invent as part of your full-time job? And isn't anything you do outside not subject to an intellectual-property assignment clause, and you retain ownership?

GIMME ALL YOUR MONEY!

Ready for one more tale of caution from my own long, long journey through side-hustle land?

Back in the mid-'90s, I worked for a regional technology consulting company in the Philadelphia area. One day about a year after I began working there, one of the partners in the firm told me that one of the local universities (Philadelphia has a lot of colleges and universities!) was looking for someone to teach a summer master's degree course in a technology area called data warehousing, which happens to be one of my specialties. (In fact, I was writing my first *For Dummies* title, *Data Warehousing For Dummies,* at the same time.)

I landed the summer teaching gig — my newest side hustle — and one night a week for eight weeks, I taught for a couple hours after a full day of billable client work. So far, so good.

Several months later, when I was trying to negotiate a salary and bonus increase — rather unsuccessfully, I might add — that same partner who let me know about the teaching opportunity had this to say: "You know, we already gave you extra money — we let you keep the teaching money last summer."

Whoa! To my mind, outside college teaching was, well, exactly that: totally outside the scope of my full-time consulting job. In fact, earlier that year, I had taught several seminars for some training company that was partnered with my employer. Those seminars *were* within the scope of my full-time job because I was assigned to deliver them and they counted toward my billable hours just as my client work did. My outside university teaching? That was a totally different bucket.

Maybe their "hand over all your money" stance was simply a negotiating posture, or maybe they truly believed that because the connection for me to do the grad-school teaching came through them, they were entitled to all my earnings, even though I was billing a full 40 hours a week, the same as every other full-time consultant there and this teaching had nothing to do with the company. In the class listing and on the faculty roster (at least for that summer) I was "Alan Simon, Adjunct Professor," not "Alan Simon from XYZ Consulting."

The matter eventually died, along with my career at that company, because I left shortly after for a larger consulting firm. But the story should serve as a lesson that you never know what curveball you may face as you proceed with your side-hustle endeavors.

You would think so, you might hope so, but you can easily walk right into a trap and risk losing ownership of — not to mention financial gain from — something you do as part of your side hustle. Videos about computer programming or some other tech topic? The software company or consulting firm or university where you work may try to claim that those videos are, in fact, within the scope of your job and you're required by your employment agreement to assign the ownership to your employer. That book about supply-chain analytics you just finished? The logistics company where you work may try to say, "Oh, no, that's ours — hand it over!"

If you're now panicky about the very idea of your full-time job and your side hustle life coexisting in the same universe, never fear: You can regain control over any brewing conflict and tip the playing field back in your favor to protect your side-hustle interests and activities (see "The employer strikes back," later in this chapter).

They're coming after you!

Not every company is maliciously trying to interfere with an employee's side hustle or to steal intellectual property and force an employee to turn over side-hustle profits. In fact, most companies operate in good faith when it comes to potential conflicts over side hustles.

Suppose, though, that an employee flagrantly uses an employer's resources — computers, Wi-Fi networks, a video-recording studio, you name it — as part of a side hustle. And suppose that the side hustle really is in direct competition with what the employer's business is. And suppose that the employee also continually does side-hustle work during company time. Wouldn't you think the company is within its rights to enforce employee agreement clauses that govern intellectual property ownership and conflicts of interest and commitment? Sure!

But what exactly can a company do to address blatant side-hustle conflicts? They could

>> Force the employee to immediately cease their side hustle — maybe permanently or at least until the two parties come to a meeting of the minds.

>> Force the employee to sign over intellectual property rights, as specified in an employee agreement. If the employee used a company computer on company time to develop an app for a side-hustle business, the employer can make a good case that they actually own the app.

>> "Claw back" profits that the employee made from their side hustle, which means that even though you've personally received the money, you need to hand it over to your employer — maybe under the premise of "repayment for unauthorized usage of company assets."

>> Perhaps worst of all, do a *forensic* (digging very, very deep!) review of even more of your past activity with the intention of seeing what else the employer may be able to gain — possibly including ownership of past work that you did even before coming to work for them!

How could an employer possibly go after something — say, a book, or a monetized series of YouTube videos — that you created even before you became an employee?

WARNING

I've seen more than a few employment agreements with an intellectual-property assignment clause that read along these lines: "I agree to assign my ownership in all intellectual property created before or during my employment with ABCDEF Corporation, except for items identified in Attachment A to this employment agreement. . . ."

Wow! If you signed an agreement that included wording similar to this *preexisting intellectual-property assignment clause*, you'd be in for a world of hurt. That book you wrote ten years ago? You just signed away your rights to the book, if your company enforces the clause. That white paper you're writing right now for some tech company? You just handed your new employer the keys to that as well.

Other than refuse to sign the employee agreement and walk away from the job offer, do you have any recourse? Sure. Take a look at the last part of that preexisting intellectual-property clause: "except for items identified in Attachment A to this employment contract. . . ."

Sometimes, your employee agreement will come with a blank "Attachment A"; other times, you need to create your own. Either way, Attachment A (or whatever terminology is used) is your escape route from potentially losing ownership of your rights to your own hard work. Don't shut off your own escape route!

REMEMBER

Use Attachment A to list *every possible piece of intellectual property you can think of* as being excluded from the employee agreement's intellectual-property assignment clause. By listing anything that you've created or "invented" in any way, you protect your ownership if any controversy ever arises between you and your employer.

TIP

Having been in the side-hustle game for my entire professional life, I have a couple of aces up my sleeve to protect my prior work. Any time in the past when I've been presented an employee agreement with a preexisting intellectual-property clause (something common in the technology and consulting world, unfortunately), I've copied and pasted from my personal computer a comprehensive list of every book, article, and presentation that I've ever done into the Attachment A portion of the employee agreement. (I also make sure to update the list with any new intellectual property since the last time I accepted a job offer.) Then, following the list of past works, I always include a final catchall line that reads: "Also excluded are all past, present, and future works that I create on my own time, using my own resources."

Basically, my message is: "Keep your mitts off my side hustles!"

A little paranoia never hurt anyone

Did you ever hear the saying that "just because you're paranoid, doesn't mean they aren't out to get you?"

When it comes to enabling your side hustle to coexist with your full-time job, a little paranoia is a good thing. Again, most employers aren't out to cheat their employees and steal the hard work from their side hustles. Some sure act like it — but most employers are fair.

Still, you should act a little bit paranoid when it comes to your side hustle. Continually ask yourself: "How could my employer make my life miserable by interfering with my side hustle, and what can I do to stop them?"

WARNING

Above all else: Don't use your company computer, your employer's Wi-Fi network, or any other company assets for your side hustle — especially on company time. In other words, be smart!

By "thinking paranoid" and reminding yourself that if you do succumb to the temptation to work on your side hustle during regular work hours, or log into your side-hustle business email from your employer's computer and send a message to a client, or anything along those lines, you're opening yourself up to a world of hurt. Maybe nothing will happen, but why take a chance? If you continually remind yourself that you need to maintain a firewall between your side hustle and your full-time job, you'll be in good shape.

The employer strikes back

What happens if (hopefully not *when*) your employer steps over the line and unfairly tries to shut down or otherwise obstruct your side hustle? Good news: You aren't powerless.

First, try to have a meeting of the minds and negotiate a solution. Maybe your supervisor just isn't aware of company policies about permissible outside work, for example. Schedule a meeting and talk it out — or at least try to.

If talking doesn't do the trick, go to your boss's boss and make your case there. True, you're treading into dangerous territory by going over your boss's head, but look at it this way: You already have a confrontation brewing by virtue of your boss trying to impede your side-hustle work. Unless you're getting tired of your side hustle and thinking about giving it up anyway, you may as well fight for your rights.

If you still don't have a resolution, check out what your employee manual specifies should happen next. Many employers have a mediation process for these types of situations, where an independent third party — perhaps someone from HR, or a manager from another organization — hears both sides and tries to negotiate a solution.

Mediation is sometimes followed by a formal grievance process — basically, the next step that raises the temperature level even more but that is sometimes necessary to protect your rights. Unlike mediation, which is often sort of a semiformal negotiation effort, a formal grievance process follows rigid steps involving exchanges of documents, presentation of evidence, and a formal hearing that is led by several people. Often, what a grievance committee rules is binding — basically, the final word inside the company that will dictate what you can or can't do with your side hustle (or anything else brought up before the grievance committee).

Whereas a grievance committee may be the final step within a company to resolve a dispute, you always have the "nuclear option" to retain an attorney and direct the matter surrounding your side hustle into the legal system.

TIP

If you find yourself unable to resolve your side hustle–related conflicts internally and do decide to go the legal route, make sure you retain an attorney who practices employment law, or who has experience representing clients with side hustle–related situations similar to yours. An attorney who specializes in estate planning or real estate or some other specialty may or may not be what you need to advocate for you and your side hustle in the face of what you believe to be unfair actions on the part of your employer.

Sometimes, an experienced attorney will give you the bad news: You may be out of luck because of the overreaching terms of the employment agreement that you signed, or because you've been "caught" using company resources, or for some other reason. Or, on the brighter side: An experienced employment attorney may tell you that even though you signed an oppressive employee agreement and that's what your boss is using to try to shut down or otherwise impede your side hustle, the laws in your state countermand the most over-the-top restrictions in the employee agreement, making them null and void. And you're actually in good shape!

REMEMBER

You may not make any friends with your company's management by filing a grievance or showing up in your boss's office one day accompanied by your attorney. But if you truly feel that you're in the right and that someone is trying to unfairly infringe on your side-hustle activity, you may as well fight for your rights — and maybe start looking for a new job, too. Or you could always kick your side-hustle work into high gear and try to make it your new full-time work (see Chapter 15).

Chapter **12**

Spinning Off Your Current Side Hustle into a New Side Hustle

S ide hustles can be like potato chips or Halloween candy. You try one, and you quickly want another. Pretty soon, you just can't stop grabbing for more and more!

Are you currently doing rideshare driving for Lyft? Go ahead and add Uber ridesharing. Rideshare driving for Uber? Now add Uber Eats delivery. Doing Uber Eats delivery? Why not also do Grubhub and DoorDash and Postmates and, well, you get the idea.

Or maybe you created a YouTube channel to capitalize on some hot new exercise trend. Why stop there? You could add another channel where you cover healthy eating tips, and then cross-market your two channels. And then some new exercise trend comes along? Hey, you already have a built-in audience, so you can jump onto this newest trend and rush out an entirely new set of videos.

No matter what your side-hustle game is, you have opportunities to branch out into new side hustles. I should know, because I've been doing exactly that for 40 years! My original consulting and software side hustle led to my first book, as well as college and university teaching. My tech and business books led to writing novels, and also to doing tech video courses. And my tech video courses became the foundation for hobby-related videos.

REMEMBER

Expanding your personal side-hustle world is yours for the asking, but you need to make sure that you carefully think through your spinoff ideas to make sure you have all your side-hustle ducks in a row!

Spinning the Side-Hustle Web That's Right for You

You're all in on the side-hustle game. Your first one is up and running, and going along great. Now you can't wait to add another side hustle — or more than one — to your personal portfolio.

REMEMBER

You typically can go one of three ways as you start looking at new side hustles:

>> Add a new side hustle that is highly complementary to what you've already got underway.

>> Head in a totally different direction from what your current side hustle is, with the intention of building a "balanced portfolio."

>> Lay the groundwork for a new side hustle as you begin to wind down your current one.

All aboard the synergy train

No matter what your side-hustle game is, you can almost always find a synergistic "Act II" to bolt onto your initial side-hustle efforts. Table 12-1 offers some ideas for new side hustles that are synergistically paired with what you may already be doing.

By day, Juliana is a midlevel marketing manager with a global consumer products company. By night and on weekends, she becomes her side-hustle alter ego and publishes tons of content about interior home design, including the following:

>> Short videos that bring her advertising-generated revenue

>> Longer courses for which people pay a couple hundred dollars per course

>> Blog posts that feature plenty of affiliate marketing links for even more revenue

TABLE 12-1 ### Pairing Up Synergistic Side Hustles

Current Side Hustle	Synergistic Side-Hustle Ideas
European travel tips blog	European travel tips videos
	Asia travel tips blog and videos
	In-depth restaurant reviews
	Personalized travel itineraries
Rideshare driving with Uber	Rideshare driving with Lyft
	Uber Eats food delivery
Instacart shopping and delivery	DoorDash food delivery
	Grubhub food delivery
Writing nonfiction business and tech books	Writing novels or short stories
	Writing business and tech articles for magazines and websites
Tech seminars and training	Seminars and training in complementary tech topics
Blogging about exercise for seniors	Blogging about diet and nutrition for seniors
Airbnb rentals for your own home when you're on vacation	Buying a second home solely for Airbnb or Vrbo rentals
Dog walking	In-home overnight pet sitting
College subject tutoring	College and graduate school entrance exam tutoring

Juliana's interior home design side hustle is tracking just as she had planned. So, now what?

Juliana thinks about it, but doesn't need to think too long. Interior home design . . . home . . . design . . . hey! What about the exterior of a home? Window shutters . . . roofing tiles . . . creative paint schemes . . . porches and porch furniture . . . the list goes on and on!

Juliana sets out to repeat her side-hustle success in an area closely related to what she's currently doing, in a quest for synergy between the old and the new within her personal side-hustle portfolio.

Building a balanced side-hustle portfolio

Sometimes, differences can be a good thing.

REMEMBER

Many people who build personal side-hustle portfolios go in the opposite direction of synergy between their day job and their side hustle. Instead, they create a *balanced portfolio* of seemingly unrelated disciplines and focus areas.

TECHNICAL STUFF

In the world of investments, you create a balanced portfolio when you combine stocks and bonds; gold and cryptocurrency; real estate; and other assets — in certain proportions — into your overall collection of investments. Even better: Your stock investments are made up of large and small companies; well-established corporations and newly public, riskier companies; and companies from a variety of industries. Basically, you're trying to spread your risk among a variety of investments and build a portfolio that will perform well in a variety of economic situations (that's the goal at least).

Sara is a software developer who works in the information technology (IT) department of a large retailer. She also teaches online computer science classes for the large state university with a campus in the city where she lives. Side hustle? Check! Side hustle that's complementary to her day job? Double-check!

So, when Sara decides to do some blogging and create video content for a second side hustle, why doesn't she stick with technology in the pursuit of synergy between her two side hustles? Well, she could — but Sara's motivation for her side hustle is not only to start a little side business, but also to devote her energies to something far, far away from her day job. What about blogging and videos about backpacking trips and camping? Aha!

Sara decides to follow the balanced portfolio approach with her side hustles. Her college teaching side hustle pays fairly well, but she does have to put in a fair amount of time for every class that she teaches. The idea of *passive income* (see Chapters 3 and 16) from her side hustles has her intrigued. And although she's spreading out her side-hustle portfolio, why not also try to monetize her passion for backpacking and camping?

Passing the side-hustle baton

Sometimes you can use a side hustle as a beginning step in the next phase of your career journey. If you sort of enjoy some aspects of your current career, but positively hate other parts of your day job, you can use a side hustle to "pivot" to continue doing what you enjoy but leave behind the less satisfying parts.

Suppose that after four or five years, Sara's passion for college teaching has hit rock bottom. She still likes the idea of sharing her insights and knowledge about various topics — tech-related and otherwise — but grading dozens of assignments and exams, holding office hours, and everything else that goes along with college teaching (even for online courses) has gotten to be a real downer.

BE CAREFUL ABOUT SIDE-HUSTLE CONGLOMERATES

At one time in the corporate world, *conglomerates* were all the rage. The largest corporations in the world would buy up companies from all sorts of industries, and plop them all under the same corporate umbrella — even though these underlying companies had little or nothing to do with one another. One of the most famous conglomerates was ITT Corporation, with underlying businesses in insurance, training and trade schools, manufacturing, and hospitality. In more recent times, General Electric had underlying businesses in consumer electronics, aviation, medical equipment, and finance.

A funny thing happened on the way to conglomerate-land, however: The trend toward packaging unrelated businesses under a single corporate umbrella fell out of favor. Back in 1995, ITT spun off various businesses. More recently, General Electric and Johnson & Johnson announced that they, too, are basically getting out of the conglomerate game.

So, what do mega-corporate conglomerates have to do with side hustles? If you pursue a strategy of building a "balanced portfolio" of side-hustle activities rather than closely related synergistic ones, be very careful not to spread yourself too thin to the point where you're having difficulty switching back and forth between unrelated activities. The basic idea of a conglomerate holds true in the corporate world, just as it does in side hustles: a balanced portfolio of business activities to lessen and "smooth out" your overall risk, in case one particular portion of your business hits a bumpy road.

The smart folks who run General Electric, Johnson & Johnson, and other corporate conglomerates now heading down the breakup path are well aware that any company — or person — can't be all things to all people. Sometimes you may need to slice off portions of your overall portfolio to be able to focus on other portions.

Ah, but Sara really likes the additional income that her teaching side hustle provided, and she's not really looking forward to giving up that money if she stops teaching on the side. No problem! Sara's new side hustle — the backpacking and camping videos — may become the successor to her original teaching gig when they start bringing in a decent amount of money.

Better yet: In addition to her "balanced portfolio" approach, Sara also decides to create a separate set of videos about tech-related topics. This way, she can have her side-hustle cake and eat it, too, by pursuing *both* the synergistic and balanced portfolio approaches at the same time as she prepares to ease her way out of teaching and head off to new side-hustle pastures. Talk about a side-hustle triple play!

At least that's Sara's plan, and the "passing the baton" concept might also apply to your own side hustles. Maybe your first side hustle isn't as enjoyable as it once was, or it's no longer earning as much money as it once did. You still want to stay in the side-hustle game, but you're looking for something new and fresh.

Putting Together Your Side-Hustle Jigsaw Puzzle

Spinning off a new side hustle requires more than just deciding to take the plunge. Just as when you started your first side hustle, you need to make a whole lot of gears work in concert with each other. Basically, you need to repeat all the planning and startup activities that you did the first time.

Additionally, you need to take a close, careful look at how a new side hustle will coexist alongside your existing side hustle — or side hustles, if you already have more than one underway — with a careful eye toward:

» Your available time

» Potential conflicts with your current side hustle

» Your overall side-hustle finances

Making sure you have enough time available

If you already had a full-time job when you started your first side hustle, you had to make sure that you had enough time for whatever your side gig would be. Suppose you worked traditional working hours and a full-time 40-hour weekly schedule, with an additional five hours a week spent commuting to and from work. This schedule left you with at most a couple hours each weekday evening; maybe an hour or so in the very early hours each weekday before you started getting ready for work; and then weekends available for your side hustle. So, you were smart, and you planned your side-hustle schedule around your available time.

And now, here comes side-hustle number two. How much time will this one take? Are you thinking about a new idea that could create a time clash with either your current side hustle or your full-time job?

For example, Terri is a full-time high school teacher who started writing a travel-related blog two years ago. She earns money from the affiliate marketing links placed in her blog. Now, she has a great idea for a second side hustle: selling travel-related clothing and accessories. She does her research and figures out how to create a simple Shopify storefront. She lines up several suppliers of clothing and goods. She's all set to go, pending what she decides for her final step: How can she best reach prospective customers?

She learns that other people who have been successful in similar side hustles have done the best using Facebook Live (www.facebook.com/formedia/solutions/facebook-live) for live selling directly to people out there in Facebook-land. "Okay," she thinks to herself, "I can do that, too."

But as Terri looks into Facebook Live, she realizes she may have some time-related issues. Apparently, the best time to go live on Facebook is between 1 p.m. and 3 p.m. local time on weekdays (www.pepperlandmarketing.com/blog/best-times-to-go-live-on-social-media). But Terri is still at school during those hours.

She digs a bit further, and the same site tells her that if she tries going live on Instagram instead of Facebook, her best time there is either noon (still a problem because of school) or between 7 p.m. and 9 p.m. local time. Aha! There's her answer!

Not so fast, Terri. She had been setting aside two nights each week to write her travel-related blog, set up the affiliate marketing links, and take care of most of her tasks for her first side hustle. She spends the other three nights each week grading student papers and exams. So, where is Terri going to find the time for her new side hustle?

Terri comes up with a solution. Right now, she spends only a little bit of time each weekend on either her travel-blog side hustle or teaching-related work that she needs to take care of at home. Her weekends are when she decompresses and recharges to get ready for another action-packed week.

However, if she's really going to go forward with this second side hustle, she needs to make some adjustments. She plans to shift some of her travel blog writing and additional work to the weekend to free up two weeknights to go live on Instagram for her new side hustle.

WARNING

Beware of shifting schedules only on paper! Terri can easily find time slots for seven or eight hours of weekend work for her travel-blog side hustle. But finding those slots on paper is one thing — what's going to happen the first time Terri wants to go for a hike or see a movie on a Sunday afternoon, but now she can't because she has to get her travel blogging done? She's already weary enough from spending five evenings a week doing either travel blogging or outside schoolwork. When she started her travel blog, she realized that the two evenings she had free from school work would now be filled with side-hustle work. Now, she's eating into her weekend free time as well.

Terri may decide to proceed with side-hustle number two despite the further erosion of her free time. For Terri, she has a goal in mind: to drop back to part-time teaching within the next three years, instead of being in the classroom full-time. To achieve this goal, Terri needs to really ramp up her outside income, and a second side hustle is a great start toward even more outside money to make her part-time teaching goal a reality.

On the other hand, Terri may decide that selling travel-related clothing and accessories via live-streaming will be one side hustle too many. She *needs* her down time, and she's insightful enough to realize that if she pushes herself too far into the side-hustle game, she'll be miserable.

TIP

Terri doesn't necessarily have to totally ditch the idea of a second side hustle selling travel-related clothing and accessories. Trying to schedule live-streaming seems to be the stumbling block here. She may have other ways to reach her prospective customers, so she starts digging again. The important thing for Terri, though, is that she was insightful enough to sniff out time- and schedule-related issues before she went too deep into her initial plans for this second side hustle.

Checking for conflicts

If your new side hustle is along the "balanced portfolio" lines and you're heading in a totally different direction from your first side hustle, you most likely will steer clear of potential conflicts between the two. If, however, you're aiming for synergy between your side hustles — books and videos; affiliate marketing links for products sold by different retailers or wholesalers; or expanding your online training and teaching into the in-person realm — you need to carefully check and make sure your side hustles aren't in conflict with one another. But if you're careful in the first place with all contracts, for anything related to your full-time job and your side hustles, you should be in good shape.

For example, when Tyler started his side hustle — writing a book on graphic design — he was smart enough to carefully avoid conflicts with his day job as a graphic artist in the marketing organization of a major software company. He used his own computer, worked on his own time, and followed all the rules to keep a firewall between his side hustle and his full-time job (see Chapter 11).

Unfortunately, Tyler wasn't nearly as careful when he signed a book contract with the small publishing firm. Otherwise, he would have spotted the overly broad "Competing Works" clause that prohibited him from not only writing a similar book about graphic design with a different publisher, but also declared videos, consulting work, and pretty much any other intellectual property Tyler might create about graphic design to be in direct competition with his book — and, thus, prohibited as long as the book was in print. Oops!

Tyler's cousin Amanda finds herself in a similar situation. Her side hustle involves taking pet photos that people submit to Amanda's website and sending those photos to an artist, who creates colorful paintings of dogs, cats, horses, goats, ducks, geese, chickens — pretty much any possible pet! — set in iconic travel locations such in front of the Eiffel Tower or the Roman Colosseum or in a hot-air balloon soaring along over midtown Manhattan or the Las Vegas Strip.

One problem, though, and for Amanda it's a *big* problem: The artist she works with required her to sign an exclusive contract that prohibits Amanda from working with any other artists as long as they have an active business relationship. This artist only draws pets in scenic locations. Amanda wants to add a new line of photos turned into art for holiday family pictures. She found an artist for this new line, but unfortunately, her side-hustle contract with the pet artist prohibits her from working with anyone else.

REMEMBER

Obviously, both Tyler and Amanda should've been much more careful, and much more discriminating, when they signed contracts for their respective original side hustles. Beyond that obvious point, however, you need to make the same diligent effort to look for potential conflicts with any new side hustle as you did for your first one.

Balancing your side-hustle checkbook

WARNING

You need to be careful when you spin off a new side hustle that you're on top of the financial commitments you might need to make. Even if your spinoff side hustle is mostly the same as your current one, your next phase could require you to make a substantially larger investment. If you can make the finances work, great! Just don't get caught by surprise.

Catalina has run an online boutique, selling women's clothing, for the past two years. As a single mother, she didn't have a whole lot of savings to invest in her side hustle, so she built her business around drop-shipping — basically, customers place an order but the goods are shipped directly from suppliers to the customers, without Catalina having to buy the inventory herself and store it in her house or maybe a storage locker. The major advantage of drop-shipping is that you can try out selling different products without having to drop a whole lot of money to buy inventory that may never actually sell. Then you're not only out all that money, but you need to figure out what to do with products you weren't able to sell.

Catalina's side hustle is going along fairly well, and now she wants to expand to new clothing lines, as well as new products: exercise gear, travel-related items, and more. Catalina has built up a fairly loyal customer base, and she's confident that she can do a decent job selling these new product lines just as well as her original women's clothing.

Overall, Catalina's idea seems like a solid one, but there's a catch: She can't find drop-ship suppliers for all these new products. Plenty of wholesalers are out there, but Catalina will need to spend money on inventory, find room in her house to store all the inventory, and now pack and ship customer orders herself.

Catalina may be able to make her side-hustle expansion work, but she needs to be careful about the financial aspects of this new side hustle. She deliberately chose a financial model for her initial side hustle where her income potential from selling items may be slightly reduced, but — most important — her financial risk in the event of side-hustle failure was minimized.

Now, even with a couple years of success behind her, Catalina needs to be careful not to head down a path that greatly increases that risk to the point where her side-hustle portfolio overall may wind up being more of a drain on her personal finances than a benefit.

REMEMBER

Have an eye toward the complete financial picture of not only your first side hustle, but every other one that comes after. In a perfect world, every additional side hustle you take on would add to your outside income over time. But make sure that you look at scenarios where a second or third side hustle totally flops — and do your best to make sure that failure doesn't take down your entire side-hustle world by tanking your finances.

Chapter **13**

Other People and Your Side Hustle

N o matter what you have in mind for your side hustle, even if you're looking at doing something totally on your own, you absolutely need to get other people involved from the very beginning to help you get going.

However, depending on the circumstances of your specific side hustle, you may find yourself with very little direct involvement with other people after you get up and running. Or, at the other end of the spectrum, almost everything you do will involve interacting with people.

Suppose your side hustle is creating and posting YouTube videos featuring a variety of tips about personal appearance (skin care, makeup, hair care, and so on). You set up a studio in a spare bedroom in your house or apartment, and that's where you record all your videos. You record each video yourself, using a remote control that controls a video camera plopped on a tripod. You then sit down at your computer in the corner of your spare room to edit each video yourself, before you upload the final edited video to YouTube. You're also computer-savvy enough to set up all the affiliate links to the products you'll feature. Basically, you're a one-person side hustle!

Not so fast!

When you first came up with the idea to record and post videos, did you discuss the idea with anyone else? A partner or spouse? A parent or child? A friend? Did someone help you put together your business plan?

How about right now, after you've been up and running for almost a year. If you're trying to set up a new affiliate link that isn't working properly for some reason, do you contact someone to help you figure out how to diagnose and then fix the problem?

You originally built your own website using a basic template, but when all of a sudden some of your web pages start looking or acting weirdly, do you reach out to a web design expert to help you get your website back in working order? Or to help you hook up your website to some new cool apps that you want to try?

And what about your customers? What's that? You're only posting videos to try to earn advertising revenue from YouTube and other platforms, so you don't really have any customers? Are you sure? Don't some of those people who watch a video send you an email or click a Contact Me link on your video post to ask you a question about some product that you demonstrated?

No matter what your side hustle is, you'll rely on other people for one or more of the following:

» To provide you with advice

» To be your partners

» To be your suppliers

» To be your customers

» To be your employees or subcontractors

In this chapter, I walk you through each of these scenarios so you can get the most from the experience and avoid some pitfalls along the way.

Give That Side Hustle Proposition the Once-Over

Your side-hustle aspirations might not even begin with that "lightbulb moment" where you suddenly have a brilliant idea for a business, or even an impulse to check out a gig-economy job. Very often, a friend or family member tells you about some fantastic side hustle they've been doing for the past six months, and how much money they're making, and what they've bought with all that money.

"Oh, by the way," your friend or relative continues, "you can get in on this side hustle, too."

Do you immediately ask, "Where do I sign?" Of course not! You need to do your homework. And in this case, your homework begins by asking some really on-point questions to dig for the real story behind the sizzle.

For example, Jennifer's friend, Melanie, is a distributor for a multilevel marketing (MLM) company that sells health and wellness foods and drinks: low-calorie meal replacement shakes, protein bars, healthy snack foods, and much more. Jennifer has bought about a hundred dollars' worth of items from Melanie each month for the past year.

One day, when Jennifer meets her friend for coffee and to pick up her latest delivery, Melanie says that she has a great idea: Why doesn't Jennifer join the MLM company herself? She can not only buy her own products that she uses each month at a discount, but she can also sell even more items to other people, just as Melanie does. Talk about a win-win!

Does Jennifer immediately respond with "Sign me up!" or "Absolutely — how soon can I get started?" Maybe a better question is *should* Jennifer respond immediately that she wants to jump aboard and is ready to start buying and selling today.

The short answer: No! Not immediately, anyway.

Of course, Jennifer needs to find out of the details about this particular MLM, as discussed in Chapter 3:

>> Is there any signup fee, and if so, how much?

>> How much product is she required to purchase each month?

>> Does Jennifer need to purchase all of that month's products first before she books any orders versus a sell-first-then-order model?

>> How much of her sales proceeds will go to Melanie, who brought her into the company, or to anyone else?

>> Can Jennifer return any unsold products?

Presume that Jennifer asks Melanie all these questions, and she's 100 percent satisfied with the answers. An hour later, after the two friends say goodbye, Jennifer grabs her phone and does some quick research about this particular MLM company and their products. The feedback from the company's distributors — all the people like Melanie — is generally positive. Even better: Jennifer isn't the only person out there buying and enjoying this company's protein bars and shakes and snacks; social media posts are filled with words and phrases like *delicious* and *filling* and *great stuff.*

Gathering your team of advisers

Advice — you need plenty of advice. You want your friends, family, and coworkers whom you've sworn to secrecy about your side-hustle aspirations to be as honest as possible with you about *everything.* You want these trusted advisers to:

>> Pick apart your overall idea and tell you if they see the same bright future that you do.

>> Critique the way in which you're planning to take your side hustle to market, such as through a particular MLM.

>> Help you run the numbers for your projected income and costs to make sure you're not being overly optimistic or forgetting key expenses.

>> Give you some ideas of additional things that you need to check out before you're ready to officially get underway.

WARNING

Before Jennifer signs on the dotted line and joins the MLM, she needs to get feedback from other people to help her make sure that this new side hustle is right for her. Jennifer needs to reach out to trusted friends and family members and gather as much input as possible about this possible new venture.

So does Arjun, who is thinking about starting a side hustle in which he will create a series of videos called "5-Minute Coding Hacks." As you can probably guess from the title, each of Arjun's videos will be exactly five minutes in length, and will feature some unique block of programming code that viewers can then incorporate into their own apps or websites.

However, when Arjun tells his sister Nyra about his idea, she points out that at least a dozen similar video series can be found on various social media platforms. She challenges Arjun: "How will your series be different?" This simple question spurs an hour-long discussion in which Arjun and Nyra discuss:

>> Ways in which his video series can be unique and differentiated from others that are already out on social media platforms.

>> His revenue model, which is based on securing enough subscribers to earn advertising revenue.

>> The frequency of his video posts. Arjun originally was thinking about posting a new video every weekday, but Nyra challenges this assumption based on what she knows about her brother's work schedule.

>> The topics he's thinking about covering in his programming hacks. Nyra is also a software developer and she helps Arjun prioritize his list, as well as remove a few that, upon second glance, don't seem all that interesting.

Then there's Lanie, who has been following a number of online boutiques for the past few years and who has put together a business plan to start her own online storefront that will sell clothing and accessories. Lanie is pretty astute, and one glorious autumn Saturday afternoon she invites her two brothers and their wives over for a cookout. After eating lunch, Lanie, her husband, and their four guests plop down onto comfortable seats in the backyard gazebo, and Lanie lays out the ground rules for the next couple of hours: "Pick my business plan apart! Challenge *everything* — the products I'm thinking of selling, my pricing, how I'm going to fill orders, my advertising strategy, my time management strategy . . . I mean *everything!*"

By the time the sun is ready to dip below the wall in the back part of Lanie's yard, about half of her business plan has been turned upside down. Her brothers, her sisters-in-law, and her husband did exactly as Lanie had asked them to do, and now Lanie is ready to start on the second iteration of her business plan.

REMEMBER

The last thing you need when you're starting your side hustle is a bunch of "yes people" automatically telling you that whatever your idea is, it's absolutely brilliant! Your side hustle will make you a ton of money! Everything you're setting out to do with your side hustle is guaranteed to happen!

Maybe you *will* make a ton of money from some unique idea or some new approach that you'll incorporate into your side hustle. Perhaps you'll soon be on your way to not only beginning a successful side hustle, but eventually turning that side gig into your new full-time career. But that path to success begins with honest input and feedback from your friends and family and advisers, even if some or many — or even all — of your initial side-hustle plans are challenged.

Lanie has it exactly right. You want your "side-hustle brain trust" to help you think through — and possibly adjust or refine — your ideas for:

>> **The very nature and merits of your side hustle itself:** First, state what your side-hustle idea is, using only a few words: "an online custom-styled boutique" or "do makeup and hair" or "record and post videos about baseball cards."

>> **How you refine your high-level idea:** If you're thinking about "an online custom-styled boutique" you quickly need to get more specific and focused for your brain trust. What are you going to sell? Are you going to preemptively purchase and stock inventory or exclusively use drop-shippers and avoid carrying inventory? What is your target market and your overall pricing strategy? Or suppose you're thinking about baseball card–related videos. What kind of baseball cards? Older ones (known as *vintage* in the hobby)? The so-called "junk wax" ones from the late '80s and early '90s? Modern cards? Your brain trust will

- Help you refine and drill into your basic side-hustle concept

- Help you decide if you're on the right track or if you need to pivot your ideas in a different direction

>> **How much funding you need to get started:** Prospective side hustlers have a tendency to underestimate how much money they'll need to get their side hustle up and running, and then perhaps to keep things moving along until business kicks in. Sitting around with trusted friends and family members — especially those with a financial background, or who may have previously done the side-hustle bit themselves — helps you catalog all the little costs that you may have otherwise overlooked.

>> **If you might be biting off more than you can chew:** Sure, that side-hustle idea sounds like a definite winner. But what about the time commitment? Do you really have enough time to do everything that needs to get done? Are you glossing over the impact on your evenings and weekends? What about that monthlong family vacation coming up in a few months that you've been looking forward to for the better part of a year — can you get all your startup tasks done before you head for the airport? And then what happens while you're gone? Other people may have a better big picture view of the time-commitment side of your side hustle than you do while you're all caught up in the enthusiasm of getting off the ground.

Deciding what to share and with whom

When it comes to sharing your side-hustle ideas, who is in your "circle of trust"? If you immediately answered "close friends and family," you may be correct — or you may not.

You need to carefully and methodically and carefully (yes, I wrote *carefully* twice, to really drive home that point!) decide in whom you should confide, especially at the earliest stages of your side hustle. After all, what's to prevent someone from hearing your brilliant idea and then thinking, "Hey, I could do that myself!"

Come on, would a close friend steal your idea and run with it on their own? Hopefully not, but that's where *you* need to make the judgment call about who you can really trust.

TECHNICAL STUFF

In the professional world, people and companies commonly use *nondisclosure agreements* (NDAs) to legally bind another person or perhaps an entire company to secrecy about a product idea, the details behind a bid and proposal submission, a possible company merger or acquisition, pretty much anything. NDAs come with a hefty load of "legal oomph" — you can wind up in pretty big legal trouble if you sign an NDA and then violate the terms and blab about something that you were supposed to have kept secret.

In the world of side hustles, NDAs have their place, but they can be overkill when you're just seeking advice from friends and family at the earliest stages of whatever you have planned. (Not to mention that handing an NDA to, say, a sibling or a parent or ne of your closest friends, can lead to some pretty awkward moments and hard feelings!)

Still, you're running a risk every time you share an early-stage idea with someone else that they could steal your idea and leave you out in the cold. Therefore, you need to have a really, really good idea of who you want to confide in and how trustworthy they are. So, if, say, one of your cousins has a reputation for not always being on the up and up in business and personal dealings, you probably don't want to share your ideas with that person — even if you think they could really help you — at least until you're far enough along with your side hustle that you have a healthy head start, should your cousin decide to poach your idea.

WARNING

Be careful about your earliest-stage "circle of trust" even beyond worries of someone stealing your side-hustle idea. Back during World War II, posters across the United States warned that "Loose lips sink ships" — in other words, if you accidentally spill defense secrets that you know, those secret plans could get back to the enemy and lead to military disaster.

In the world of side hustles, loose lips also, well, I can't think of a catchy rhyme equal to that long-ago World War II–era saying, but you get the idea. You tell a friend about a unique idea you have for a podcast that's all about the 1950s, Baby Boomers, and the early days of TV. (It's already been done. . . .) Your friend happens to have dinner and drinks with a couple of other people the next weekend, gets a little careless when they all start talking about joining the "Great Resignation" and quitting their full-time jobs, and all of a sudden blurts out, "You know, my friend has a great podcast idea. . . ." Could one of your friend's friends — someone you've never met — poach your idea? Or could someone that one of them knows steal the idea because it's being passed around, and before you know it, someone else rushes out a '50s-related podcast before you get yours going?

Don't be scared off from seeking advice from others at the earliest stages of your side-hustle planning. Just be careful. Every single person you discuss your idea with should have something to offer you: online marketing expertise, or painful experiences from having tried something similar that didn't work out, or just being a great sounding board who isn't afraid to share their opinions with you.

Howdy, Partner!

Bringing a partner into your side hustle is a major step that can help you get to that magical next level — or, on the other hand, it might drive your side hustle into the ground. Likewise, joining someone else's side hustle as a partner may be the opportunity of a lifetime, or turn into the nightmare that never ends.

Partner doesn't necessarily mean a partner in a tax-filing sense (for example, a legal partnership that files IRS Form 1065 and distributes K-1s). Think of *partner* in a more general sense: someone with whom you will share responsibilities in some manner and likewise share in the success (or failure) of your side hustle.

Hiring an employee or a subcontractor to offload some of your work is one thing; bringing a partner into your side hustle is on a totally different plane, with many considerations to think about.

What does a potential partner offer?

Are you a techie who needs someone with business skills to help you get that side of your side hustle squared away? Are you an introvert who really needs someone extroverted to take the clever scripts that you write and be the face of your side hustle in your YouTube videos?

Are you looking primarily for an investor to help you get your side hustle off the ground? Maybe you're already well underway and your delivery service is going so well that you need someone to help you start up operations in the next city you've targeted on your business plan.

You can always add employees or subcontractors — or both — for the "arms and legs" to help you out. Someone whom you're seriously considering bringing on as a partner needs to have a solid *value proposition* (the value provided by some person or aspect of your business). In other words, this person needs to be more than just a friend or acquaintance with whom you think you'd like to work — if you don't have a solid idea of exactly how the two of you would work together, the partnership won't be any help.

How do the two of you get along?

Not everyone in business needs to be the best of friends, but you definitely don't want to bring on a side-hustle partner with whom you frequently argue or who just generally rubs you the wrong way. Even if that person has tremendous skills in some area that you desperately need, you likely would be making a gigantic mistake joining forces if you already have an underlying layer of contention every time you get together.

TIP

Look for little signs that could be a tipoff to potential trouble down the road. For example, suppose one of your personal hot buttons is people who, when you're in a conversation either in person or on the phone, frequently interrupt you as you're finishing a sentence — or maybe even in the middle of something you're saying — and talk right over you. Then suppose you have a friend who, in almost every respect, would be the perfect complement to you in your side hustle . . . except that person *always* interrupts you, and you find yourself gritting your teeth and seething. Danger, danger, *danger!* You already have some serious barriers that you need to overcome in order for the two of you to work well together. Maybe you can still find a way to make a side-hustle partnership work, but (to use one more cliché) you're facing some pretty stiff headwinds!

How does a potential partner get along with other stakeholders?

Do you and your current side-hustle partner get along fantastically? That's great! What happens, though, if you're thinking about bringing someone else into your business? You and that third person may get along superbly. But you need to make sure that both of your partners also will get along *with each other.*

After all, the three of you will be working together very closely, and the last thing you want is for personality clashes between these other two partners to submarine your overall business.

Suppose your online boutique that you began with a friend who also works at your day job company has been in business for a year. The business is growing, and the two of you agree that it's time to bring in a third partner to help take things to the next level.

You contact your best friend from college, because the two of you had talked for years about starting a business together. Unfortunately, she had too many things going on when you started your side hustle, which is why you turned to your friend from work.

You get along with your side-hustle partner, and you've never had a discouraging word with your college friend. But how well do the two of them get along?

TIP

Make sure that the two of them spend enough time together for all of you to be 99.9 percent confident (or pretty darn close to that number) that if your side-hustle duo becomes a side-hustle trio, you won't soon find the business embroiled in interpersonal drama.

What are this person's weaknesses?

You identify potential partners for what they bring to your side hustle. But what are that potential partner's weaknesses?

TECHNICAL
STUFF

In the business world, companies often do performance reviews for an employee in which they not only evaluate how well that person did against a sales quota or some type of job-quality target, but also dig into that employee's personality and motivations. The idea is to really *know* what makes an employee tick — not only how to maximize an employee's strengths, but also how to understand an employee's weaknesses.

You need to have the same deep insight into a prospective partner's weaknesses as you decide whether you should bring that person into your side hustle — and if so, what tasks you should give to your new partner.

For example, Jay has been creating and posting videos about health cooking tips for six months. In front of the camera and behind a stove, Jay is a natural: outgoing, friendly, a crystal-clear speaker, and a great chef. But on the tech side, Jay struggles with the video editing. He's thinking about farming out that task to someone from Fiverr or another job task website, but before he posts the job, his friend Todd hits him up with this idea: Todd would come on as a partner and take care of all the video editing, as well as the social media marketing, search engine optimization (SEO), and other online marketing tasks. Basically, Jay could concentrate on planning and recording the videos and leave all the online-related tasks to Todd.

At first, Jay thinks Todd's idea is fantastic. The two of them have been friends since college, and they've always gotten along fairly well. But then Jay remembers something: Todd doesn't exactly have a "task completion ethic." He's a pretty good techie, but over the years, Todd has unashamedly told Jay about the trouble he's gotten into at work for not finishing assignments. Todd describes himself as more of a "tech explorer." He likes to *start* a particular assigned task, but when he comes across something of interest — whether it has anything to do with his assignment or not — he's just as likely to go off on a tangent, stay up all night wired on caffeine, and explore the outer limits of some particular tech aspect in a quest for knowledge.

Jay should really think twice about entrusting his video editing and online marketing to Todd — friend or not. This particular weakness of Todd's could very possibly be the undoing of Jay's side hustle, not to mention their friendship.

WITH FAMILY LIKE THIS . . .

Actor George Clooney once played a character named Michael Clayton in a movie called, well, *Michael Clayton*. In the movie, George's character is a New York City lawyer who also has a side hustle going: a restaurant that he opened with his brother as a partner.

Sounds like a solid idea, right? After all, you should have a pretty good idea of a brother's — or sister's — strengths and weaknesses, and how the two of you can best work together.

Unfortunately, in the movie Michael Clayton's brother steals a lot of money from the restaurant because of personal addiction problems, which causes the restaurant to fail. Pretty bad, right? Unfortunately, things actually get worse from there. Some "unsavory and dangerous characters" are after George Clooney's character to repay $75,000 that he had borrowed for the restaurant, and these people aren't the type to take "I don't have the money, sorry" for an answer!

Michael Clayton is forced to go to the partners at the law firm where he works full-time to ask for a loan to bail out his side hustle, which basically is to pay off these dangerous people and keep from winding up in *real* trouble.

And this is only a subplot in the movie! (*Michael Clayton* is a great movie, by the way.) You get the idea, though: You need to be *very* careful about who you go into business with for your side hustle — even family members and friends you may have known your entire life. You also need to be careful about what you tell anyone — even family members and friends — about what you're setting up during the earliest stages of your side hustle activity.

The prime directive here: You almost certainly will need to work with or even just talk with other people for various reasons related to your side hustle, but be extremely cautious, almost to the point of being paranoid.

What other alternatives do you have?

REMEMBER

A side-hustle partner is a serious matter. Before taking the plunge, look at alternatives such as:

>> Hiring a part-time (or even full-time) employee

>> Finding subcontract help on Fiverr, Freelancer, Upwork, or some other job site

>> Reaching out to a local university to see if an undergraduate or even graduate program course is looking for projects

>> Checking into small business loans, if your primary reason for adding a partner is to infuse capital into your side hustle

You may still find that adding a partner to your side hustle is the right thing to do. But before everyone signs on the dotted lines, check out a few other options.

How will the financial picture of your side hustle change?

A partner almost always has a financial stake in some business venture, including a side hustle. Suppose you start your side hustle on your own, and from the moment you begin posting videos or selling athletic wear or doing small software development jobs or whatever your side hustle happens to be, the spoils are all yours. Oh, yeah, the costs are all yours, too.

How would things change with a new partner? Would you share the proceeds 50/50? The costs 50/50? Or, as the founder, would you retain a majority stake in both the income and the costs?

Any and all possibilities are open to you. Just make sure that you're crystal clear going into any partnering discussions exactly what you are — and are not — willing to give up. Prepare to negotiate, but also be prepared to walk away if you can't make the financials work to your satisfaction. After all, this was your side hustle to start with!

How will the voting and ownership of your side hustle change?

Suppose you decide that you and your new partner will share both revenues and costs 50/50, because you're sharing the efforts more or less equally as well. So far, so good.

But what about making major decisions? Suppose you want to spin off the partnership into new activities, or maybe even an entirely new side hustle (see Chapter 12). Or suppose you want to pull the plug and move on to something else (see Chapter 14). Or, on the really positive side, someone comes along and wants to acquire your side-hustle business. Jackpot!

Not so fast. Suppose you want to do A, but your partner wants to do B. You're sharing revenues and costs equally — did you decide to share voting rights equally as well? If so, how do you break a tie, because that's what 50/50 ownership between two people gets you!

Very often, a solo partner joining an already-existing business (side hustle or not) winds up with a 49 percent voting share at the most, with the solo founder retaining a 51 percent voting share. From the perspective of the side hustle that you conceived and grew before a partner joined, a 51/49 split in your favor seems like a fair deal, right? And maybe it is. But from the flip side (see the next section), signing up for a two-person partnership where you can *always* be outvoted could be a problem.

TIP

You can avoid both a 50/50 stalemate and a 51/49 "someone always wins, someone always loses" situation with a little bit of creativity. For example, as the founder, you may retain decision-making rights for key business decisions, such as accepting a buyout offer or major expansions. Your partner, however, has majority decision-making rights for other matters — marketing and technology, hiring employees, or things along those lines. You can set up decision-making however you like —just make sure you write everything down in your official contracts!

Joining Someone Else's Side Hustle as a Partner

Your friend Jiao has had a pretty solid home pet-sitting side hustle underway for the past two years. She contacts you and pitches you this idea: Just as she is still doing her day job, you don't have to quit your full-time job either. But why not join up with her pet-sitting side hustle as a partner?

Before you instantly shout "Absolutely!" (and presuming you like hanging around with pets anyway), you need to do a little bit of thinking about the offer — basically, the alter ego of the same questions you need to ask if you're thinking about bringing on a partner to *your* side hustle.

Why are they asking you?

Does someone just need "arms and legs" — basically, help managing the workload? Do you have any particular skills or knowledge that is in short supply with the person asking you to come aboard as a partner? Are they looking primarily for an infusion of money?

REMEMBER

Just as you need to be crystal clear what the value proposition is for potential partner for your side hustle, you need to ask yourself the same questions before you sign on the dotted line for someone else's business. If you're just providing "arms and legs" — additional labor — that may work. But more productive side-hustle partnerships work when the skills and knowledge of the various partners complement each other and help overcome any potential weaknesses.

What do you offer?

Jiao states her proposition very clearly. True, you can help her take on more pet-sitting jobs than she can do alone. But her website isn't exactly in great shape, and she's falling behind on the accounting and record keeping. Basically, Jiao really needs your help for a variety of tech and business tasks above and beyond the actual pet sitting.

Okay, are those skills in your wheelhouse? Do you have strong tech skills for website maintenance and social media marketing? Do you know enough about accounting to take on what Jiao wants to send your way?

TIP

Make sure that whatever your potential partner spells out for you is, indeed, something that you can provide and do a great job.

How will the compensation and ownership be set up?

How do you feel about the financial and ownership split that's being offered to you? Will you be required to regularly kick in money to fund the side hustle, but might you always be outvoted on key decisions?

WARNING

Basically, are you getting a fair deal? If you don't think so, and if you can't negotiate financial and ownership terms that you feel are fair to you, then you're better off not taking the partnering plunge. You may find different ways to work together with your friend on this particular effort; or you may mosey off to greener side-hustle pastures on your own.

Can you be kicked out?

One of the advantages of joining up as a partner in an existing side hustle, versus coming on board as an employee, is that you're immune from being fired or otherwise shown the exit door.

Or *are* you immune?

One morning at the local coffee shop, Hannah begins talking with another woman who introduces herself as Fawn. About ten minutes into the conversation, Fawn mentions that six months earlier, she started a web marketing company to help small businesses with their targeted social media advertising. Hannah mentions that she went back to college when her kids were grown and off on their own, and she just graduated with a business computing degree and a certificate in digital marketing. Hannah adds that unlike the "kids" she graduated with, she isn't looking for a full-time tech job. Instead, she's looking at a couple of different entrepreneurial ideas that she can do part-time, and she already has one of them underway.

Before the conversation has finished and the coffee has had a chance to get cold, Fawn throws out this idea: Maybe Hannah wants to partner up with Fawn's social media marketing company as part of Hannah's side-hustle portfolio.

Over the next few weeks, the two share ideas. Then Fawn makes the offer: Hannah, with the formal business computing education and a business degree that Fawn doesn't have, would come aboard Fawn's side-hustle business as an equal 50/50 partner. Fawn has some pretty big plans for her little business, and having a partner with the title of executive vice president would help give her side hustle that extra credibility for someone looking to invest or even buy it out down the road.

Hannah's radar lights up just a little. She just met this other woman not that long ago, and now Fawn is offering to bring her in as an equal partner? Something doesn't sit quite right, but on the other hand, why look the proverbial side-hustle gift horse in the mouth?

Anyway, the two of them get working and start visiting clients, but more than a month after Fawn's surprise offer, still no partnering paperwork. Even more worrisome: Every time Hannah brings up the paperwork, Fawn gets snappy and becomes far less friendly than when the two of them chatted congenially over coffee about their respective side hustles.

Finally, Hannah receives an email from Fawn's attorney with the partnering agreement. She reads it over and, what do you know, the agreement contains traps, both obvious and (as Hannah finds out after she spends $5,000 for an attorney to review the agreement and then tell her *not* to sign it under any circumstances!) hidden.

That 50/50 ownership split that Fawn verbally offered? The contract specified a 51/49 split — in Fawn's favor, of course. Voting rights? Solely with Fawn. But beyond those two glaringly obvious discrepancies, Hannah's attorney points out a total dealbreaker couched in legalese. Basically, at any point in the company's lifespan, Fawn can fire Hannah and not owe her a single penny. As Hannah's lawyer explains during a $400-per-hour phone call (!) "Fawn could accept a buyout offer from some other company, but the day before the deal closes, she could fire you, and she wouldn't owe you anything."

Needless to say, Hannah walks away from the whole deal, and never does business with Fawn again. True, she wasted a couple hundred hours over a few months that she could have devoted to her own ongoing side hustle, and maybe jump-started another one. But at least she bailed before it was too late!

Can you wind up on the hook financially?

Oh, yeah: Hannah's attorney pointed out one more dealbreaker buried in this side-hustle partnering contract from you-know-where. Even though Fawn could fire Hannah at any time, when you unpack the legalese, Hannah could be on the hook for 49 percent of the company's bills — even after being fired, if those expenses were incurred while Hannah was still a part of the company. And worst of all: Hannah could be long gone from the company, but if Fawn's company was ever successfully sued for something that happened while Hannah had a 49 percent ownership stake, even if the lawsuit happened several years later, Hannah would be on the hook for 49 percent of the judgment, as well the legal bills to defend against the lawsuit.

You get the idea. Side hustles are supposed to be, well, not necessarily fun, but at least rewarding. Joining up with someone else's in-progress side hustle may sound at first like a way to jump right into something without all the startup work, but you need to be very, very careful before taking the plunge, especially with someone whom you haven't previously worked with or even known for that long. But even with family members and longtime friends, be careful!

Your Side-Hustle Supply Chain

If you're doing rideshare driving for Lyft or Uber, or delivering restaurant meals or groceries, or doing dog walking or pet sitting, your side hustle doesn't really have a supply chain. If you're recording videos or writing books or blogs, you really don't have a supply chain either. The same applies if you're providing professional services on the side — tech consulting or software development, accounting, résumé writing, college entrance exam tutoring, and so on.

But if you're selling physical products, you absolutely do have a supply chain, even if your side hustle pales in comparison with even a modest-size retailer. And where you have supply chains, you have suppliers. And where you have suppliers, you have people. And with people at your suppliers, you need to be on top of those relationships every bit as much as with potential partners.

For example, Erica runs an online boutique, specializing in women's clothing and accessories. A couple of months ago, she decided to add a line of custom-designed seasonal T-shirts to her items for sale. On her Shopify website, Erica will put up Valentine's Day T-shirts in mid-January; Christmas T-shirts in mid-November in time for the holidays; graduation-related T-shirts in the spring; and so on.

She found a reasonably priced supplier through a website for clothing wholesalers and put everything in place for this T-shirt company to fill orders in a timely manner, given the seasonality of these specialized shirts.

Even though Erica's side-hustle boutique does a little bit of drop-shipping (wholesalers directly filling orders and shipping products to customers, rather than Erica having to carry inventory), this particular T-shirt supplier will send the shirts directly to Erica, who then will pack the orders and ship them to customers along with anything else they may have ordered.

But from the very first order for the upcoming Valentine's Day, this wholesaler has been nothing but problems. On the good side — that is, the customer side — a decent number of orders for the first batch of seasonal T-shirts comes in. Nothing that will buy her a new car or pay for a vacation to Paris, but a few dozen orders. Not too bad for the first try!

The expected delivery day arrives, and Erica's mailbox is empty. The next day: same thing. Now, Erica emails the T-shirt supplier, who replies later in the day with "I shipped them last week." Worried that the T-shirt shipment is lost in the wilds of a post office somewhere, Erica asks her T-shirt wholesaler to send her the package tracking number so she can try to figure out where the shirts actually are.

Crickets.

The next day, Erica asks again. This time the wholesaler sends a fuzzy image of a tracking number, and — big surprise! — when Erica enters it into the postal service's tracking system, she's informed that no such tracking number exists.

Long story short: The T-shirts finally arrive a week later, and Erica still has to ship them to her customers, most of whom selected regular first-class shipping rather than Priority Mail or even Priority Mail Express. Erica figures she has no choice but to eat the additional shipping cost, and she sends every package out Priority Mail.

Guess what: The next time Erica offers seasonal T-shirts, for Halloween later in the year, the same problems happen! The missed delivery date; the tracking number that really isn't a tracking number; the T-shirts finally showing up a week late; and having to eat the cost of additional postage to get the shirts to her customers in time for Halloween.

Erica decides to try one more time, a few weeks later for the upcoming Christmas season. Yeah, you've seen this movie before. Exact same results!

REMEMBER

Depending on the specifics of your side hustle, you may find yourself dependent on suppliers — make that *people* — who could be great to work with or, on the flip side, could be a total nightmare. You could have all your side-hustle ducks in a row for an online retail business — a slick website, great social media marketing technology, a great product mix at the right prices, and a loyal customer base — but those folks who are upstream in your supply chain could cause your best-laid plans to stumble and fall. Be ready, and have contingency plans in place!

Interacting with Your Side-Hustle Customers

Your customers can be your strongest advocates for your side hustle or your worst nightmare. Especially in this era of viral social media, you need to be very careful in how you relate to your customers.

REMEMBER

If you have a retail-oriented side hustle, just remember: The customer is always right, even if the customer is wrong. Basically, even if a customer is absolutely unreasonable in demanding a refund or gets a refund but refuses to return supposedly defective products, be very careful in going head-to-head with such a customer.

The largest retailers can get past angry posts that social media — ahem — "aficionados" delight in spreading around. But a small retailer, especially one that's a side hustle, has much more difficulty overcoming a viral campaign besmirching a company's or even a person's name.

TIP

When any potentially confrontational situation with a customer is bubbling to the surface, always ask yourself a couple of questions:

>> What's the absolute worst outcome here?

>> What could I do or say to unfortunately bring about that absolute worst outcome?

>> On the other side of the coin, what could I do or say to *avoid* bringing about that absolute worst outcome?

If you don't have a retail-oriented or service-oriented (consulting, tutoring, financial advice, pet-sitting, and so on) side hustle, you don't have customers, so none of this applies, right?

Not exactly. Even if you're creating and posting ad-supported videos for "the masses," you might still find yourself interacting with sort-of-customers. For example, someone emails you to let you know that they really liked your latest video. Or maybe someone else contacts you to let you know that they spotted a mistake in one of your videos. No matter what the reason for someone contacting you may be, take the time to email or otherwise contact them with a reply. If someone asks you a question, do your best to answer it. If someone points out some possible error or problem in your content, politely thank them and let them know you'll check it out.

WARNING

If someone gives you a bad review for a video course, do *not* point out the flaws in their logic or otherwise "defend yourself and your work." Ask yourself the same three questions listed earlier, even for interacting with people through general feedback-oriented contacts.

Divvying Up Your Side-Hustle Workload

Your side hustle needs help! But not to fix problems or save it from ruin. Everything is actually going very well, and you need some assistance — basically, additional arms and legs.

You have two primary choices: hiring employees or engaging with subcontractors.

Hiring employees brings a hefty administrative burden (see Chapters 10 and 15). You will need to:

>> Establish a payroll

>> Withhold and submit income and payroll taxes

>> Take care of state unemployment payments

>> Offer at least some benefits

On the other hand, subcontractors are transitory in nature. You may use some of them only once, others every so often, or others perhaps on a regular basis.

As soon as you begin dealing with either employees or subcontractors, your side hustle has "grown up" from its earliest stages, whatever that may have been. You need to treat your employees and subcontractors fairly, cordially, and professionally. But at the same time, you need to be clear-headed about work quality, attendance, meeting deadlines, and everything else that goes into your business and that you expect from yourself.

REMEMBER

If you're not ready to take on a people management "burden" as part of your side hustle, you have a couple of choices. You can throttle back your side-hustle activity to the point where you can once again handle it all on your own. Or you could bring on a partner (as discussed earlier in this chapter) solely for the purposes of running your side hustle as a business, while you focus on the areas you're passionate about.

Chapter **14**

Deciding When to Change Directions or Pull the Plug

Your side hustle is moving ahead in lockstep with your plans and expectations. You're having a lot of fun. In fact, you're getting ready to add one or two new side hustles to your little portfolio. Maybe you're even seriously thinking about leaving your full-time career and turning this particular side hustle into *the* hustle.

Or not.

Perhaps your side hustle has taken a turn for the worse. Where did your customers go? Where did your side gigs go? Where did your money go?

Maybe all is well with your side hustle, but an even more promising one just crossed your radar, and there's no way to do both, so something's gotta give!

If you're right on track with your side-hustle plans with clear sailing ahead, then bravo! Enjoy the feeling of having your side-hustle aspirations come to life. At any point along your side hustle's life span, however, you may be asking yourself a rather tense question that you definitely need to answer.

That question?

"Okay, so what do I do now?"

Sign, Sign, Everywhere a Side-Hustle Sign

You built much of your side hustle's plans around a business school concept called a *value chain* (see Chapter 4). Figure 14-1 shows the framework of your side hustle's value chain using an organization diagram.

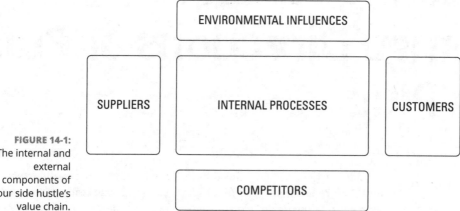

FIGURE 14-1:
The internal and external components of your side hustle's value chain.

REMEMBER

Your side hustle value chain isn't only for your planning efforts. You should keep an eye on each of the major components — customers, suppliers, environmental factors, and competition — for some early warning signs you'd better pay attention to. The following sections walk you through these components.

Changes in your customers and markets

Quick — what fashion trends dominated when you were in high school? If you went to high school way back in the '70s, you're probably thinking bell-bottom jeans, platform shoes, and tie-dyed T-shirts. If your high school days were during the '80s, "preppy" and "really bright colors" probably spring to mind. Now jump forward into the 2010s, and if that's when you were in high school, you probably remember denim vests, black boots, and sports jerseys.

Our tastes in clothing change over time. Sometimes a trend just runs its course, while in other cases the advertisers and marketers do their best to convince us that most of our wardrobe is now obsolete, and we need to break out our wallets and buy the latest trendy clothes.

Clothing isn't the only type of item that goes in and out of style. In the movie *Sideways*, Paul Giamatti's character famously yells outside of a restaurant that he's not going to drink any Merlot wine, and if anybody orders Merlot, he's leaving. Well, what do you know? Sales of Merlot dropped soon after the movie came out, while sales of Pinot Noir (the "star wine" in the movie) rose significantly.

If your side hustle is built around selling products, you need to have your finger on the pulse of consumer tastes. The retail marketplace is littered with stores that didn't adapt to the changing tastes of consumers quickly enough — or at all. The last thing you want is to build a successful side hustle only to watch it all fade into oblivion because you didn't adjust your product offerings quickly enough.

You could also face the opposite situation, where suddenly everything clicks in your favor and your customers are buying everything that you put up for sale. Maybe you've luckily stumbled into the right products, at the right time, and you're simply riding the wave of good fortune. Or maybe you've tweaked something in your marketing and advertising, or adjusted your pricing, or made some other adjustment that is now paying gigantic rewards.

Either way, you need to start digging into the data and analytics behind your changes in fortune — whether good or bad — so you can either correct the problems or keep doing even more of what's going right for you.

Both Breanna and Sarah have side hustles — they run online boutiques where they sell fashion items to the world at large. Breanna buys clothing and accessories from wholesalers, while Sarah makes jewelry.

For the past three months, Breanna's business has been way, way down. She's been buying the latest fashions that she can afford from wholesalers, but the inventory is piling up in her spare bedroom. Even the seasonal T-shirts that she put on sale for Valentine's Day barely sold, unlike last year when Breanna sold out weeks before Valentine's Day and had to stop taking orders.

Sarah has a different situation on her hands for her customers. All of a sudden, her orders have doubled, and she's having lots of trouble making all the jewelry within the two-week time frame boldly listed on her website.

Breanna's situation? Bad! Sarah's situation? Good . . . sort of. "Good" because business is booming, but "sort of" because she's not really sure if she can make all the jewelry to fill all the orders within her promised time frame.

Good or bad, both Breanna's and Sarah' situations fall into the "Customers" section of their respective side-hustle value chains.

Breanna needs to dig into a whole lot of data to figure out not only what to do, but what's really going on with her boutique. Is Breanna's problem:

>> Her social media ads are suddenly not being shown as frequently.

>> Potential customers are seeing her ads, but they're just not clicking on them.

>> The guy she hired to redesign her website actually made it too confusing for customers, and people are just saying "Oh, forget it!" and shopping elsewhere.

>> A couple of styles of blouses are still selling, but almost everything else isn't moving.

Sarah should be happy about all the new business for her jewelry, but she needs to do some data digging as well. Maybe she increased the money she was spending on Instagram ads a couple months ago, or maybe she added teaser videos for her jewelry on YouTube and TikTok. Is her sudden increase in orders the result of an advertising change? Or did she launch a couple of really stylish new bracelet-and-earrings combinations that suddenly everyone wants to buy from her?

Wait a minute! If Sarah's business is humming along, why does she need to dig into "the story behind the story" of why her business is suddenly doing so well? That's a great question — and I have a great answer: If Sarah can figure out the *root causes* of what has triggered her business success, she can continue doing more of the same. True, Sarah has no guarantee that her secret recipe for success will work forever — but at least for the near future, she can be fairly confident that she has identified certain levers to pull that will likely result in sales.

REMEMBER

The actual steps that Sarah and Breanna take for their respective side hustles aren't the important point. What *is* important is that both Sarah and Breanna need to take note of the changes in their customers' activity and buying habits, and then make whatever adjustments are necessary to their side hustles.

Supply-chain changes

Even if you did a fantastic job setting up your supply chain when you opened for business, you never know when hiccups will develop among your suppliers and wholesalers. Wholesalers can suddenly change their pricing, or all of a sudden they're days or even weeks late on almost every one of your orders. One of your suppliers may go out of business or stop carrying the products that you buy from them. Then what?

Breanna did it! She found a new web developer on Fiverr to redesign her website. She dumped a bunch of clothing items and accessories that weren't selling and found a bunch of new blouses and dresses and T-shirts that instantly started selling great.

Are Breanna's side-hustle problems over? Not quite, unfortunately.

Two of her best suppliers suddenly go out of business. Another supplier tells Breanna that prices are going up 15 percent across the board, and Breanna is certain that she can't simply pass those price increases on to her customers without seeing a big drop-off in business. Suddenly, Breanna's problems have shifted from the customer side of her side hustle value chain to the supplier side.

Back to the drawing board. Breanna finds new suppliers who can provide her with dresses, blouses, and other clothing items that are pretty close in style and quality to the ones that she used to get from her now-out-of-business previous suppliers. She decides to replace the jewelry items that are now 15 percent more expensive with similar items that are slightly lesser in quality, but which Breanna can price in line with her other accessories.

REMEMBER

No rest for the weary! Even though Breanna's boutique business is her side hustle rather than her full-time job, it still is a business, and Breanna needs to be on top of the end-to-end supply chain, from her suppliers to her customers, the same as a gigantic department store would — just on a smaller scale.

Climate change, the side-hustle version

REMEMBER

You need to have your radar on alert for potential problems — and also possible opportunities — in more than just the supplier and customer components of your value chain. Environmental influences, both good and bad, can affect your side hustle, too.

The whole world was impacted in numerous ways by the COVID-19 pandemic. Not only were our daily lives heavily affected, but so were businesses large and small — including side hustles.

TIP

Even beyond once-in-a-lifetime (hopefully!) events such as a pandemic, your side hustle may be impacted by all sorts of environmental influences such as:

>> A new child

>> An aging parent

>> Your spouse getting a job offer that requires moving to a new city

>> Earning a promotion in your day job that will require significantly more hours and a lot of travel that you didn't have to do before

You took environmental influences into account when you created your original side-hustle business plans (see Chapter 4). As your side hustle marches on, though, you need to be aware of new or changing environmental situations that can impact your side hustle — a little or a lot!

A year before the pandemic suddenly began, Gina started a really challenging side hustle. Ever since she was young, Gina loved baking, and always dreamed of opening a bakery. Professionally, though, Gina's job working the 3 to 11 p.m. shift at a large retailer's distribution center was about as far away from her baking passion as anything she could imagine.

Still, side hustles come in all shapes and sizes and aren't necessarily restricted to certain times of the day or certain days of the week. Gina pulled together her savings and borrowed money on a Small Business Administration (SBA) loan to lease a small location in a high-traffic shopping center and then remodel that location as a bakery. She worked at her regular job Mondays through Fridays, which was perfect for what she had in mind.

Gina opened her bakery with hours between 7 a.m. and 1 p.m. on Thursdays, Fridays, Saturdays, and Sundays. She would only have horrendously long workdays two days a week (Thursdays and Fridays, when she would close the bakery at 1 p.m. and then run home for about half an hour before heading to her regular job). On weekends, she would still get to the bakery around 6 a.m. — the same as Thursdays and Fridays — but after she closed up each weekend day, she could go home and try to relax for a little bit. She was able to hire two part-time bakers to arrive even earlier than Gina did to get a head start on baking the day's pastries, bagels, breads, and other goodies.

Gina's double life between her regular job and her bakery side hustle was busy, but fulfilling, and it went along more or less smoothly until the COVID-19 pandemic hit. Gina's city initially issued a lockdown order preventing people from leaving their homes other than to go to jobs that had been deemed essential. Even after the lockdown order ended, though, most people stayed home almost all the time. Almost nobody was going to restaurants or bakeries.

Fortunately, Gina quickly adjusted her overall side-hustle strategy by taking two important steps:

>> She immediately applied for a Paycheck Protection Program (PPP) loan that provided funds to cover the payroll for her two employees. Eventually, Gina applied for forgiveness of the loan amount under the terms of the Coronavirus Aid, Relief, and Economic Security (CARES) Act. (See Chapter 8 for more on watching for special financing programs for your business.)

>> From the time she opened her bakery, almost all of Gina's business came from walk-in customers, with only a few takeout orders a day. Now, though, Gina realized that her business would only be able to survive through takeout orders. She hired a web developer on Upwork to quickly build a website and storefront for her bakery. She began advertising in local newspapers and through social media that she offered takeout services. She got permission from the owner of the shopping center where her bakery was located to block off two of the parking spots in front of her store for five-minute pickups, and she began offering curbside services. Now, customers didn't even need to come into the bakery to pick up their orders.

Gina made it through the worst of the pandemic, and as it turned out, her bakery gained a lot of loyal customers — so many that she's seriously thinking about leaving her day job and trying to make her bakery side hustle her full-time business (see Chapter 15).

Don't look now, but you've got company!

Most side hustles are different than larger businesses when it comes to new competitors coming onto the scene.

Think about all the well-known retail businesses that have seen their fortunes plummet. From department stores such as Sears, Kmart, and JCPenney to clothing chains and even entertainment-oriented businesses such as Circuit City and Blockbuster, new competitors arrived on the scene and eventually took tons of business away from those former retail stars, or even drove some out of them out of business.

Could your side hustle suffer the same fate as those giant retailers? Possibly — but unlikely. For one thing, your side hustle won't have shareholders or equity owners who live and die by quarterly earnings, no one who might see "only" a 5 percent or 10 percent sales increase versus the same quarter last year as a disaster that will require layoffs and store closures to prop up earnings data in response to sales being stolen away by competitors.

WARNING

Still, your side hustle isn't immune from being impacted by competition, so stay alert and keep an eye on the new kids on the block.

Sarah makes custom jewelry that she sells online. Will the sudden appearance of another custom jewelry maker have a significant impact on Sarah's side hustle? Perhaps, but more likely, as long as Sarah's jewelry reflects her unique design style, her business won't be impacted too much, if at all.

Of course, if someone copies Sarah's styles and then undercuts Sarah's pricing, suddenly Sarah would have a competitor-related problem on her hands. So, Sarah does need to have competitors on her side-hustle radar.

Interestingly, competition impacts a side hustle more in the online world, especially when side hustlers are trying to monetize themselves. Suppose you were an early side hustler in the "van lifestyle" genre of online videos. For a while, viewers interested in watching someone ride out a winter storm in a van, or vicariously exploring Yellowstone, Yosemite, and other national parks while living out of a van, or learning how to most efficiently pack as much stuff as possible into a van would very likely watch your videos. And all along the way, you'd make money from ads that were placed on your videos or affiliate marketing links that you would use to try to get people to buy the products you use.

Before long, though, dozens or even hundreds of other people started doing their own van lifestyle videos. Now, someone who is checking out the van lifestyle has a ton of YouTube channels and TikTok videos to choose from. Your advertising revenue? Down. Your affiliate marketing revenue? Also down. So yeah, competition can impact your side hustle, causing you to go back into planning mode to figure out what to do next, such as:

>> Switching to focus on a very narrow niche that none of your newcomer competitors is addressing, such as "eating vegan while living the van lifestyle" or "exploring with my dogs while living the van lifestyle"

>> Ditching the whole "van lifestyle" business and finding a different focal point for your videos — sort of working backward through what Chapter 2 covers where you know you're going to do lifestyle-oriented videos, but now you need to figure out what those videos will be about

>> Sticking with the whole "van lifestyle" video side hustle because you enjoy it, but just accepting that you'll make less money, at least from your videos

So switching, ditching, or sticking — your choice.

The Biggies: Time, Money, and Fun

Take a step back from and above the four components of your side hustle value chain where you'll find signals indicating that you need to adjust your strategy. Ask yourself a couple of questions about time and money.

Time is — or isn't — on your side

Your side hustle is up and running. Okay, great. But are you getting enough sleep, or are you dead-tired almost every day? When's the last time you went to a theater to see a movie? Do you still have time to work out, or go hiking, or just go for a long walk? Are you tempted to violate the side-hustle equivalent of the separation of church and state — that is, sneak in side-hustle work while you're at your day job (a big no-no; see Chapter 11).

REMEMBER

You absolutely need to be alert for signals coming from your suppliers, your customers, environmental influences, and the competitive landscape. But one of the most powerful signals that could tip you off that you need to adjust your schedule is when your side hustle is negatively impacting many other aspects of your life, possibly including your day job.

Checking the cash register

So, how's the side hustle business? Making any money?

Maybe money isn't the primary motivator for your side hustle. Some people jump into a side hustle as a head start on a career change, with money only a secondary factor and maybe not even an important factor (see Chapter 1).

If, however, you're like most other side hustlers, you're trying to make some money. If you're doing ridesharing or delivery services or other gig-economy jobs for a side hustle, you still have some costs to cover such as extra fuel or washing and detailing your car if you're doing ridesharing. Also, the more you use your car for business, the closer you get to that point where some expensive vehicle repair rears its ugly head. For the most part, though, every hour you spend on your side hustle will be profitable, even if you're not getting rich.

If, however, you're running an online boutique or a bakery or renting out vacation real estate through Airbnb or Vrbo, then you're definitely trying to make money, or at least not *lose* money. Maybe your Airbnb rental income will, by design, barely cover the mortgage and other expenses on the property, but you're counting on that rental house increasing in value over the next five or ten years, so you'll make your money when you sell the place.

If, however, you set up an online business to sell handmade leather goods (wallets, briefcases, purses) that you buy from wholesalers, and not only are you not selling many but you've laid out more than $15,000 for inventory that's sitting in your spare bedroom, well, that's not a good sign, business-wise. But it *is* a sign that you need to make some big-time adjustments to your side-hustle strategy.

A great time was had by all

"It's not supposed to be fun — that's why they call it work."

Yeah, the long-time mantra of those who will tell you that you go to work each day, you don't go to "fun" each day.

Don't believe it, at least when it comes to your side hustle. True, some side hustles may be more business than fun. But unlike your day job, where you may need to suck it up and do a job you don't really like because you have to make a living, nobody is forcing you to do a side hustle — at least for the most part.

REMEMBER

Maybe you're doing ridesharing or delivery services or some other gig-economy job because you need the money. Maybe your full-time hours were cut or you lost your job. Maybe your spouse lost their job, and you're both doing side gigs to make up the lost income. In these situations, you can suspend the "should be having fun" guideline for side hustles.

But if you don't *have* to do a side hustle out of financial necessity, then the "fun factor" really needs to be there, even if you're not making a whole lot of money or your side hustle is really eating into your free time.

Roll with the Changes

The signals are all flashing red: Side-hustle change is in the air. Now what?

You could:

>> Shift your current side hustle into a different but related one.

>> Drop some aspect of your overall side-hustle portfolio while leaving the rest intact.

>> Add a new side hustle that complements what you already have going.

Musical chairs

As time flies, you may come to the point where you need to make some adjustments to your overall business model, even if you're sticking with your same overall theme. Go back to your original side-hustle flowchart where you started with an overall theme and then narrowed down your options into a specific business idea (see Chapter 2). Basically, you're going to work your way back *up* that step-by-step decision-making process and hopefully find a side-hustle cousin to your current business model.

For example, Sandy's side hustle is buying bargain-priced baseball and sports cards on eBay and other websites, at estate and garage sales, and wherever he can find stashes of those long-hidden gems. Then he resells the cards at a profit — or at least that was his plan.

At the beginning of the COVID-19 pandemic, when Sandy jumped into this particular side hustle, his strategy worked pretty well. But soon, sports card prices began skyrocketing, meaning that Sandy got squeezed on a couple of different fronts. First, people became aware that their own cards that they hadn't looked at in years were worth a whole lot of money, and they wanted a lot more to sell those pieces of cardboard than they would have only a few months earlier. Also, a whole lot of people had the same idea that Sandy did, which meant that he now faced significantly more competition when it came to trying to find cards at a reasonable price.

Looking back at Sandy's side-hustle value chain, he was picking up signals of changes in both his suppliers and his competitors.

What to do, what to do. . ..

Sandy has no intention of resigning from the sports card side hustle game. But maybe, just maybe, this buying-and-flipping strategy has played itself out. Sandy decides to start recording a podcast where each week he reviews different aspects of the sports collectible marketplace, looks at some particular past year's set of cards, talks about trends in the hobby, and other topics along those lines.

During the sports card resurgence that began with the COVID-19 pandemic (people staying home, having more spare time, looking for nostalgia-related items as sort of mental comfort food, and so on), a lot of returning collectors just like Sandy did exactly what Sandy is thinking about doing: started recording and publishing podcasts. Some of those podcasts have sponsors, so the side hustler is presumably making a little bit of money along the way; others are just doing their podcasts mostly for fun. So, Sandy isn't too far off base with his thinking.

Addition by subtraction

You know that saying about your eyes being bigger than your stomach when it comes to piling food onto your plate? Sometimes your appetite is bigger than your ability to successfully handle everything that you put on your plate. You have all these great ideas, but you only have so much time and energy.

As much as it pains you, sometimes the best adjustment to make to your side-hustle strategy — at least for now — is to remove some of those different ideas from your overall portfolio so you can do better with those you leave untouched.

Mark started a side hustle to record and post videos about small-business accounting topics on his YouTube channel and then monetize those videos through ads. Then he decided to create a series of paid courses about small-business accounting and other financial topics that he would publish on Udemy. He decided to add a twice-weekly blog to his portfolio.

Before he knew it, Mark was getting about four hours of sleep a night because of all the time he needed to create and publish all this content. More important, he wasn't making all that much money from his paid courses. Web analytics indicated that his blog wasn't getting a whole lot of traffic, and even those readers typically went next to check out news or sports scores, not to check out Mark's videos or to his paid courses.

Mark decided to streamline his side-hustle portfolio. The paid courses? Leave the ones he had already created, but hold off on creating any more, at least for now. The blog? Once every two weeks would be fine, given that it really wasn't doing anything for him; maybe even switch to once a month, and maybe next year drop the blog.

Sometimes the best change in your side hustle strategy is to take a few things off the table so you can avoid being spread too thin and instead focus on the best one or two parts of your portfolio.

Addition by addition

You might find yourself headed in the reverse direction to "addition by subtraction" — *adding* new things to your side-hustle portfolio in the quest for synergy.

Are you doing videos about an accounting or other business topic? Add more videos. Or start writing a blog. Or add some paid courses on Skillshare or Udemy or some other learning platform.

Selling jewelry? Add clothing to your online boutique. Selling clothing? Add jewelry.

Suppose that Mark's original YouTube channel didn't get a whole lot of traffic at the beginning. Mark wonders if the trick is to try to drive more traffic there by making himself more visible on social media. He starts doing frequent posts and articles on LinkedIn.

Soon, the LinkedIn activity drives a fair amount of traffic to Mark's YouTube channel, and some of the feedback he receives through comments on his videos and even direct messages is along the lines of "Do you have any courses available? This stuff is great!" That's when Mark checks out Udemy or Skillshare or Teachable to see what might be the best platform to publish a couple of paid courses.

REMEMBER

In this alternative universe's Mark (versus the one where he's taking components of his side hustle portfolio off the table; see the preceding section), Mark's strategy change comes in the form of *adding* new types of content in the quest for synergy among those different components.

Turn Off the Lights, the Party's Over

You actually have one more option for your side-hustle strategy change: Quit!

REMEMBER

If you decide to pull the plug on your side hustle, make sure that you neatly close up shop instead of leaving behind a mess. If you're doing gig-economy jobs such as ridesharing or delivery services, or even weekend bartending or yardwork, you probably have minimal closing-up stuff to take care of. If, however, you're running a business, you may need to:

>> Get rid of unsold inventory.

>> Ease yourself out of relationships with other people and businesses.

>> Close out any of your business financials.

Cleaning out your closet

REMEMBER

If you ultimately decide to call it a day with your side hustle, you can still try to recover some of your investment money by selling off your business assets, including any unsold product inventory. True, part of the reason you may be leaving the side hustle behind is that you couldn't sell enough of the products to keep your business going. But you can do the side-hustle equivalent of a "going out of business" closeout sale to try to bring in at least a little more money on your way out the door.

For example, nothing Sylvia has tried has been able to get her business working. More important, she has no free time, is losing money, and isn't having any fun. She's stuck with a ton of unsold inventory that's cluttering up several rooms in her house. She's had it with the whole side-hustle game — she wants out. She can certainly shut down her website and storefront and stop doing social media marketing. But what about all that unsold inventory?

She can take it to a local charity or thrift store, drop it off, and wash her hands of all those unsold items. Hopefully, the thrift store can sell the goods or a charity could just give away clothing or other items to needy people.

REMEMBER

Sylvia could also sell off some or even all of her inventory through a site such as Poshmark, which carry second-hand items at relatively lower prices than full retail. Sylvia almost certainly won't make a profit from the inventory she's dumping, but she may be able to recoup some of her costs.

Saying your goodbyes

If you have contractors you use on a regular basis for your business, make sure you don't just drop off the face of the earth. Contact each one and say that you're no longer going to be doing your side hustle.

If you have employees, give them plenty of notice that they'll no longer have jobs.

Tell your suppliers that you're shutting your business. If you do lawn and yard services or clean pools, tell your customers that you'll no longer be available.

If you have a few loyal customers for your online business, give them a heads-up that you're shutting down your website.

REMEMBER

Don't leave people hanging — you wouldn't want them to do that to you!

Tidying up the financial side

Close your business bank accounts. Make sure that you file any final tax returns and designate those returns as "final." Shut down your S corporation or LLC (see Chapter 7) or even a sole proprietorship that will no longer actively be in business.

Get help from an accountant or attorney if necessary to make sure that you're officially closed for business with the tax authorities so you don't get any rude surprises down the road in the form of taxes or fees for a business you no longer own.

TIP

Sometimes you're better off leaving your business open for a year or two but in a "dormant" state because of any lingering tax or legal considerations. Consult an accountant or attorney to help determine the best timing for when to close bank accounts and file final tax returns and legal forms.

Chapter **15**

Deciding What to Do If Your Side Hustle Gets Really Successful

Your side hustle may remain exactly that — a side gig — for as long as you're creating online content, or making and selling products, or doing a little bit of weekend bartending or landscaping. Or your side hustle could be headed for the big time.

Your day job? Hey, that's all in the past. You've moved on to bigger and better things — your side hustle is now your full-time hustle!

Is Your Side Hustle Ready For the Big Time?

Chances are, you're thinking about putting all your eggs into your side-hustle basket for one or more of the following reasons:

>> You want to spend even more time on your side hustle than you already are.

>> You've already made enough money from your side hustle; and along with your savings, you don't really need to stay at your full-time job anymore.

>> You hate your full-time job, and you're looking for an escape hatch.

More time!

Sometimes, you just *know* that if you could only spend more time with your side hustle, you could turn it into a fantastically successful business. Sure, you like having your cake and eating it, too — the security of your full-time salary existing side-by-side with the rewards of your side hustle.

Still, you can't help but wonder: If you could put even more time into your side gig, where could you take it? Unless someone figures out a way to put more than 24 hours in a day, or if you could get by on only 30 minutes of sleep each night, the only way to find that extra time is to take the plunge and go full-time with your side hustle.

Breanna's online boutique side hustle is going great! She always knew she had a good eye when it came to fashion, but apparently, she's a natural! Almost every single clothing item and piece of jewelry that she decides to buy from one of her suppliers and list on her Shopify site sells out. She's making good money from her side hustle, too.

In fact, the only frustration Breanna has these days when it comes to her side hustle is that she wishes she had more time to spend on it. If she had more time, she could

>> Find even more products from even more suppliers.

>> Try out some new ideas, such as putting together outfit ensembles or maybe even experiment with a subscription model similar to what Stitch Fix does.

>> Try to expand from just selling online to some in-person selling through consignment stores or a pop-up booth during the holidays.

"If only I had more time," Breanna thinks to herself a couple times a day. "I could really make something out of this boutique. . . ."

You have your money bases covered

What happens if your side-hustle income no longer complements your day-job salary, but actually is more — maybe significantly more! — than what you make from your full-time job? Should you continue doing your day job?

Maybe — or maybe not.

If you get to the point where your day-job salary becomes your side money and you're making the big bucks from your side hustle, you might be tempted to say goodbye to your full-time job and go full-time with your side hustle.

When Miguel started creating and posting bartending-related videos on his YouTube channel, he had a hunch he could make some money from the advertising and the affiliate marketing links. But he never dreamed that he would actually be making at least twice as much money every month from his side hustle than he was from his full-time job as an accountant!

For the past two or three months, as the clock ticks past midnight on the nights that Miguel is editing his videos and he realizes that he still has a couple hours of work ahead of him, Miguel can't help but ask himself the same question: "Why am I still doing my day job?"

Miguel is pretty happy making a lot of money from both his full-time job and his side hustle. He lives fairly modestly, even in somewhat expensive Boston. His apartment is a bit pricey, but he doesn't need to own a car because he mostly uses mass transit to commute to and from work and to go out on weekends. If he needs a car to drive out of the city, he usually rents a car from Zipcar for a couple of hours or maybe longer for a weekend trip. But he's been investing a lot of his "extra" money each month, and his stocks and crypto investments have done great for the past couple of years.

Truthfully, Miguel could leave his full-time job tomorrow and easily get by on what he's making from his YouTube channel and his bartending videos. Maybe he would make even more videos or try to come up with another related side hustle with the 40-plus hours he would have. More likely, though, he would record, edit, and post his videos during what used to be his full-time job hours or maybe even in the early evenings. But he could say goodbye to two or three nights a week where he would only get a couple hours of sleep, plus have more weekend time available to do fun things.

He's already making enough money from his side hustle, so why not let his bartending videos be his one and only hustle?

Get me out of here!

Have you ever had a job that you once enjoyed, but because of changes in the company's management you now have the worst job in the world? That morning alarm every workday taunts you and might as well be saying "Get out of bed, you fool! You thought yesterday was a horrible day at work? You haven't seen anything yet!"

Sure, you can start circulating your résumé and interviewing for a new job. But if you have a side hustle going, you may have another escape hatch out of that job from hell by turning your side hustle into your full-time business. Maybe you can expand what you're already doing, or perhaps you can plop a few complementary side-hustle activities alongside your current gig. Either way, now you can see the light at the end of the horrible-job tunnel.

For more than a year, Jack taught information technology (IT) classes at the local community college alongside his day job as a software developer in Scottsdale, Arizona. Then he switched to teaching at one of the big universities in the Phoenix area, where he's been an adjunct faculty member for the past nine months. Jack makes decent money from his teaching gigs, but more important, he found that he really enjoys teaching college-level classes.

Four months ago, the Scottsdale app development company where Jack works was bought out by a private equity firm, which installed its own management team. As Jack takes stock one blazing hot July morning, with the Phoenix-area temperatures way above 100 degrees for the 20th straight day, he can't help but admit to himself: "I absolutely hate my job!" The new management team is the worst one Jack has ever worked for during his 20 years in the tech field. Jack is hardly alone among the app company's developers, and he's well aware that more than half of the people he works with are circulating their résumés and looking to jump ship as soon as they find new jobs.

Jack has his résumé out with a couple of headhunters, but he's also thinking about a different idea. The academic department through which Jack is an adjunct faculty member still has a lot of teaching slots open for the coming fall semester's classes. Jack knows that the university's policies allow for an outside faculty member to teach up to six classes in an academic year on a contract basis.

Even though Jack could try to join the university as a full-time, non-PhD faculty member, by teaching on a contract basis he isn't subject to university rules that would restrict him from teaching elsewhere or that would limit the number of hours he could spend on outside activities such as consulting.

Jack sends a few emails and then braves the stifling midsummer Arizona heat to go to a few meetings. By the end of July, he has a plan in place. He signs on to teach the maximum six classes at the university, and he also arranges to teach four more classes — two each semester — at the community college where he previously taught. Then he tentatively has four more classes lined up for next summer: two at the university, and two at the community college.

Jack's teaching schedule looks overloaded when he thinks about teaching 14 classes starting in late August and going until the following August. But half of those classes are online, with prerecorded videos and no set time that he needs to be in front of students, either in person or via Zoom.

Jack decides he can turn his teaching side hustle into a full-time gig and bail from his current job that's getting worse by the day. The total of all of his contract teaching payments will still be a little short of his full-time salary, but Jack is confident that he can make up the difference with a little bit of consulting work here and there. And he also has some ideas for software-related courses that he can record, edit, polish, and then publish on Skillshare, Teachable, or Udemy to also bring in some money.

Most important to Jack: He can run far, far away from a full-time job that he hates through the side hustle that he began a couple of years ago and taking it to the next level.

Your Side-Hustle Business Plan, Take 2

TIP

When you're evaluating how to turn your side hustle into your full-time hustle, you use the same process that you used for your initial side-hustle planning (see Chapter 4):

>> Brainstorming

>> Looking at your side-hustle value chain

>> Contemplating best-case and worst-case outcomes

>> Checking out your timeline

>> Digging into the finances

Letting your brain storm again

You have the itch to go full-time with your side hustle, but right now you're at the "impulse" stage. You have a basic idea, but have you really thought through all the ins and outs?

REMEMBER

Just as when you planned for your side hustle in the first place, begin with some freewheeling brainstorming rather than a formal, highly structured business-planning methodology. Build your brainstorming around the five Ws and their one H cousin:

>> What will your side hustle turn into if you go full-time?

>> Who else now needs to be involved?

>> Where will you operate?

>> When will you make the transition to going full-time, along with key milestones along the way?

>> How will you make the transition from side hustle to full-time hustle?

>> Why are you contemplating going full-time?

What's new?

REMEMBER

Just as when you did your original side-hustle planning, you already have a head start on the "what" portion of your brainstorming.

For example, Breanna envisions her boutique carrying more products that she'll get from more suppliers. She clearly sees new channels to reach customers: putting her clothes and accessories into consignment stores and doing holiday pop-up booths. In Breanna's case, going full-time means "more" on a bunch of different aspects of her boutique business.

Miguel might do more videos than he's doing right now, or he may not. Miguel's version of going full-time is different from Breanna's in one important aspect: Breanna will take the hours that she "saves" from leaving her current full-time job and fill most or all of that time with boutique-related activities. Miguel plans to dramatically scale back his total number of work hours each week to a number that leaves him with more free time. So, in Miguel's case, his side hustle–turned–full time hustle won't change all that much, at least for now. What *will* change is the rest of Miguel's life, giving him a lot more free time.

Jack's vastly expanded teaching gigs will sort of be like Breanna's plans, by "repurposing" the hours he no longer has to spend at his day job into expanding his side hustle into full-time contract teaching. But Jack will add a brand-new side hustle to his portfolio with some consulting and contract software development and a couple of online courses alongside his teaching.

TIP

Going full-time with your side hustle typically follows one of three patterns:

>> Dramatically expanding what you're already doing (Breanna)

>> Pretty much doing exactly what you're already doing at more or less the same level of activity, but taking your full-time job off of the table to give you more free time (Miguel)

>> Expanding what you're already doing, but adding a new side hustle to hopefully make up some of the money you're leaving behind by quitting your full-time job (Jack)

Who will be involved?

With more time available for your side hustle, you can spend all those hours doing much more with your side hustle, right?

At least that's how the math looks at first glance. Realistically, going full-time with your side hustle may also be the catalyst to bring other people onboard, such as:

>> A partner

>> Employees or subcontractors

>> Outside advisers

REMEMBER

You'll find all sorts of guidance in Chapter 13 to help you decide if you should bring other people into your side hustle, and if so, what to do and what not to do. Very often, the trigger point that has you reaching out to other people is making the jump from side gig to full-time gig.

Spreading your side-hustle wings

As you transition your side hustle into your full-time hustle, you'll typically find yourself headed into greatly expanded — or even brand-new — areas of your business. These changes could mean that your side-hustle "footprint" grows along with your business. You don't want to expand just for the sake of expanding, but quite possibly you won't be able to go full-time without venturing into new physical locations.

As an example, if Breanna's full-time aspirations become a reality, she'll be carrying two or even three times as much inventory as she currently has stashed in her spare bedroom. She'll be packing and shipping two or three times more orders than she currently does. Maybe, just maybe, shifting from a side-hustle boutique to a full-time one means that Breanna needs to look for an outside location that can serve as a combination warehouse and shipping center.

Jack's side-hustle shift may take him in the opposite direction of Breanna. All of Jack's teaching for the past couple of years, at the community college and the university, has been on the schools' respective campuses. He has always worked onsite at the app company's office for his full-time job. Now, though, maybe Jack needs to convert a spare bedroom into a home office to support both his teaching and the consulting and contract software work that he plans to begin as a new side hustle.

REMEMBER

Going full-time with your side hustle may not mean any changes at all to the "where" factor for your business. If you're currently doing "gig economy" delivery services, for example, and you add ridesharing and even more delivery services after quitting your full-time job, you're still jumping in your car and doing a heck of a lot of driving. Or in Miguel's case, he'll still be recording and editing his bartending-related videos at home — it's not like he'll now need to rent out a professional recording studio.

Whatever your particular going-full-time aspirations may be for your side hustle, give some thought to what might — or might not — change in where you do your work as a result of that shift.

Your side-hustle calendar: Spring ahead

WARNING

Making the leap from side hustle to full-time gig never happens in a vacuum. You need to pay careful attention to key milestones, dependencies, and considerations from your full-time job — *before* you quit! — as well as from your life in general.

Take a look at:

>> Key money-related milestones at your full-time job

>> Your spouse's or partner's job and career timeline

>> Upcoming personal and family events and situations, both definite and possible

YOUR JOB AND CAREER MILESTONES

Maybe you can't wait to hit the ejection seat and bail out of your full-time job to get going full-time on your side hustle. You have all your ducks in a row, and you could quit your job tomorrow.

Should you?

Suppose you're six months away from being fully *vested* (basically, qualified) to receive your company's matching contribution to your retirement account, such as a 401(k) plan. The rules at your company are that they'll fully match the amount of money that you contribute, but you aren't fully vested until you've been working there for five years. If you leave before that five-year point, you'll get your own contributions and whatever profits you've earned from those investments, but you'll be out of luck for the company's contributions that they've been setting aside. Sorry!

Or suppose that your employer is one of those that still has an old-fashioned pension plan. Or maybe you work for a governmental agency, where you receive a pension after 20 or 30 years on the job. If you quit before you're pension-eligible (or if you're fired), you aren't eligible for any pension payments.

REMEMBER

Pay careful attention to milestones such as retirement fund vesting and pension eligibility as you're contemplating leaving your full-time job. Maybe you have all your going-full-time ducks in a row — but why throw away tens or even hundreds of thousands of dollars by leaving several months or even several years too early?

You can always come up with a plan B to help realize your side-hustle aspirations even while you stick it out at your full-time job a little while longer. Hire some help or bring on a partner. Or maybe your aspirations for going full-time have to wait a little bit longer.

YOUR SPOUSE'S OR PARTNER'S CAREER MILESTONES

If your spouse or partner is up for a big promotion next year that would bring a big raise, that extra money could help you say goodbye to your own full-time job as you take your side hustle to the next level. Maybe you should hold off on quitting your job for a little while longer, just until your spouse or partner gets that promotion and raise.

PERSONAL AND FAMILY SITUATIONS

Kids headed off to college next year? Or kids in college for another year or two, and then you're no longer paying big tuition bills? Do you have an aging parent who needs to go into an assisted-living facility for which you'll be paying part of the bill?

REMEMBER

Before you quit your current job to go full-time with your side hustle, make sure you take a look ahead to what your money picture may look like over the next few years, not just how your finances are today.

Shuffling your side-hustle deck

So, what changes will you need to make in how your side hustle will operate after you've gone full-time?

>> Will other people be packing and shipping orders, rather than you?

>> Will you have to rent time at a recording studio to record your videos?

>> Will you need to upgrade your website software in anticipation of significantly higher traffic and more orders?

TIP

Many of the "how" questions about a possible new, full-time incarnation of your side hustle will be answered along with the other parts of your brainstorming. But you should take a little bit of time to double-check your thinking, and make sure that you didn't forget anything else as you've been letting your mind roam free, dreaming about glory days to come.

One more time: Why?

REMEMBER

You may be thinking about going full-time because you're confident that you can turn today's side hustle into a really, really successful business. Or maybe you're so totally overloaded that something's gotta give, and it's going to be your full-time job. Or perhaps you despise your full-time job with white-hot hatred, and you're looking to your side hustle as a "port in the storm" to be able to quit.

Maybe you're fully aware of your motivations as you began this journey into contemplating a full-time future for your side hustle. Or maybe the "why factor" was only swirling around in the back of your mind, and you didn't quite fully grasp onto what's been driving you down this path of going full-time.

WARNING

If your motivations were hiding under the surface, dig them out and go face-to-face with your reasoning. Make sure you're crystal clear about what you're looking for from a full-time future for your side hustle. Otherwise, you run the risk of getting too far down the road without really knowing where you're going, which could lead to some big problems as you take those final steps to going full-time.

Updating your side-hustle value chain

If the business-school side of side-hustle planning wasn't a whole lot of fun for you the first time around, I apologize in advance. But you do need to go back to the drawing board and take a look at your side-hustle value chain (see Figure 15-1) and turn the high-level thinking from your brainstorming into the fleshed-out details for your:

>> Customers

>> Suppliers

>> Environmental influences

>> Competition

>> Internal processes

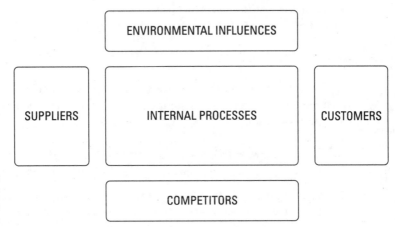

FIGURE 15-1:
Revisiting your
side-hustle value
chain.

Take a look back at Chapter 4 and the details about each component of your side hustle value chain, because you'll be making another pass through each of these segments related to your side hustle.

TIP

Depressed at the thought of heading back into business-school stuff? Don't be! For one thing, you already went through this exercise when you were planning your side hustle. If you'd done a poor job at mapping out your side hustle's value chain, you most likely wouldn't be at this stage, looking at taking your side hustle to the big time! And for another thing, that first time around, you already did a great deal of the work that you'll need to do. This time, you're taking what you already have and looking at the *delta* — what needs to change to realize the vision about which you just finished brainstorming.

High hopes versus dashed dreams

Time for a touch of euphoria, followed by a stone-cold look at a deflated, depressing future.

When you were planning your side hustle the first time around, you let your hopes soar and imagined the brightest possible outcome for what you were about to undertake. So, once again, ask yourself one simple question: After you cut the strings to your full-time job and dive head-first into turning your side hustle into a full-time venture, what do you see as the best possible outcome?

Breanna has a crystal clear vision of her utopian future. Her boutique expands from only being online and run out of her house, to an expanded online presence accompanied by occasional in-person selling through consignment stores and seasonal pop-up locations, to eventually having multiple retail stores in several states, accompanied by one of the best retail websites that features all sorts of cool virtual-reality shopping. Oh, yeah — Breanna's company will be widely regarded as one of the top fashion and accessory retailers across the United States, and maybe even across the world!

Ah, to dream!

WARNING

Breanna also needs to steady her nerves and bravely come face-to-face with the worst possible outcome from jumping into the boutique world on a full-time basis. Are you ready?

> » She tries to expand too quickly, choosing the wrong suppliers and maybe also the wrong products, and sales go nowhere. Then they begin to decline.

> » Breanna's business starts losing money, and she no longer has her full-time job to help cover her business expenses as she did when she was first getting started.

> » Eventually, she gives up and — after losing a lot of money — needs to find a new full-time job.

Which outcome is more likely for Breanna? Honestly, she has no way of knowing with absolute certainty at this point. Her real-world future will probably wind up somewhere in between turning her business into a world-renowned retailer and losing everything. But with a clear eye as to the best and worst possible outcomes, Breanna can do her best to move forward with the right mix of optimism and caution as she begins to pivot her business from side hustle to full-time.

What about *your* dreams and aspirations? You want to be optimistic, but jumping from side hustle to full-time job doesn't come with guaranteed success. Brace yourself and stare into the abyss that is filled with broken side-hustle dreams, and be realistic about *your* worst-case outcome. If you keep one eye on the dark side, you'll be on alert if your full-time adventures even begin to touch on your personal worst-case scenario.

Looking at Key Financial Considerations

WARNING

Unless you're already independently wealthy and you're just looking for some sort of side hustle to do full-time to keep yourself busy, you need to look at how your finances will likely change as a result of going full-time with your side hustle.

If you already do a good job at personal and family budgeting, you have a head start when it's time to start examining the financial considerations of leaving your day job and taking your side hustle into full-time land. If you're sort of allergic to budgeting, I have bad news for you: You'll have to sharpen that pencil and fire up that spreadsheet, because you need to dig into the financial realities of saying goodbye to your day job.

Miguel's bartending-related videos are doing so well that he's ready to say goodbye to being a corporate accountant. Right now, he's in pretty good financial shape, banking about $11,000 a month after covering all his personal and business expenses.

But Miguel's financial success is coming at a big price, in the form of long, long hours between his full-time job and his side hustle. He's gone through all the planning steps to go full-time, and so far all looks good. Now he needs to run the numbers, which are shown in Figure 15-2.

The first big difference you see in Figure 15-2 between the now-versus-future sides of Miguel's finances is a pretty big drop in his monthly income. No full-time job? No full-time salary. Miguel is playing it safe, so he builds the first version of his financial model presuming that he won't make any more revenue from his side hustle when it's his full-time gig than he does now. Realistically, he can probably devote more time to increase his revenue, but because Miguel's major motivation to wave goodbye to his day job is to have more time, he wants to see how his finances look if he keeps his side-hustle activity exactly the same even after he quits his job.

For the most part, Miguel's expenses will remain the same. He'll no longer be contributing to his company's mandatory retirement plan through payroll deductions, so that will be less money on the personal expense side. However, he'll no longer have company-provided health insurance where his employer pays most of his premium, so he needs to *add* an expense for health insurance.

CURRENT			GOING FULL-TIME		
Monthly Income			**Monthly Income**		
Salary from full-time job		$7,500	Salary from full-time job		$0
Revenue from YouTube channel		$20,000	Revenue from YouTube channel		$20,000
Total monthly income		**$27,500**	**Total monthly income**		**$20,000**
Monthly Expenses - Personal			**Monthly Expenses - Personal**		
Apartment rent		$2,200	Apartment rent		$2,200
Car payment		$0	Car payment		$0
Utilities		$700	Utilities		$700
Groceries		$600	Groceries		$600
Restaurants		$800	Restaurants		$800
Paycheck deductions (health insurance, retirement, etc.)		$1,875	**HEALTH INSURANCE**		$500
Average monthly other expenses		$1,500	Average monthly other expenses		$1,500
Total monthly personal expenses		**$7,675**	**Total monthly personal expenses**		**$6,300**
Monthly Expenses - Video Business			**Monthly Expenses - Video Business**		
Social media advertising, etc.		$500	Social media advertising, etc.		$500
Website hosting, cloud storage, etc.		$1,000	Website hosting, cloud storage, etc.		$1,000
Other general expenses		$500	Other general expenses		$500
Tax payment reserves		$6,500	Tax payment reserves		$6,500
Total monthly business expenses		**$8,500**	**Total monthly business expenses**		**$8,500**
Total monthly personal and business expenses		**$16,175**	**Total monthly personal and business expenses**		**$14,800**
Average Monthly Net Income		**$11,325**	**Average Monthly Net Income**		**$5,200**

FIGURE 15-2:
Miguel's side hustle: part-time with his day job versus going full-time.

TECHNICAL STUFF

Ideally, Miguel should also open a retirement investment account for self-employed individuals, such as a SEP-IRA, to replace his company's retirement plan. Very often, though, someone starting a brand-new business venture skips doing retirement investing for a year or two until a business really gets going. Why? To have additional funds available to buy inventory, do more social-media advertising, or cover dozens of other business expenses.

WARNING

You don't want to wait too long to start some type of self-employed retirement fund. Every year you don't plop additional money into a retirement fund can cost you in the long run because you'll miss out on that money turning into even more money over the years.

The bottom line: Presuming Miguel keeps his income from his videos at the same level, he'll still be about $5,200 ahead each month in revenue versus expenses. Not bad!

But what happens if, say, Miguel's YouTube channel revenue gets cut in half, to $10,000 a month? Figure 15-3 shows the gloomier — but not necessarily doomsday — financial picture.

Miguel now projects that he'll *lose* about $1,100 a month on average. The silver lining in the numbers shown in Figure 15-3 is that with significantly less revenue, he doesn't need to set aside nearly as much money as he did before for federal and state income taxes and any other taxes he needs to pay.

CURRENT			GOING FULL-TIME	
Monthly Income			**Monthly Income**	
Salary from full-time job	$7,500		Salary from full-time job	$0
Revenue from YouTube channel	$20,000		**Revenue from YouTube channel**	**$10,000**
Total monthly income	**$27,500**		**Total monthly income**	**$10,000**
Monthly Expenses - Personal			**Monthly Expenses - Personal**	
Apartment rent	$2,200		Apartment rent	$2,200
Car payment	$0		Car payment	$0
Utilities	$700		Utilities	$700
Groceries	$600		Groceries	$600
Restaurants	$800		Restaurants	$800
Paycheck deductions (health insurance, retirement, etc.)	$1,875		**HEALTH INSURANCE**	$500
Average monthly other expenses	$1,500		Average monthly other expenses	$1,500
Total monthly personal expenses	**$7,675**		**Total monthly personal expenses**	**$6,300**
Monthly Expenses - Video Business			**Monthly Expenses - Video Business**	
Social media advertising, etc.	$500		Social media advertising, etc.	$500
Website hosting, cloud storage, etc.	$1,000		Website hosting, cloud storage, etc.	$1,000
Other general expenses	$500		Other general expenses	$500
Tax payment reserves	$6,500		**Tax payment reserves**	**$2,800**
Total monthly business expenses	**$8,500**		**Total monthly business expenses**	**$4,800**
Total monthly personal and business expenses	$16,175		Total monthly personal and business expenses	$11,100
Average Monthly Net Income	**$11,325**		**Average Monthly Net Income**	**–$1,100**

FIGURE 15-3: Miguel's full-time side hustle with only half the revenue.

In Miguel's case, he could absorb an $1,100 loss each month for a while because he's been saving and investing a ton of money each month for a while. Even better, his investments have done great. So, he can definitely cover the shortfall, if his revenue happens to fall off.

REMEMBER

Run the numbers for *multiple* scenarios if you're thinking about ditching your full-time job. Look at a best-case but still realistic scenario with an increase in your side-hustle income as a result of the additional time you'll have. But also look at gloomier scenarios where your income from your side hustle drops off. What then?

Leaving No Going-Full-Time Stone Unturned

Do you have health insurance through your full-time employer? Is the health insurance for you only if you're single? Or for your spouse and maybe also your children?

What about saving for retirement? Does your company offer a 401(k) plan or equivalent retirement fund where they match your contributions?

Do you get a quarterly or annual bonus above and beyond your base salary? Is it a relatively small token amount? Or do you rely on your bonus to cover the family vacation every year?

WARNING

Don't overlook the so-called "fringe benefits" or other components of your compensation at your full-time job when you're digging into the pros and cons of leaving to take your side hustle full-time. Paying for health insurance can be pricey, especially if you're covering your entire family.

Take the time to walk through all the benefits your company offers, and decide how (or if) you'll cover them yourself after you go full-time.

Also, do your best to leave your job on good terms, even if you really do hate it and can't wait to quit. Ever since the Great Resignation began during the COVID-19 pandemic, I've talked with a lot of people who quit their jobs to follow a dream and start a few side hustles in place of their full-time jobs. Many of them have said that when they handed in their resignations, their employers worked out a deal with them to continue working part-time on a contract basis, either for a short while or for a longer period of time. Basically, for each of these people, a former full-time job turned into a side hustle as part of an overall portfolio of work. If you can work out a deal like that, it might make the transition into going full-time with your side hustle a smoother one.

The Part of Tens

IN THIS PART . . .

Make money from side hustles without a lot of ongoing work.

Get help for your side hustle.

Adjust your side-hustle plans.

Chapter **16**

Ten Tips on Earning Passive Income from Your Side Hustle

Passive-income side hustles sound like a dream come true — at least on paper. After all, doesn't the term *passive income* mean that you basically sit around and collect money for doing nothing (or almost nothing)?

WARNING

Not so fast! Passive-income side hustles are probably the most misunderstood aspect of the whole side-hustle game. The following ten tips are crucial to helping you work passive-income side hustles into your own portfolio while at the same time avoiding the traps that are waiting to grab you.

Remember That "Passive" Does Not Mean "No Work Required"

The biggest misconception about passive-income side hustles is that you collect money for doing little or no work, ever. So basically, as the classic rock band Dire Straits would put it: "Money for nothing."

REMEMBER

A passive-income side hustle is one where your effort and work do *not* move in lockstep with your earnings from that particular side hustle. (See Chapter 3 for a deeper discussion of how passive-income side hustles differ from labor-based side hustles.)

Presume that you create a single online course that you upload to a learning platform such as Skillshare, Teachable, or Udemy. Your course gets very popular, very quickly — and before you know it, you're pulling in around $5,000 every month! Month after month, you really are just sitting back and collecting the income for little or no additional effort.

Notice, though, how I specifically noted "for little or no *additional* effort." What about all the hours you put into creating that course in the first place? Creating slides and scripts, doing screenshots, recording and editing your videos — all together, you may have spent 200 or 300 hours, or even more, getting to that point where you *then* could sit back and just count the incoming money, month after month.

Watch Out for Get-Rich-Quick Schemes

WARNING

Passive-income side hustles are a magnet for get-rich-quick schemes and outright scams.

The sneaky folks who try to separate you from your money are well aware of the seductive appeal of "lots of money in exchange for little or no effort." The same traps that you need to sidestep when it comes to your personal finances and investments are waiting for you in the world of side hustles. If you do your homework and evaluate side-hustle opportunities with a clear head and a critical eye, you can avoid making some really bad mistakes that you'll almost certainly regret when some too-good-to-be-true side-hustle idea turns out to be exactly that: too good to be true.

Recognize That Some Side Hustles Are Mislabeled as Passive Income

If you tap away at your computer or phone keyboard, you'll find some so-called passive-income side hustles that aren't really "passive" at all. For example, you may come across opportunities where you can earn money by watching videos or completing surveys or taking photos — with every one of those side hustles pitched as a way for you to earn passive income.

In reality, every one of these so-called passive side hustles actually requires you to actively *do something* in lockstep for whatever sums you will earn. The distinction — and the confusion, whether deliberate or not — with these types of side hustles is that you don't need to have any particular skills or training for whatever it is that you do in exchange for whatever money you earn. Unlike, say, a YouTube channel that you create to teach photography techniques or provide home landscaping ideas, you don't need to have any particular skills or background to watch videos or answer surveys. But you'll still need to continually *do the work* in order to earn money from one of these side hustles.

REMEMBER

Think of these types of side hustles as being more in the category of "anyone can do it . . . even you!" rather than a truly passive side hustle.

Know the Difference between Investment Ideas and Passive-Income Side Hustles

Don't be surprised to see investment ideas pitched as side hustles under the premise of:

>> First, make an upfront investment.

>> Then, just sit back — you don't have to do anything.

>> Eventually, sell that investment for more than you put in and — presto! — passive income.

For example, is real estate an investment or a side hustle? The answer: Either, and it all depends on the details and specifics!

TECHNICAL STUFF

If you plop a sizable chunk of money into a real estate mutual fund or a real estate investment trust (REIT), I would argue that you're investing in real estate rather than using real estate as the vehicle for a side hustle.

On the other hand, if you purchase a second home in your city with the intention of renting out that property, and if you're responsible for keeping the plumbing and electrical and landscaping all in tip-top shape, well, to me that sounds more like a side hustle.

Admittedly, though, you'll find a fine line between true investments and side hustles. More important than splitting hairs over definitions and distinctions is knowing that your overall personal portfolio will likely include both investments and side hustles, all coexisting with one another under your keen eye.

Pay Attention to Your Fans

Many passive-income side hustles are built around creating online content that you hope will bring in a steady stream of money, month after month. Sometimes your content will take the form of a paid course that you upload to Skillshare, Teachable, Udemy, or some other learning platform. In other situations, you'll create content for a platform like YouTube that will be available for free, but that you'll try to monetize through ads or affiliate links.

No matter what shape your online content takes, if the money starts rolling in, so too will the "fan mail" in the form of comments posted to your latest content, or emails, or people commenting on social-media posts that you make to publicize your latest drop. Some of the feedback will be general comments like "Great job!" or "Love it!"; in other situations, viewers will ask you questions.

Engage!

You don't need to further comment on every "Loved it!" piece of feedback, but you should "like" those comments to signify to your loyal audience that you are, indeed, paying attention to their feedback. Then, for specific or general questions you get via email or perhaps through a learning platform's direct-messaging capability, make sure to reply promptly and do your best to answer the question posed to you. The worst thing you can do is ignore a viewer — especially someone who might have paid for your course — when someone asks you a question or seeks advice. A passive-income side hustle does *not* mean "no further work or involvement required after I publish or post something, ever!"

You do need to be careful not to allow someone to maneuver you into doing a bunch of free consulting or anything along those lines. Think in terms of "up to three minutes" — if you can answer someone's question or provide the advice they're asking in three minutes or less, then share your thoughts. Anything more than that, be diplomatic and offer a tidbit or two in a response but then write something such as "What you're asking about would take a couple hours to explain, because it's much more advanced material than I covered in this course. Here are a couple of things to think about, and here's where you can look that might have the answers you're looking for."

Weather the Storm of a Failed Side Hustle

Wow, what a colossal waste of time your latest video course turned out to be! You may have hit the jackpot with your course about selling childhood collectibles, and the whole passive-income side-hustle business seemed so easy. So, of course, you created and uploaded a brand-new course — this time, about jumping back into a childhood hobby during your retirement years.

Unfortunately, this course was a bust. After a full year has passed, you've barely earned enough to go out for a nice dinner. Guess what: It happens. Sometimes, you'll spend 200 or 300 hours — or even more — and expect to see your efforts generously rewarded, month after month, with plenty of passive income. But the waterfall of money never comes about.

The very principle of passive income means that you'll invest a fair amount of effort or money (or sometimes both) upfront, in anticipation of a regular flow of money going forward. Not every video course or book or other passive-income side hustle will pay off.

TIP

If you strike out, don't be afraid to try again — but make sure that you do a deep-dive, postmortem analysis of your failed passive-income side hustle to try to figure out why it didn't work as well as you had expected.

Find the Right Flavor of Passive-Income Side Hustle

The word on the street is that real estate can be a great passive-income side hustle, especially in a city or town with a hot housing market. But even if you decide that you're heading down the real estate path for your side hustle, you'll still have a variety of choices from which to choose.

Maybe you buy a single family house in your own neighborhood, or a couple of miles away, or even across town. You intend to spend a hundred hours over the next couple months fixing up the place, and then you're going to rent out the house. Along the way, you — and you alone — will be responsible for all the maintenance. Does the plumbing spring a leak? You'll either fix the leak yourself (if you're handy) or call a plumber. Does the grading in the backyard start sinking to the point where a heavy rain causes a lot of standing water against the house? Congratulations! You're the one who needs to arrange to get the grading fixed and prevent the house's foundation from water damage.

Now you may be thinking: Wait a minute! I really don't want to be responsible for all that maintenance. So, is a real estate–oriented side hustle out of the question?

Not at all! You can join forces with a couple of other people and go in together on a house purchase. Maybe someone else is handy and will take care of all the maintenance (or at least be in charge of calling a plumber or appliance repairperson or landscaper when needed), while you're in charge of collecting the monthly rent from your tenant.

You don't even need to buy a new property to tap into the world of real estate side hustles. During your family's annual winter and summer vacations, you list your house on Airbnb or Vrbo. You won't bring in as much money from your real estate side hustle as you would by purchasing and renting out an entire house, but you also need a much lower upfront financial investment and — usually — significantly less time investment along the way to earn that passive income.

REMEMBER

Regardless of your passive-income side-hustle interests, you'll often find different "flavors" from which to choose. So, do your homework!

Be Prepared for the Financial Ups and Downs of Passive-Income Side Hustles

Your video course catches fire, and for the next six months you earn close to $10,000 in passive income every month. Wow!

But suddenly your course goes cold — ice cold. Your passive income the next month drops to barely $1,000, which is still better than the following month, when you barely early $500. For the next couple months, you stay around that $500 level, and you figure, okay, you had a good run, even though it was a short run.

All of a sudden, your course gets popular again — *very* popular! Your passive income rockets all the way up to $5,000, and then stays at that level for a few more months.

REMEMBER

Passive-income side hustles often gyrate back and forth, up and down, on the income side. Unlike a side hustle where your income goes in lockstep with your ongoing efforts, you've already made your upfront investment of time, and now your successes are largely up to the fates. True, you can try to influence the fates of your passive-income side hustle. Maybe you came out with a new course, and this one becomes so popular that viewers go and check out your earlier course that had gone cold. Or you write a new book that readers enjoy so much they start buying earlier books that you had written, which had all but stopped selling.

Get ready for the ups and downs of passive-income side hustles. Sometimes you're on top of the world, just sitting there and raking in the money — but the money flow can quickly slow or even come close to a full stop. But the good news is that the gyrations work the other way also, and a passive-income side hustle that you've all but given up for dead can come roaring back to life.

Calculate Your Passive-Income Side-Hustle Life Span

You're all aboard the passive-income side-hustle train, and you love the idea of publishing video courses. Sure, each one takes a good bit of time to create, but then you can just sit back and let the money flow into your pockets.

But for how long?

Every passive-income side hustle has a life span associated with it. If you're doing a video course about the latest version of a hot new software package or some other time-sensitive tech topic, your video may remain current and relevant for up to a year — but then it can quickly become obsolete. Maybe you can redo some or all of your course for a new version of some software product, or maybe technology has marched on by, and the tech world has moved on to newer and more powerful technologies.

On the other hand, a video about landscaping designs or photography tricks or the best little-known places to visit in Italy could remain relevant for years!

REMEMBER

Even if you're only creating a single video course or writing a single book as your side hustle in anticipation of passive income, you need to create a mini business plan that reflects your best estimates of the life span of that particular content. You don't have a crystal ball, of course, but you do know whether a particular topic has a relatively short life span — basically, a built-in expiration date — or could conceivably have some pretty long legs and earn money month after month.

Stack Your Passive-Income Side Hustles

TIP

Here's a recipe for passive-income side-hustle success: Produce a few longer-life-span videos or books or whatever you create, intermingled with some shorter-duration ones. And better yet: Have the plans in place to succeed your shorter-duration content with new shorter-duration content when something becomes obsolete and stops earning you money.

Build yourself a "stacking portfolio" of passive-income side hustles — some shorter duration, others longer term — and regularly measure your income versus your overall objectives. Then make adjustments as necessary: Add new content, remove or revise underperforming content, and in general, keep a good eye on how your passive-income side-hustle portfolio is chugging along.

Chapter **17**

Ten Leading Gig Economy Platforms

When I started my first side hustle way back in 1982, I offered computer consulting, software development, and tech training services. Thinking back, the most difficult part of ramping up my side hustle was building relationships with computer stores and other businesses to offer my services.

If only the gig economy had existed all those years ago! I could've marketed myself through one or more of the leading job-and-task-matching platforms. But good news for you and your side hustle: These job-and-task-matching platforms *do* exist today, and you can put yourself out there as quickly as you can sign up and either post your services or find someone looking for the type of services you provide.

Take a look at ten leading platforms, listed here in alphabetic order, that you can use right now. You don't need to limit yourself to just one platform, either — spread your bets across at least a couple!

TIP

As time goes by, keep your eyes peeled for new platforms that may hit the scene and quickly become wildly popular. You want to keep your side hustle where the action is!

By the way, looking for help for your side hustle? You can turn to these same platforms to find someone to help you with website design, social-media marketing, blog writing, Shopify site creation, and much more.

Angi

You might know Angi (www.angi.com) more by the platform's former name: Angie's List. Angi specializes in physical labor services, both skilled and unskilled. (Note that *unskilled* isn't a negative term; instead, it refers to labor services that don't require any particular training. Think "moving heavy furniture" versus "rewiring a house.")

If your side hustle falls into one of the following categories, take a look at joining and posting on Angi:

>> Electrical work

>> General "handyman" services

>> Lawn and yard care

>> Plumbing

>> Remodeling

>> Roofing

Fiverr

For your side hustle, are you doing techie stuff such as website design, social-media advertising, or software development? Then take a look at Fiverr (www.fiverr.com) for listing your services.

How about music and audio services such as doing voice-overs or playing background music for commercials or videos? You can list your side hustle on Fiverr.

Planning on helping other people write business plans or draft contracts or write their résumés? You should consider posting your services on — wait for it — Fiverr.

For pretty much any sort of service-related side hustle, Fiverr should be a strong player for listing your services.

FlexJobs

FlexJobs (www.flexjobs.com) specializes in "high-quality remote and flexible jobs" in a variety of career fields: accounting, project management, social-media marketing, supply chain, and many more. Even though many of the jobs listed on FlexJobs are full-time, career-type jobs (that just happen to be flexible in terms of being able to work remotely or to have a highly flexible schedule), many of the listings are contract-based, both shorter and longer duration.

So, if you want to do some project management for your side hustle, check out listings on FlexJobs. Setting up shop as an accountant? Check out listings on FlexJobs. Specializing in social-media marketing? Check out, yeah, you know where this is going.

Freelancer

In many ways, Freelancer (www.freelancer.com) is similar to Fiverr. You can post your services for graphic design, search engine optimization, blog or ad copywriting, legal contracts, and many other specializations. You're now "out there" for the world at large to find you.

You can also target your services geographically — in India, for example, or only in the United States. Or you can make yourself available to the world at large.

Guru

Guru (www.guru.com) is another site where you can make yourself available for techie work, administrative services, design and graphic arts, accounting or finance, or other specializations.

As with other sites, the major categories are broken down into subcategories where you can more precisely target prospective customers for your side hustle. For example, if you're a writer, you can be a "writer at large" or you can specialize in editing, copywriting, or proofreading; writing articles or blogs; or providing translation services for already-written works in one language that someone wants to translate into another language.

99designs

Let's say you provide graphic design services, and you specialize in creating really slick logos. In addition to listing your logo design services on Fiverr, Freelancer, and other sites, you can also watch for "contests" that businesses post on 99designs (https://99designs.com).

You watch for a business to post that they're looking for a logo, along with some general guidelines and preferences. You fire up your graphic-design software, give it that old side-hustle effort (a cousin to "that old college try"), and submit your best work. If they choose your design, you've got the gig!

99designs does contests for website design and other graphics work, and they also support more traditional listings where you post your side hustle, show off your portfolio, and then businesses come directly to you. But the contest aspect of 99designs is particularly intriguing for side hustlers who like a good challenge and are willing to do some design work with no guarantees that they'll win the contest and the job.

TaskRabbit

If you're side hustling in the realm of physical labor — helping people move, painting, mounting TV sets on walls, hanging pictures, doing yard work, and so on — then hop over to TaskRabbit (www.taskrabbit.com) and post your services.

TIP

You can even offer up local grocery shopping and delivery services just as you would through Instacart.

Toptal

Toptal (www.toptal.com) is similar to Fiverr, Guru, and other sites if you're offering techie, accounting and finance, and similar business services. According to their website, freelance side hustlers use Toptal to land gigs not only at small companies but also at global corporations such as Kraft Heinz and Bridgestone.

So, if you have business services to offer for your side hustle, sign up!

Upwork

Upwork (www.upwork.com) is another gig-economy marketplace where you can post your availability for work in software development, project management, writing and editing, legal assistance, and other business disciplines.

ZipRecruiter

You may be familiar with ZipRecruiter (www.ziprecruiter.com) because they advertise fairly heavily on cable news, radio, and other media channels. You may think of ZipRecruiter in terms of playing matchmaker for full-time, career-type jobs. But ZipRecruiter is also a great place for freelancers to connect with companies looking for part-time or even full-time — but shorter-duration — contract work.

TIP

Filter your job searches by Contract or Temporary under the All Employment Types drop-down to limit your results to contract jobs suitable for your side hustle. Or you could even add "part-time" to your search criteria if you want to broaden your side-hustle portfolio to include longer-term, steady work alongside the ebbs and flows of your other side-hustle gigs.

Chapter 18

Ten Signs That You Need to Adjust Your Side-Hustle Strategy

Very little remains the same in life, and that applies to side hustles, too. As life — and your side hustle — continue heading down that long and winding road, pay attention to key signs that tell you that the winds of side-hustle change are blowing.

You're Not Making Any Money

If you got into the side-hustle game to make money, you're not alone. Maybe you're after a small amount of money each month that you intend to stash away to pay for your annual family vacation. Or you could be trying to hit the big time and build up a sizable business.

But whatever your intentions and financial goals were, small or large, they're just not coming to fruition. Perhaps what you're trying to sell just doesn't have the target market size that you originally thought. Or perhaps the market is there, but you need to adjust your advertising and promotion strategy to reach prospective customers.

Or maybe — just maybe — you need to go back to the drawing board and perhaps even bail out of one particular side hustle and look for a different one. Whatever your particular situation happens to be, if you intended to make money from your side hustle but you're seeing little or no income — or worse, spending a fair amount of money each month but not seeing any return — you need to revisit your side-hustle strategy.

You Don't Have Enough Time

Suppose you jumped into the world of e-commerce for your side hustle and started an online business. You originally budgeted 20 hours a week, give or take a little, to devote to your side hustle. But you actually find yourself needing to spend 35 or 40 hours a week — sometimes even more — on your side hustle, and that's on top of your regular job, the time you spend with your family, and even just a little bit of downtime to decompress and reenergize.

Why is your side hustle taking up so much more time than you anticipated? Perhaps the administrative side of your e-commerce business is more complex and time-consuming than you had originally thought. Maybe you're doing your own website work and doing online ads, and that's what's taking up so much time. Maybe your suppliers and wholesalers are habitually late with shipments or sending you defective merchandise, and you're spending many hours every week fighting with those other businesses, as well as trying to do right by your customers.

Or, on the more positive side, maybe your business has really taken off. You had budgeted ten hours a week for packing orders and printing shipping labels, but double or triple the business means double or triple the time you need to spend preparing and shipping customer orders.

What to do, what to do. . . .

Hire additional help. Find new suppliers who are more responsive and don't have nearly as many quality control issues. Subcontract your website and online advertising work. If you find that you're running out of time to keep your side hustle moving forward, you need to adjust how you're running one or more aspects of your business.

The Overall Environment Is Shifting

Even if your side hustle is humming along and you're making money every month, you still need to pay attention to the overall environment in which your side hustle exists. An occasional hiccup is one thing; a seismic earthquake, side-hustle style, is something significantly more significant that you need to deal with.

Three years ago, Leila signed up with one of the hottest multilevel marketing (MLM) companies around. She got in fairly early and has made some decent money, month after month, selling kitchenware. In recent months, though, Leila's income has dropped off dramatically. She's not the only member of this MLM experiencing an income decline, either. Across the entire United States, this MLM is rapidly becoming old news, with newer competitors taking away business.

Leila can certainly just stay the course and hope her kitchenware sales start to improve and her side hustle income goes back up. Maybe the side hustle fates will shine down on her. Or perhaps it's time for Leila to start looking for a new side hustle if the decline in her income is because she's trying to sell products that just aren't selling anymore.

You Experience a Major Life Disruption

Life is filled with twists and turns — many of them unanticipated. Family members become ill or even pass away. An investment that is a significant part of your retirement nest egg suddenly crashes in value. Your spouse is offered the job promotion of a lifetime, but accepting that promotion requires moving 1,000 miles away. You have a baby and find yourself with less time on your hands.

TIP

Any life disruption — positive, negative, or neutral — should lead to you to immediately and thoroughly examining your side-hustle strategy.

Perhaps the result of that disruption-triggered strategy review is that you actually don't need to adjust anything at all. Great! But if you don't at least take a look and *consider* possible adjustments, you risk running into complications or even problems down the road.

An Even Better Side Hustle Has Surfaced

Maybe you've seen the well-traveled meme where a guy is walking down the street with a woman — presumably his girlfriend — but his head is pivoted back to gawk at another woman. You'll see this meme used over and over as a spot-on visual cue for getting distracted by something different.

In fact, you could label the two women on that meme "your current side hustle" and "another side hustle that looks even more promising"!

Tara's side hustle is in the MLM realm. She's sailing right along, with no overall slowdown in business. Tara should just stay the course with her side hustle, right?

Well, maybe. Suppose Tara hears about a brand new MLM with some really cool products and a novel marketing strategy. Or maybe Tara hears about some other side-hustle opportunity that isn't even structured as an MLM — say, a longtime friend is looking for a partner for her online boutique to help take it to the next level.

Regardless of the particulars, one thing is clear to Tara: A new opportunity is even more promising than what she's doing right now!

Can she do both? Should she throttle down on her current MLM-based side hustle so she can jump into a new opportunity? Should she totally quit what she's doing now and go all in on a brand-new side hustle?

REMEMBER

You almost certainly will, on a regular basis, find out about new and potentially more promising side hustles than what you're currently doing. Whether you try to squeeze both of them into your overall side-hustle portfolio, or dump your current one in favor of the newest shiny object, you need to thoroughly explore multiple options and courses of action. Regardless, when a promising new side hustle squeezes into your field of view, you need to at least consider adjusting your side-hustle strategy.

A Key Supplier Can't Deliver

One thing about supply chains: They can be your best friend or your worst enemy.

If you have reliable, trustworthy, and financially friendly suppliers for your side hustle, you're golden! But you still need to pay attention to delivery times, product quality, and other facets of that supplier–retailer relationship that's so critical to your side hustle's success.

On the other side of the coin, suppliers who promise certain delivery times but are frequently late, or who regularly have quality problems in whatever they send you, or who arbitrarily and dramatically increase their wholesale prices can be your worst nightmare. Or perhaps the supplier issues you suddenly face aren't necessarily malicious — say, the supplier increases their minimum order size to a level that doesn't make sense for your smaller-scale side hustle.

Whatever the particulars of your supplier problems may be, a supplier that doesn't deliver should immediately trigger an adjustment of your side-hustle strategy. Whether you scramble to find new suppliers (though you should have already had some backups on your radar) or you need to go back to the drawing board on your entire end-to-end side-hustle strategy, you need to do something — anything! — other than just sitting around and hoping that the situation will get better.

You've Achieved Your Goals Sooner Than Planned

When you do your side-hustle planning, you set a timeline for major milestones that you hope to achieve. Sometimes, you'll fall short; other times, you'll actually wind up achieving your goals sooner — maybe much sooner — than you planned. Then what?

Carl began creating and posting YouTube videos about sports card collecting. His original business plan called for around 2,000 subscribers at the six-month point. To Carl's immense surprise, he actually has more than 10,000 subscribers — the number his business plan showed for the two-year point — and he's pulling in four times as much money in ad-sharing revenue as he originally anticipated at this phase of his side hustle. Woo-hoo!

Carl could, of course, just stay the course and keep doing exactly what he's doing. Or perhaps sports cards are much more popular than he had thought, and consequently he has even greater opportunities and profit potential from his side hustle than he ever dreamed.

Carl definitely needs to get out his business plan, open up his spreadsheet, do some research, and revisit his original side-hustle strategy. What opportunities are available to him at the 10,000 subscriber level that weren't available if he had only met his original projections? Spin-off podcasts? Specialized affiliate marketing programs? Simulcasting in podcast form and selling sponsorships?

REMEMBER

If your side hustle turns out to be a home run, don't spend all your time celebrating. Even if, in the end, you decide to let things run at your current level of activity and investment, at least take a look at adjusting your strategy.

A Business Partner Has Let You Down

If you do a side hustle totally on your own, the only person who can let you and your business down is, well, you. If, however, you have a partner on whom you depend for side-hustle success, you always run the risk of that partner not only letting you down, but potentially taking down your entire side hustle. Even with relatives and close friends, you need to be on alert.

Tina and Cheryl have been friends since college. Then, ten years after graduation, they decided to start an interior design firm on the side of their respective full-time jobs. If all goes according to plan, at the two-year point they'll both quit their regular jobs and go all in on this joint side hustle to turn it into a full-time business.

For the first year, everything goes according to plan. They do some of the interior design jobs together, while in other cases Tina takes one gig while Cheryl focuses on another. Their customers seem pretty happy, and they've picked up a few referrals. So far, so good!

Then, all of a sudden, Cheryl heads to the side-hustle dark side. She schedules meetings at the homes of prospects and current clients but often doesn't show up. She's habitually late on design plans, pricing estimates, arranging for subcontractors — everything!

The reasons that Cheryl has, all of a sudden, let down Tina and put their joint side hustle at risk are unimportant, at least when it comes to the most critical and immediate task at hand for Tina: She needs to adjust her side-hustle strategy. Maybe Cheryl will come around, but could these client-facing issues happen again down the road? If Tina decides to continue partnering with Cheryl, what new backup and contingency measures does Tina need to put in place in case another "dereliction of duty" were to occur? Does the ownership structure and financial split between Tina and Cheryl need to be adjusted?

Tina also needs to consider the side-hustle nuclear option: dissolving her partnership with Cheryl.

In any event, Tina needs to get cracking on revisiting her side-hustle strategy.

Your Early Test Phases Don't Prove Out

Early in your side-hustle journey, you do a test-drive for your business idea, or your gig-economy work. In a perfect world, the success you see during your test-drive will be an indication of whether you're on the right track with your idea and if all the plans you've put in place will bring you success.

What should you do, though, if your side hustle test-drive is a flop?

Keri jumped into the world of e-commerce to create a small retail presence as a side hustle. Her business plan called for between four and six months of testing out all aspects of her business before taking things to the next level. Keri's business model is based around selling products that are fulfilled through drop shipping: sent directly from someone else to her customers, without Keri having to stock inventory, or to handle the packaging and shipping herself.

Keri finds someone to build a Shopify site for her. She lines up several drop shippers for the items that she wants to start selling, places some search engine and social media ads, and opens her virtual doors to the world.

Crickets.

Keri does make a few sales here and there, but her results are far, far below what even the most pessimistic scenario in her business plan called for.

Now what?

Maybe Keri is trying to sell the wrong products. Or maybe she has a good product mix, but the wrong target market. Perhaps she has the right products for the right market, but isn't reaching potential customers.

Something needs to be fixed before proceeding. Or maybe Keri should just call it a day and move on to a different side hustle. Regardless, it's back to the drawing board for Keri's side-hustle strategy.

You're Not Happy

No matter how successful you are or aren't in your side-hustle endeavors, you're not happy. In fact, you're miserable. You began with such high expectations, none of which have come to fruition. Or maybe you've met — or even exceeded — every goal you intended to achieve, but you still cringe at the thought of checking your email or voicemail, or talking to a customer or supplier, or going in front of a classroom, or presenting to a client, or, well, pretty much anything even remotely connected to your side hustle.

If you're not happy, you absolutely need to adjust your side-hustle strategy. Maybe that adjustment will be moving into some different kind of side hustle or throttling way back on your current level of activity to free up some time. Maybe you need to cut into your profits to add someone to help you with some of your tasks. Or maybe you need to rid yourself of a toxic partner or employee, a problematic supplier, or a difficult customer.

Or you might decide to pull the plug on the world of side hustles, having discovered that at least at the moment, the game isn't one that you want to play.

REMEMBER

Whatever you need to do to rid yourself of side hustle–induced unhappiness, do it!

Index

building
  balanced side-hustle portfolios, 231–232
  business plans, 89–94
  craft jewelry, 66–69
  products, 104–107
  timelines, 78
  travel-related lifestyle videos, 62–65
  videos to monetize online content, 100–104
business assets
  compared with investments, 34
  monetizing, 33
  selling off, 272
business deductions, 183–184
business liability insurance, 154
business name, choosing, 130–131
business plans
  about, 89–90, 279
  brainstorming for, 280–284
  business processes, 93
  creating, 89–94
  customers, 92–93
  elevator pitch, 90–91
  financial aspects, 93
  key players, 92
  major milestones, 91–92
  mitigation, 93–94
  overview, 90–91
  risks, 93–94
  schedule, 91–92
  time commitment, 91
Business Process Change, 3rd Edition (Harmon), 81
business processes, in business plans, 93

business structure
  C corporation, 124
  choosing, 123–130
  limited liability company (LLC), 127–128, 180, 191–192
  limited liability partnership (LLP), 124
  partnership, 126–127, 180
  S corporation, 129–130, 180, 189
businesses
  choosing name for, 130–131
  choosing structure for, 123–130
  legal issues, 135–139
  running side hustles like a, 123–139
  technology and, 131–135

C

C corporation, 124
calculating
  estimated income taxes, 193–194
  passive income side hustle life span, 299–300
callouts, in leases, 138
career
  milestones, as a component of scheduling start of side hustles, 283
  as a reason for having a side hustle, 15–16
CARES (Coronavirus Aid, Relief, and Economic Security) Act, 159, 175
CC&Rs (covenants, conditions, and restrictions), 137–138
certificate of formation, 128
Cheat Sheet (website), 4

checking
  for conflicts, 236–237
  propositions, 240–246
choosing
  business name, 130–131
  business structure, 123–130
circle of trust, 245
city taxes, 193
climate change, 263–265
COGS (cost of goods sold), 152
collaboration, 56–57
collecting
  payments, 161–162
  teams, 242–244
commercial zone, 136
company premises, using your employers', 218–219
company time, using your employers', 218
company Wi-Fi networks, using your employers', 214–216
compensation, partners and, 252
competition, changes in, 265–266
comps, 149
computers, using your employers', 213–214
conducting delivery services, 107–109
conflicts
  about, 201–202, 278–279
  approval of outside activities, 211–213
  avoiding, 201–228
  avoiding employer tricks, 219–228
  checking for, 236–237
  of commitment, 205–210
  conflicts of commitment, 205–210
  conflicts of interest, 204–205

employer issues, 202–210
  of interest, 204–205
  noncompete clause, 203–204
  using employer resources, 213–219
content, presenting, 61–62
contracting, to provide services, 28–29
controlling
  failure, 58–60
  success, 275–290
Coronavirus Aid, Relief, and Economic Security (CARES) Act, 159, 175
Corporation Commission filings, 153
cost of goods sold (COGS), 152
covenants, conditions, and restrictions (CC&Rs), 137–138
COVID-19 pandemic
  about, 19–20
  Great Resignation and, 290
  lending programs and, 159, 175
  tax filing extensions during, 194
craft jewelry, creating and selling, 66–69
creating
  balanced side-hustle portfolios, 231–232
  business plans, 89–94
  craft jewelry, 66–69
  products, 104–107
  timelines, 78
  travel-related lifestyle videos, 62–65
  videos to monetize online content, 100–104
Creating a Business Plan For Dummies (Curtis), 94
criticism, 57
Curtis, Veechi (author), *Creating a Business Plan For Dummies*, 94

customer relationship management (CRM)
software, 133

customers
in business plans, 92–93
changes in, 260–262
interacting with, 256–257

D

date, marking for launch, 113–114

day job conflicts
about, 201–202, 278–279
approval of outside activities, 211–213
avoiding, 201–228
avoiding employer tricks, 219–228
conflicts of commitment, 205–210
conflicts of interest, 204–205
employer issues, 202–210
noncompete clause, 203–204
using employer resources, 213–219

DBA ('doing business as') names, 130

decentralized finance (DEFI), 34

delivery services, conducting, 107–109

delta, 285

Diamond, Stephanie (author), *Social Media Marketing For Dummies*, 118

direct deposits, 161

direct payments, 161

dividing workloads, 257–258

documentation
about, 163–164, 166
analytics, 170–173
archives, 173–178
backup and catchup plan, 168–169
catchup plan, 168–169
foundational documents, 164–166
official records, 166–168

tax documents, 164–166
technology for, 169–170
tools for, 169–170

'doing business as' (DBA) names, 130

drop shipping, 45, 255

E

elevator pitch, in business plans, 90–91

employee agreements, 225

employees, paying, 162

employers
avoiding tricks of, 219–228
navigating issues with current, 202–210
using resources of, 213–219

ending side hustles, 259–273

environment, adjusting side hustles due to, 309

environmental influences, 82

error and omissions (E&O) insurance, 154

establishing success criteria, 97–98

estimated income taxes, calculating and filing, 193–194

expenses, planning, 151–156

experience, as a reason for having a side hustle, 13–15

extrovert, 52–53

F

Facebook, 118

Facebook Live, 235

failure
managing, 58–60
weathering, 297

family situations, as a component of scheduling start of side hustles, 283–284

"fans," 296–297

Returnly, 116

SBA loan programs, 158

Shogun themes, 117

Shopify themes, 117

Side Hustle Nation, 7

Small Business Administration (SBA), 127

state filing requirements, 128

TaskRabbit, 304

Toptal, 304

Upsell Product Add-Ons, 116

Upwork, 305

USA Today, 7

Wishlist Plus, 116

Wondershare, 168

for your side hustle, 132–133

ZipRecruiter, 305

introvert, 52–53

inventory, selling, 272

investments

active investors, 160

compared with assets, 34

compared with passive income side hustles, 295–296

passive investors, 160

Investopedia, 18

IRS (Internal Revenue Service)

Form 1040, 188–192

Form 1065, 180, 191–192

Form 1096, 195

Form 1099-MISC/-NEC, 185–187, 191, 195–196

Form 1120-S, 180, 189

Form K-1, 180–181, 190–192

Form W-9, 196–197

Schedule C (IRS Form 1040), 188–189

Schedule E (IRS Form 1040), 190

J

job milestones, as a component of scheduling start of side hustles, 283

jock tax, 184–185

Johnson & Johnson, 233

JOVIAL, 14

K

key players, in business plans, 92

Kim, Seoyoung (author), *NFTs For Dummies*, 37

knowledge, as a reason for having a side hustle, 13–15

Krasniak, Michelle (author), *Social Media Marketing All-in-One For Dummies*, 118

L

launching

about, 111

backup supply chain, 117

marking the date, 113–114

pre-, 112–113

publicizing, 114

social media and, 117–118

sticking to the plan, 115

technology and, 116–117

three-month checkup, 120–121

troubleshooting, 118–120

Laurence, Tiana (author)

Blockchain For Dummies, 2nd Edition, 37

NFTs For Dummies, 37

legal issues

budgeting for, 154

for taxes, 183–187

for your business, 135–139

S

test-drives
  about, 95–96
  adjusting side hustles due to better, 313
  establishing success criteria for, 97–98
  examples of, 100–109
  fun and, 98–99
  length of, 99–100
  questions for, 96–97
themes, 117
three-month checkup, 120–121
Thumbtack, 151
time
  adjusting side hustles due to, 308
  changes in availability of, 267
  commitment of, in business plans, 91
  needed for side hustles, 234–236
  for side hustles, 276–277
  using your employers', 218
timelines, creating, 78
TIN (taxpayer identification number), 196
Tip icon, 3
tools, for record-keeping, 169–170
tools of the trade, budgeting for, 152–153
topical areas, for side hustles, 24–27, 35–38
Toptal, 304
tracking payments, made to others, 194–197
trade name, 130
transaction privilege tax (TPT) license, 154, 198
transforming brainstorming, into value chain, 81–86
transportation expenses, budgeting for, 155
travel expenses, budgeting for, 156

travel-related lifestyle videos, creating and monetizing, 62–65
troubleshooting launching, 118–120
Tyson, Eric (author), *Small Business Taxes For Dummies,* 3rd Edition, 182

U
Uber, 155
UNIVAC, 14
updating value chain, 285
Upsell Product Add-Ons, 116
Upstart, 159
Upwork, 305
USA Today, 7

V
value chain
  about, 260
  updating, 285
value proposition, 246
vehicle expenses, budgeting for, 155
Venmo, 161
Venmo for Business, 162
verifying
  for conflicts, 236–237
  propositions, 240–246
videos
  creating to monetize online content, 100–104
  using your employers' resources, 216–217
virtual reality (VR), 160
volunteer work, 13
voting, partners and, 250–251, 253–254

About the Author

Alan Simon is the managing principal of Thinking Helmet, Inc., a boutique consulting firm that specializes in enterprise data management, business intelligence, and analytics.

He also teaches technology-related courses in the business school of a leading university. Alan also writes technology and business books . . . and novels . . . and does video courses . . . and used to be a farmer. . . .

When it comes to side hustles, Alan has been in the game since the dawn of his professional life in the early 1980s, when he started a consulting firm on the side while he was a U.S. Air Force officer. Even now, with what has traditionally been the "retirement zone" fast approaching, Alan has several new video series in development that will soon join his side-hustle portfolio.

Alan is a native of Pittsburgh, Pennsylvania, and currently lives in the Phoenix, Arizona, metro area.

Dedication

This book is dedicated to my wife, Erica Bianco Ellis, who has been my biggest supporter and inspiration since the day we met.

Author's Acknowledgments

I would like to thank several people for their contributions to *Side Hustles For Dummies*. First and foremost, thanks to my wife, Erica, who is my chief editor and adviser for everything I write, as well as my coauthor on several of my novels. Erica has several of her own side hustles going, and her experiences provided great content and examples for this book. She also was a great sounding board for much of this book as I wrote it. To put it bluntly, and to say it once again: Everything I've written in recent years (not to mention my life) is better than it would otherwise have been, all because of Erica!

Thanks also to Steve Hayes, Zoë Slaughter, Elizabeth Kuball, and the great *For Dummies* team at John Wiley & Sons. I had just completed *Data Lakes For Dummies* when I came up with the idea for *Side Hustles For Dummies*. The team at Wiley liked the idea, and the rest is history. As always, they've been great to work with.

Thank you to my agent, Matt Wagner, of Fresh Books, Inc. The first book Matt sold for me was *Data Warehousing For Dummies* back in 1996 — in fact, he contacted me to let me know that the publisher was looking for someone to write that title. We've worked on many projects together since, including *Side Hustles For Dummies.*

Finally, thanks to Eden Lustig, a long-time friend who has also traveled the side hustle road, who served as the technical editor of this book.

Publisher's Acknowledgments

Associate Editor: Zoë Slaughter
Project Editor: Elizabeth Kuball
Copy Editor: Elizabeth Kuball
Technical Editor: Eden Lustig

Production Editor: SaiKarthick Kumarasamy
Cover Photos: © Dragana Gordic/Shutterstock

Leverage the power

Dummies is the global leader in the reference category and one of the most trusted and highly regarded brands in the world. No longer just focused on books, customers now have access to the dummies content they need in the format they want. Together we'll craft a solution that engages your customers, stands out from the competition, and helps you meet your goals.

Advertising & Sponsorships

Connect with an engaged audience on a powerful multimedia site, and position your message alongside expert how-to content. Dummies.com is a one-stop shop for free, online information and know-how curated by a team of experts.

- Targeted ads
- Video
- Email Marketing
- Microsites
- Sweepstakes sponsorship

20 MILLION PAGE VIEWS EVERY SINGLE MONTH

15 MILLION UNIQUE VISITORS PER MONTH

43% OF ALL VISITORS ACCESS THE SITE VIA THEIR MOBILE DEVICES

700,000 NEWSLETTER SUBSCRIPTIONS TO THE INBOXES OF *300,000* UNIQUE INDIVIDUALS EVERY WEEK

# of dummies

Custom Publishing

Reach a global audience in any language by creating a solution that will differentiate you from competitors, amplify your message, and encourage customers to make a buying decision.

- Apps
- Books
- eBooks
- Video
- Audio
- Webinars

Brand Licensing & Content

Leverage the strength of the world's most popular reference brand to reach new audiences and channels of distribution.

For more information, visit dummies.com/biz

PERSONAL ENRICHMENT

Staying Sharp
9781119187790
USA $26.00
CAN $31.99
UK £19.99

Facebook
Carolyn Abram
9781119179030
USA $21.99
CAN $25.99
UK £16.99

Guitar
Mark Phillips
Jon Chappell
9781119293354
USA $24.99
CAN $29.99
UK £17.99

Investing
Eric Tyson, MBA
9781119293347
USA $22.99
CAN $27.99
UK £16.99

Beekeeping
Howland Blackiston
9781119310068
USA $22.99
CAN $27.99
UK £16.99

Digital Photography
Julie Adair King
9781119235606
USA $24.99
CAN $29.99
UK £17.99

Meditation
Stephan Bodian
9781119251163
USA $24.99
CAN $29.99
UK £17.99

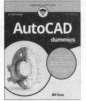
Pregnancy ALL-IN-ONE
9781119235491
USA $26.99
CAN $31.99
UK £19.99

Samsung Galaxy S7
Bill Hughes
9781119279952
USA $24.99
CAN $29.99
UK £17.99

iPhone
Edward C. Baig
Bob "Dr. Mac" LeVitus
9781119283133
USA $24.99
CAN $29.99
UK £17.99

Crocheting
Karen Manthey
Susan Brittain
9781119287117
USA $24.99
CAN $29.99
UK £16.99

Nutrition
Carol Ann Rinzler
9781119130246
USA $22.99
CAN $27.99
UK £16.99

PROFESSIONAL DEVELOPMENT

Windows 10
Andy Rathbone
9781119311041
USA $24.99
CAN $29.99
UK £17.99

AutoCAD
Bill Fane
9781119255796
USA $39.99
CAN $47.99
UK £27.99

Excel 2016
Greg Harvey, PhD
9781119293439
USA $26.99
CAN $31.99
UK £19.99

QuickBooks 2017
Stephen L. Nelson, MBA, CPA, BS in Taxation
9781119281467
USA $26.99
CAN $31.99
UK £19.99

macOS Sierra
Bob "Dr. Mac" LeVitus
9781119280651
USA $29.99
CAN $35.99
UK £21.99

LinkedIn
Joel Elad, MBAs
9781119251132
USA $24.99
CAN $29.99
UK £17.99

Windows 10 ALL-IN-ONE
Woody Leonhard
9781119310563
USA $34.00
CAN $41.99
UK £24.99

SharePoint 2016
Rosemarie Withee
Ken Withee
9781119181705
USA $29.99
CAN $35.99
UK £21.99

Fundamental Analysis
Matt Krantz
9781119263593
USA $26.99
CAN $31.99
UK £19.99

Networking
Doug Lowe
9781119257769
USA $29.99
CAN $35.99
UK £21.99

Office 2016
Wallace Wang
9781119293477
USA $26.99
CAN $31.99
UK £19.99

Office 365
Rosemarie Withee
Ken Withee
Jennifer Reed
9781119265313
USA $24.99
CAN $29.99
UK £17.99

Salesforce.com
Liz Kao
Jon Paz
9781119239314
USA $29.99
CAN $35.99
UK £21.99

Coding
Nikhil Abraham
9781119293323
USA $29.99
CAN $35.99
UK £21.99

dummies.com

dummies
A Wiley Brand

Learning Made Easy

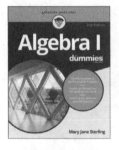

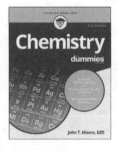

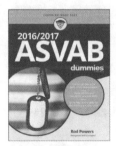

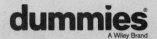

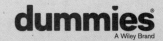